I0815051

The Architecture of Ramses Wissa Wassef

The Architecture of Ramses Wissa Wassef

Conchita Añorve-Tschirgi
Ehsan Abushadi

Photographs by
Nour El Refai

The American University in Cairo Press
Cairo New York

First published in 2021 by
The American University in Cairo Press
113 Sharia Kasr el Aini, Cairo, Egypt
One Rockefeller Plaza, New York, 10th Floor, NY 10020
www.aucpress.com

Dar el Kutub No. 23528/18
ISBN 978 977 416 924 3

Dar el Kutub Cataloging-in-Publication Data

Añorve-Tschirgi, Conchita
The Architecture of Ramses Wissa Wassef / Conchita Añorve-Tschirgi, Ehsan Abushadi.—Cairo: The American University in Cairo Press, 2021.
p. cm.
ISBN 978 977 416 924 3
1. Wissa Wassef, Ramses, 1911–1974
2. Architecture—Egypt
I. Abushadi, Ehsan (jt. auth.)
613.23

1 2 3 4 5 25 24 23 22 21

Designed by Fatiha Bouzidi
Printed in China

Contents

Acknowledgments 1
Preface 3

Part 1: Ramses Wissa Wassef **5**
Introduction 7
Architect and Artist 17
Architectural Legacy 23
Professorship 27

Part 2: A Descriptive Catalog **31**

EXTANT 33
Ramses Wissa Wassef Art Center **33**
Village Art Studio and Gallery—Phase 1 34
Solar Kiln 38
Village Art Studio and Gallery—Phase 2 39
Habib Georgi Museum 45
Chicken Coops and Toolshed 53
Silos 54
Cérés Wissa Wassef Villa 55
Seven Weavers' Houses 58
Second-Generation Weaving Workshops 63
Engineer Mounir Nosshi Villa 64
Temporary Chapel 67
Posthumous Additions 67

Churches **69**
Church of the Archangel Michael in Shubra 69
Dominican Fathers Priory Chapel Renovation 73
St. George and St. Abram Church in Heliopolis 80
Church of the Virgin Mary in Zamalek 87

Sanctuary of Archangel Michael Coptic Orthodox Church in Damanhur 97
Stained-glass Stucco Windows at St. Mina Coptic Orthodox Church 102

Residential **108**
Wissa Wassef Aguza Residence 108
Ina Makkar House 116
Mohie al-Din Hussein House and Studio 121

Educational and Cultural **123**
Jardin d'Enfants at the Lycée Français du Caire 123
Lycée Franco-Égyptien d'Héliopolis 130
School in Old Cairo 136
Mahmoud Mokhtar Museum 140

Other **146**
Al-Chark Insurance Company Building Renovation 146
Stained-glass Stucco Windows at the Social Building, Egyptian Shooting Club 152
Nematalla Louis Mausoleum 156
Al-Dar Restaurant 158
Lounge Ceiling at the Palestine Hotel 161

NONEXTANT 163
Churches **163**
Evangelical Presbyterian Church 163
St. George the Martyr Coptic Orthodox Church, Giza Diocese 166
Two Martyrs Cyrus and John Coptic Orthodox Church 169
St. Joseph Church 172
St. George Monastery on the Nile Bank 174
Evangelical Church, Community Center and Offices 175
Coptic Catholic Patriarchate Church 178
Cathedral of St. Mark and Anba Ruways Compound 180
Heliopolis Church Theater and Club Extension 183
Iconostasis at the Coptic Catholic Church of Faggala 186
Unidentified Church Community Services Building 188
Unidentified Church 1 188
Unidentified Church 2 191

Residential **194**
Villa Fikry Boutros 194
Villa al-Amira Naima Ibrahim 196
Augonie Abdel Sayed and Habib Georgi Beach House 199
Berlanty Youssef Beach House 201
Apartment Building on Sheikh Rihan Street 203
Apartment Building on Clot Bey Street 205
Building Number 34 and 36 207
Zeinab Badawi House 208

Adam Henein House and Atelier 209
Abul-'Enein Weekend House 212
Student Project: Villa 213
Unidentified Apartment Building 1 215
Unidentified Apartment Building 2 216
Unidentified Villa 1 217
Unidentified Villa 2 218
Unidentified Villa 3 219
Unidentified Villa 4 220
Unidentified Villa 5 222

Educational and Cultural 224
Graduation Project: Old Cairo Potters' House 224
Small Renovation at Collège Français du Daher 226
Faruq I University Dormitory 227
School for Art and Handicrafts in al-Qubba 231
Ismailiya Secondary School 233
American Mission for Girls: Experimental Project for Farming 235

Other 237
Banque Misr Building and Hotel Competition 237
Garage and Atelier Magar 240
Interior Design and Stained-glass Panels for the Grand Reception Hall at the Cairo Governorate Headquarters 241

Glossary 245
Notes 247
Bibliography 255
Figure Credits 259

Acknowledgments

This book would not have been possible without the unending support of Ramses Wissa Wassef's family, who provided invaluable information on his life and work: Sophie Habib Georgi, his loving wife, who has been waiting years for this book to come to life; Suzanne and Yoanna, his dear daughters, who preserved his work; Ikram Nosshi, his son-in-law, who was instrumental in the research for this book, providing continual insight and feedback; as well as Ramses Nosshi and Taya Doss, two of his grandchildren; and Bassem Badie Habib, his nephew.

The presentation of Wissa Wassef's architecture works would not have been possible without the support of the American University in Cairo's Rare Books and Special Collections Library staff: Shahira El Sawy, former dean of Libraries and Learning Technologies; Balsam Saleh, the current curator of the Regional Architecture Collection, for her invaluable and prompt aid; Dalia Nabil, the former curator; and Ahmed Kadry, Mohamed Saleh, and Mohamed Farag, who facilitated the digitization of Ramses Wissa Wassef's archive.

It is very significant to note that Philip Croom, associate dean for the Rare Books and the Special Collections Library, had a decisive involvement that led to this book. His advice and inputs were extremely valuable when the whole idea was only a vague concept in the authors' minds. He has been a constant support in the creation of this book.

We would like to thank the American University in Cairo Press and the people who placed their faith in our book proposal: Nadia Naqib, who provided much support; Neil Hewison; and Nigel Fletcher-Jones.

We were privileged to be granted the use of photographs from the Aga Khan Documentation Center, with the cooperation of Lobna Montasser and Matt Saba. Likewise, Michel Hanna and S.G. generously allowed the inclusion of their own photographs.

Research on Ramses Wissa Wassef's built works was made possible through invaluable discussions and information on the projects with the following: Sami Shaker, Adam Henein, Nessim Henein, May al-Ibrashy, Alfonse Ghatass, Sameh

Fayek, Marianne Makar, Mervat Nasr, and Fikry Boutros.

We would like to thank all the individuals who put great efforts into facilitating site visits: Samer Benjamin, Nadia Fanous, David Ashraf, Ashraf Yousef Moawad, Hanaa Ragaie, Waseem Magdy, Wasseem Morcos, Aliaa el-Dardiry, Sherif, and Ahmed.

Our deepest gratitude goes to the people who granted us access to the projects: Anba Abraam Emil, of the Alexandria Patriarchate; al-Qummus Sergious Sergious, of the Cairo Patriarchate; Abuna Girgis Tawfik; Abuna Youhanna; Abuna Mina; Frère René du Grandlaunay; Frère Jocelyn Dorvault; Abeer Tawfik; Kamal Maher; Milad; and Milad.

Special thanks go to the St. George and St. Abram Church in Heliopolis, the Church of the Virgin Mary in Zamalek, the Archangel Michael Coptic Orthodox Church in Damanhur, the Church of the Archangel Michael in Shubra, the Dominican Fathers Priory, and the St. Mina Coptic Orthodox Church in Fleming.

Most importantly, we extend our gratitude to all the family and friends who have supported us along the way. On Conchita's side, Dan Tschirgi, for his unending moral support as well as the indispensable contribution he made by reading this manuscript when it was just taking shape. Thanks also to the Moons trio, who have always illuminated Conchita's life: Luna Llena, Luna Morena, and Luna Chiquita. And to the Lonely Star who got lost in Conchita's firmament. On Ehsan's part, it is very important to recognize the invaluable support of Mohamed Hamad, her loving spouse; her parents and siblings, who have always encouraged her pursuits: Begoña Colilla, Amr Abushadi, Nora Abushadi, Youssef Abushadi, and Ines Abushadi; her in-laws, Mona AbdelKader and Fouad Hamad; and all the friends who have supported her—particularly Reham Hamad and Maya Kazamel, who helped make sense of scribbled handwriting, and Heba El Sawy for always lending an ear.

Preface

The fundamental purpose of this book is to make known the complete architectural works of Ramses Wissa Wassef in the form of a descriptive catalog. Each project is presented via a concise description that conveys substantive information, permitting the reader to engage and understand the contribution of one of the most notable Egyptian architects of the twentieth century. In other words, the present effort constitutes a *catalogue raisonné*.

The initiative and inspiration for compiling this descriptive catalog was the lack of sources providing a comprehensive and correct presentation of Ramses Wissa Wassef's architecture, particularly in a visual format. This book does not present an in-depth architectural or sociocultural analysis of Wissa Wassef's projects but rather offers, in each case, a short description accompanied, when available, by basic background information. On some occasions, much of the background information is based on anecdotes and recollections provided by members of the Wissa Wassef family and other reliable sources.

The information presented here primarily includes Ramses Wissa Wassef's unpublished architectural plans, drawings, and sketches, as well as archival photographs, complemented by new images by Nour El Refai, which are a valuable contribution to the book and demonstrate the splendor of Wissa Wassef's work as well as its current state.

This volume offers a complete list of Ramses Wissa Wassef's buildings, and the material presented here invites us to try to understand fully the prodigious mind of the architect. But most important of all is the fact that extant projects still remain as a unique example of authentic Egyptian architecture from the twentieth century, a time when the Egyptian architectural identity was being put aside in favor of a Western and global architecture.

Very little has been written about this pioneering architect's *oeuvre*. What can be found in print mainly comprises analyses and commentaries on some of his more prominent works, or his use of vernacular architecture with a focus on passive design for the local climate. In contrast, a great amount of literature exists emphasizing his role as a protector of the arts, in view of the Ramses Wissa Wassef Art Center.[1]

Ramses Wissa Wassef's works have become a visual culture reference for a part of Egyptian society. Wissa Wassef himself always made it a point to study the architectural systems of the past. He always took very seriously the great ancient builders, in stark contrast to what is often seen today. The more recent practice of architecture has all too frequently taken a turn totally opposed to what Wissa Wassef advocated. He had argued, through the physical medium of the buildings he created, in favor of an architectural style that would recover the aesthetic sense that had once been Egypt's.

The fundamental goal of publishing this book is to ensure that both the general and the specialized reader have the opportunity to get to know Wissa Wassef and his creative gift of architecture. What is presented in the following pages is the product of a years-long effort by the authors to understand, list, discover, and track the architectural projects created by Wissa Wassef during his active career from 1935 until his untimely death in 1974. The point of departure was the archive in the Regional Architecture Collection of the Rare Books and Special Collections Library at the American University in Cairo, where Conchita Añorve-Tschirgi received the archive in 2004 and curated it until 2017.

A large component of the work that went into the creation of this book was the identification of Wissa Wassef's projects, their location, and their status. This often relied on traditional research methods such as conducting interviews, making enquiries, and consulting the existing literature, but also involved integrating contemporary technology, such as manipulating images with Photoshop, to provide increased legibility of text that may have become faint over time, or using Google Earth and Google Maps to pan entire neighborhoods in search of the buildings. These were complemented by long exploratory walks to confirm the location and existence of the projects.

This book, however, aims to go beyond being a *catalogue raisonné*. Ultimately, it hopes to do justice to the work of one of the most creative, honest, and influential architects that Egypt—and, by extension, the modern Middle East—has produced.

PART 1

Ramses Wissa Wassef

Young Ramses (second from the left) with his family, c.1928.

Introduction

The Egyptian architect Ramses Wissa Wassef was born in Cairo on November 9, 1911, into a prominent Coptic family, and he died at the relatively young age of sixty-three on July 13, 1974. His mother, Berlanty Youssef Mekheal, was a woman of the Egyptian upper class who presided over a multilingual household in which French was the preferred language of daily use,[1] although English and Arabic were also spoken fluently as required. His father, Wissa Wassef El-Beblawi (1873–1931), was born in Tahta, in the governorate of Sohag. El-Beblawi's family moved to Cairo in 1880, where he was educated in the best schools in Egypt. He pursued higher education in France (1889), and upon completing his qualifications became a teacher in Alexandria. Frustrated with the British colonial administration of schools, however, he decided to study law. Wissa Wassef El-Beblawi became the first Egyptian Mixed Tribunal lawyer in Cairo. He became an eminent lawyer while always maintaining an active status in politics, leading him to become a prominent figure in the Wafd Party, which then led the push for Egypt's full independence from British rule.[2]

Wissa Wassef El-Beblawi was an intellectual and a patron of the arts as well as social, educational, and cultural projects, becoming active in Cairo's cultural scene.[3] These interests were evident in the development of the personalities of his children: Isis, Cérés, Ramses, Oziris, and Horus. Ramses Wissa Wassef and his siblings were all well versed in the arts, among them painting, sculpture, and music. The family circle laid great stress on critical thinking and liberal ideas. His upbringing did much to inspire the young Ramses Wissa Wassef to appreciate the beauty and harmony that marked his childhood environment while simultaneously garnering a consciousness of the deep social, political, and cultural challenges confronting Egypt. Issues such as sociopolitical oppression, social justice, and economic welfare were frequent topics of discussion between father and son.[4]

From childhood, Ramses and his siblings demonstrated an inclination to cultivate key values that would serve as lodestones for the rest of their lives; among them were respect for others and pride in their country and culture.

The emphasis given to artistic expression in Ramses Wissa Wassef's childhood home strongly helped incline him to pursue a career linked to the arts. At a very young age he developed the skill to sketch accurate and well-proportioned drawings of various animals and other forms. Later, his ability and skill led him to experiment with bas-reliefs. In this way, the young sculptor emerged into the light of day, developing an urge to devote himself to sculpture as a career option.[5]

Following lengthy and detailed discussions with his father and long hours of solitary reflection, Ramses Wissa Wassef eventually decided to pursue a career in architecture. Ramses was an innately consummate artist and, as Ikram Nosshi relates, "this was a decision for which [Ramses] had reason to be pleased, as he grew more and more aware of the fact that architecture 'in code' was also a universal art."[6] According to family members, it is almost certain that Ramses would have turned to sculpture had pursuing a career in architecture fallen through.[7]

The Wissa Wassef family was quite conscious of the way they instilled moral values and aesthetics in their children, putting emphasis on their own Egyptian roots and culture. When the European neoclassical style in architecture reached the height of its popularity in Egypt, Ramses's father, Wissa Wassef El-Beblawi, chose to acquire in 1922 a residence in Giza following a neo-Islamic style with a strong Moroccan influence.[8]

In 1929 Ramses went to study architecture at the École des Beaux Arts de Paris; among his professors was Roger-Henri Expert, who would supervise his graduation project. At school he kept imprinted in his mind the beauty of his home country, being inspired by it. Once in direct and sustained contact with his mentors in Paris, Ramses absorbed their influence and proceeded to analyze architecture in a light that was different from that applied in Egyptian universities. In his projects at school, Ramses re-evaluated the authenticity of Egyptian architecture and art.[9]

The result—rendered in his graduation project, Old Cairo Potters' House (1935; see chapter 2, Old Cairo Potters' House)—made it more than clear that he had a comprehensive understanding of Egyptian art, architecture, and context. This work allowed him to develop a new way to search for an authentic Egyptian architecture. Inspired by his love of sculpting, he designed a house to improve the environment in which potters created. The house was equipped with a kiln and individual pottery studios, as well as offering spaces for leisure and well-being. Although following the concepts of people-centered architecture, stylistically he was starting to develop the emergent and unique style of his later years, which Leïla el-Wakil has labeled "modern Arab."[10]

After graduation Ramses Wissa Wassef returned to Cairo, and by 1936 he had started working with the French architect Jacques Hardy, who was one of the partners of Parcq & Hardy. Together, Hardy and Wissa Wassef worked on the designs for the Lycée Franco-Égyptien d'Héliopolis, commissioned by the Mission Laïque Française. Ramses would go on to take more commissions from the Mission Laïque Française,

Wissa Wassef El-Beblawi residence in Giza.

Jardin d'Enfants under construction at the Lycée Français du Caire, Bab al-Luq.

most significantly the kindergarten (Jardin d'Enfants) at the Lycée Français du Caire located in Bab al-Luq.[11]

Ramses Wissa Wassef met Habib Georgi[12] in 1945, when Ramses joined the Coptic Studies Institute to teach Coptic architecture. Despite their age difference, they developed a very close friendship, sharing the same principles and vision as regards children's education. They firmly believed that children are born with an innate capacity to develop art as a means to awaken their intelligence, and to improve the quality of communication between human beings. In the case of Georgi, he went further, believing that the ancestral skill is inherited by the youth.[13]

Habib Georgi El Taweel (1892–1965), better known as Habib Georgi, being a pedagogue, shared the same preoccupations as Ramses. He put his experiment into practice teaching sculpting to children, aiming to reveal their power of creation. Aided by his wife Augonie Abdel Sayed, he started instructing young children from a studio in their house in 1936. These children were creating from their heart, having had no previous artistic education. Similarly, Ramses launched his experiment using weaving to awaken the children's senses at the School in Old Cairo, 1941, and then again at the Ramses Wissa Wassef Art Center in 1951. In all cases the results were a great success; however, the School in Old Cairo did not continue, due to a change in management.

Ramses Wissa Wassef met Sophie (b.1922), the daughter of his friend and mentor Habib Georgi, in 1948, and the two got married that same year. Sophie also had a passion for the arts—particularly watercolors, from which she took great pleasure. She was a full-time art teacher, and later became an art inspector for governmental schools at the Ministry of Education.

The newlywed couple lived at the Wissa Wassef house in Giza until 1963. They had two daughters: Suzanne (b.1950) and Yoanna (b.1952). Sophie recalled that Ramses was such a rational person that she wholeheartedly believed in his projects and dreams. Likewise, Ramses supported his wife and her artistic expression.

Ramses Wissa Wassef (third from left) and Habib Georgi (left), among the people in this photograph.

Ramses Wissa Wassef and his wife Sophie Habib Georgi, a few months after their marriage, in the garden of the Wissa Wassef El-Beblawi residence, c.1949.

This point was especially valid following 1951, the year when Ramses and Sophie embarked on the creation of the Ramses Wissa Wassef Art Center (RWWAC), which would become an ongoing project that continued to develop through Ramses's lifetime and afterwards. Incrementally they acquired land in Harraniya for this purpose. The art center became a laboratory for Ramses's ideas, as well as a synthesis of his intricate personality, his artistic expression, and the climax of his experimentation as an architect; it became the crowning project of his career. The center has been described by Adelina Picone as Ramses's "Utopia,"[14] although it may be a stretch to characterize it thus given the project's organic growth and the difference between being detail-oriented and a formalist, the latter of which Ramses was not.

In this project there was sufficient spontaneity and freedom in the planning and execution to express Ramses's artistic and architectural identity. Even more important was the realization of his noble goal of helping the children of Harraniya. It was for them that he launched this experiment of faith, compassion, nurturing, and love. The child-artists working in weaving were not only allowed to be free; they were respected and urged to execute in tapestry their own designs, coming directly from their subconscious mind. While the dream may have begun with Ramses's faith in the innate inclination of children to engage in artistic expression, its immediate consequences were fully practical. The first generation of learners at the center comprised fifteen children from the nearby village of Harraniya. Today, many of the first youthful weavers who passed through the Ramses Wissa Wassef Art Center have become internationally recognized artists in their own right.

Sophie Habib Georgi's participation in the art center was instrumental, going beyond artistic advising. She took the initiative of focusing on the project's social component, which gave the center its holistic approach toward education. She personally supported Ramses all the way through, without interfering with the young artists-to-be in a direct way, respecting the noninstructive teaching philosophy.[15] This included preparations for the exhibitions where the tapestries were put on display. She also advised the community of Harraniya in various aspects, mostly focused on well-being. Given the lack of access to medical care, a clinic had been set up at the center where the villagers could access check-ups and consultations. Additionally, Sophie ran the canteen, which offered nourishing meals while providing valuable nutrition education.

Following Ramses's death in 1974, she took full control of all responsibilities for the first-generation weavers until 1984, while Suzanne and Yoanna were responsible for the second-generation weavers. To this day, Sophie still oversees the last two active weavers who were part of the first-generation group of fifteen children, now well over seventy years old. Later on, her daughters Suzanne and Yoanna took full responsibility for the center's activities.

Sherban Cantacuzino points out that the Ramses Wissa Wassef Art Center was designed and created with three essential intangible elements that were consciously planned to have a positive effect on the Harraniya community. These were: a) the social aspect; b) the buildings' sculpture-like impact on the viewers' perceptions; and c) the spiritually peaceful overall atmosphere projected by the complex.[16] These attributes were well thought out and executed by

Ramses in order to encourage young artists to express their innate creativity. This remains the norm today, and the center continues operating with the same vibrant energy it has always shown.

Ramses Wissa Wassef received two highly recognized awards for his work. The first was the Egyptian National Award for Arts, bestowed on him in 1960 for the stained-glass stucco windows made for the Church of the Virgin Mary on Mar'ashli Street in Zamalek.[17] The second was the Aga Khan Award for Architecture, presented posthumously in 1983 for his architectural, educational, and social work at the Ramses Wissa Wassef Art Center. As the awarding committee stated, the accolade was granted:

> For the beauty of its execution, the high value of its objectives, and the social impact of its activities, as well as its influence as an example. For its role as a center of art and life, for its endurance, its continuity, and its promise.
>
> The project is perfectly adapted to its environment, enhancing the role of earth as a building material, and demonstrating imagination in the organization of volumes and in the subtle use of light. The quality of the spaces, the generosity of the forms, and the ambiance created by light all reflect architectural excellence.
>
> The Ramses Wissa Wassef Arts Center has a social as well as a sculptural and spiritual dimension. It has provided a place, supportive as well as poetic, where the young tapestry weavers of the community have been free to develop a local craft that supports the village with products of great excellence and renown.[18]

OPPOSITE:
Portrait of Ramses Wissa Wassef.

Primary School in Old Cairo, 1941.

Architect and Artist

In 1935, Ramses Wissa Wassef's graduation project, Old Cairo Potters' House, allowed him to graduate with a degree in architecture from the École des Beaux Arts de Paris. Since his days as a student in Paris, he focused tightly on defining and defending his professional style. In his graduation project, he demonstrated his determination to incorporate the Egyptian tradition into his architectural repertoire.

With this initial project, Wissa Wassef made perfectly clear his interest in the revival of the arts and crafts in Egypt in a wholesome approach, and in creating a people-centered architecture. The Potters' House was an ode to the craftspeople of Egypt, demonstrating his overwhelming faith in the creativity of the nation's artisans. This can be inferred from the fact that this project was rooted within the area where Cairo's potters had worked for centuries, while providing the artisans with dignified places to work and live that suited their needs. It was a project that looked to the future of crafts and artisans.

Following in the footsteps of his graduation project, Wissa Wassef stayed away from the fine arts, classical models promoted in many architecture schools of his time.[1] It seems he consciously disdained replicating the nineteenth-century quasi-Haussmann European architecture prevailing in Cairo at the time.[2] However, taking the Egyptian tradition as his basis, he did integrate other styles into his architecture and explored combinations, even including in his early work elements of Art Deco.

Wissa Wassef was capable of creating a unique architectural mode of expression that, to varying degrees, was a tribute to art and sculpture. An artist and sculptor at heart, he began developing sculptural elements in his buildings, even sometimes adopting sculpting as an architectural creative process. It is known that in at least three projects Wissa Wassef created clay models to develop the forms of his buildings: the School in Old Cairo (1941), Seven Weavers' Houses (1970), and the Church of the Virgin Mary in Zamalek (1957).[3]

Wissa Wassef joined the faculty ranks at the Faculty of Fine Arts in Zamalek, Helwan University, Cairo, in 1938. It was there that he met many distinguished colleagues—among them Hassan Fathy, who would become a close friend. For a period of time, Fathy would visit Wissa Wassef at the Giza residence on a daily basis at 5 p.m., whereupon they would enjoy tea and engage in long conversations. They would often take walks together, exploring the traditional architecture of Cairo.[4]

The much-publicized 1941 Faculty of Fine Arts trip to Upper Egypt, and more specifically Nubia, which would inspire Fathy and his pursuit of the vernacular, was also an epiphany for Wissa Wassef. During this trip, the faculty and student participants had the opportunity to study Nubian buildings and the main elements of their composition: vaults, domes, claustra, and detailed patterns ornamenting their façades. While rediscovering the beauty of these harmonious constructions, they learned about the use of local building materials derived from the earth: limestone, mud brick (adobe), and lime for the ornamental designs.[5] This was the first encounter of the faculty and student architects of that generation with sustainable architecture. These vernacular elements from Egypt's millennia-old architectural expression would metamorphose into one of Wissa Wassef's main professional tools.

Wissa Wassef, like Fathy, inferred that these houses were the product of an accumulated wisdom that responded to the climate and the economic realities of its residents, achieving aesthetic and physical benefits via architecture.[6] Wissa Wassef was inspired to study in more depth the climatic qualities of both these houses and those found in Historic Cairo. On the path toward creating sustainable architecture, Wissa Wassef looked beyond their building materials to study their passive cooling and lighting systems. The knowledge for constructing such structures had been bequeathed by ancient generations to the modern inhabitants of the Egyptian lands. Wissa Wassef returned from this trip so ecstatic that when he built the Old Cairo School (1941), he immediately put into practice the knowledge he had acquired in Nubia.[7]

This project, in a modest way, gave birth to the incipient signs of what over the years would become Ramses Wissa Wassef's signature vernacular-inspired architecture. The Old Cairo School offered him an opportunity to test his notion that education could be dramatically improved by combining academic instruction with practical apprenticeships. In this case, Wissa Wassef introduced weaving tapestries as an educational foundation, for which purpose he had to learn this craft himself. Students were encouraged to portray scenes from their daily lives.

It was during this project that Wissa Wassef explored the overlapping roles of architect, educational reformer, and promoter of the arts. He immediately recognized that here, perhaps, was the opportunity not only to align his love of architecture, art, and education but also to revive the Egyptian tradition. Unfortunately, according to Picone, the plan foundered on the rocks of Egypt's unimaginative outlook on education at the time. The committee charged with directing the school's educational efforts proved to be more interested in rapidly raising pupils' literacy levels and in vocational skills that they could easily grasp and quickly start making a living from.[8]

First small carpet woven by Ramses Wissa Wassef before embarking on teaching the children, c.1941.

Mar'ashli Church under construction, c.1957.

Wissa Wassef studied the properties of the building materials used in sustainable architecture through observation, discussions with master builders, and experimentation, and he perfectly understood the advantages, benefits, and drawbacks of building with them. Thus he was aware of the benefits as well as the limitations of utilizing adobe in construction, and did not limit his projects to adobe, but used limestone and red brick as well. This was true for many of his projects, but especially so in the case of the house he built for his sister Cérés: the dwelling appears at one with the earth, as if growing from it.

Despite Wissa Wassef's passion for building with local materials, he also designed projects to be built with concrete. Often, this would arise due to the size of the building, in the case of the churches in particular, the stipulations of construction permits, or client desire. Yet in many cases when dealing with concrete, Wissa Wassef did not conform to the typical slab-and-column skeleton, and truly innovated with the forms that could be molded using concrete. Perhaps the best example of this is the 1957 construction of the Church of the Virgin Mary in Zamalek.[9]

As Wissa Wassef was developing his use of traditional building materials, he was also exploring artistic and sculptural elements and details in contemporary architecture grounded in the Egyptian tradition—designing around and with natural light, shadows, ventilation, degrees of transparency, and massing. These aspects often manifested themselves in the form of shafts, oculi, claustra, *mashrabiya*s, and stained-glass stucco windows. These are playfully explored in many of his buildings, including churches and the Ramses Wissa Wassef Art Center in Harraniya, particularly the 1967 museum honoring his father-in-law, the sculptor Habib Georgi.

To complete the holistic spatial experience Wissa Wassef was creating, he would often design many of the architectural and interior complements, including furnishings, woodwork and carpentry, carved panels, the stained-glass stucco windows also known as *qamariya*s or *zugag mu'ashshaq*,[10] lighting units including candlesticks, pottery and tiles, mosaics, and more. Quite often he would make the stained-glass stucco windows and pottery himself. In other cases, he would give the design to a craftsperson to implement, which was the case with some stained-glass stucco windows and carved stone. This demonstrates how Wissa Wassef could not separate the artist from the architect, an approach that is clearly manifested in his work.

PAGE 22:
Wissa Wassef Aguza residence in its original form before later expansions.

Light and shadow at the weaving workshops.

Architectural Legacy

The initiative taken in the 1940s by Wissa Wassef, alongside a few others, to adopt an architecture using local materials and adapting to local climatic needs following the path of what is today called sustainable architecture, was a step well ahead of its time.[1] Today, the strategy would be recognized and applauded as a conscious effort to preserve the planet's finite resources through means that would also enhance the affordability of construction. Aimed at supporting a revival of the use of adobe and stone, the movement stemmed from the social concerns of thinkers like Wissa Wassef. The initiative led to a trend that was propelled by a group of architects and intellectuals who feared that the unity between human beings and art and architecture had become predominantly lost.

These thinkers were trying to solve the affordable-housing problem while simultaneously exploring Egypt's architectural identity. They were concerned over the evident loss of national identity in architecture and the arts. The bulk of Egypt's population was surrendering to the overwhelming presence of foreign influence in both spheres. Wissa Wassef and Fathy, among other thinkers, formed part of the group called the Friends of Art and Life, founded by Hamed Said.[2] This group voiced intense opposition to the passive acceptance by others who remained enthralled by the influx of European styles into Egypt.

Unfortunately, the tendency to use industrialized materials is strongly rooted in people's ideas of progress and socioeconomic status. The phenomenon of abandoning the use of resources native to Egypt as building material came to a head in the 1870s during the time of Khedive Ismail (1863–79) who, in his thrust to Europeanize the nation—or, more accurately, to use Paris as a transformative model—caused a 180-degree turn in Egypt's approach to architecture.[3]

The struggle to find an authentic Egyptian architecture is still relevant today, as Egypt's current reality remains stuck in the habit of copying outmoded European architectural models (quasi-Haussmannian and neoclassical styles), or postmodern and hypermodern styles. Many of today's Egyptian architects continue imitating the same classical paradigms that were popular during Wissa Wassef's youth. It seems that builders, designers, and property owners retain an almost irreversible fascination with replicating dated

European architectural stereotypes whose glory is long past. The architectural models prevailing in today's Egypt have little to do with the realities of contemporary Egyptian society, and even less with the identity sought by such visionary thinkers and reformers as Wissa Wassef and others.

This concern for an authentic Egyptian architecture also applied to Coptic Orthodox churches. Wissa Wassef saw the need to establish guidelines for the design of contemporary churches to preserve their identity while providing innovation. He submitted a proposal to establish such guidelines to the General Congregation Council with the intention of creating a committee that could address this. It was intended for the committee to be made up of architects, engineers, and other specialists to provide a holistic approach.[4]

In view of the previously mentioned concerns, it is sad to compare Wissa Wassef's buildings with other contemporary ones that followed regressive tendencies, having little or nothing to do with Egyptian values. The trajectory taken by today's Egyptian architecture has, in the main, so completely captured the mentalities of the designers and builders serving as its proponents that property owners now accept it as definitive of refined taste. Thus both groups have collaborated in foisting upon Egypt the ersatz form of European architecture that currently dominates the residential refuges of the country's nascent middle class. Proof of this is all too readily available from casting a glance at the growing residential neighborhoods found in New Cairo.

It is undeniable that the buildings created by Wissa Wassef, and other visionaries like him, were from the start identified by all—their builders and foreigners alike—as constituting a true modern Egyptian architecture. Ironically, many contemporary architects are unaware of the true depth of this architecture and often dismiss it as stereotypical. This, in short, is an architecture that responds to human needs with the comfort of sustainable structures built with noble materials such as adobe and stone.

Wissa Wassef was one of the few who understood and appreciated the true value of the architectural legacy the ancient and medieval Egyptians had left to their modern descendants. Wissa Wassef was heavily influenced by the beauty and splendor of Historic Cairo as well as by the Nubian architecture of Upper Egypt. In his unpublished observations and reflections, he insisted that the skills and knowledge of those ancient Egyptian artisans, as well their use of local materials, were vital for the continuation of a contemporary architecture that could properly be cataloged as Egyptian.[5] This, of course, could only be accomplished by reviving the experiences acquired through generations and consciously preserving the continuation of a millennial tradition of construction, while turning to innovation.

Wissa Wassef's professional formation at the École des Beaux Arts de Paris placed him in the vanguard of those who could decipher the architecture of the ancients and thereby create a contemporary architectural language that could legitimately be considered as modern Egyptian. Before his career took off, Wissa Wassef was already exploring this: as El-Wakil asserts, the young architect-to-be had "reinvented the Arab Tradition."[6]

Following his visits to many Cairo neighborhoods and sites in Upper Egypt, Wissa Wassef understood the architectural characteristics required for an authentic modern Egyptian architecture: design, form, traits, materials, colors, the use of light as an outstanding element in architecture, and, above all, the rendering of the final building in harmony with

Egypt's ecology and identity. Other Egyptian thinkers of the same period sought to follow the same path, but with only limited success.

It can be argued that Wissa Wassef's philosophy revolved around his well-focused and self-controlled personality. Humility was his professional trademark from the start. He committed himself to studying the lessons of the past and put them into practice in his time. He was exceptionally honest with himself and others, suggesting that this was the source of his renunciation of self-glorification, public recognition, and monetary reward.

Wissa Wassef was more of a quiet and thoughtful observer than an intrusive personality, a characteristic that has sometimes been misunderstood. At times, some felt intimidated by his silence. He was actually a very inclusive person, a key trait that he proved by his innovative and creative ideas in favor of people. Always wanting to improve people's lives, he paid great attention to detail, ensuring that his architecture was people centered. This, indeed, was the reason he began to experiment in participatory or inclusive design. The main point of this approach was to empower those who participated in the process of creating dignified shelter.

When building the Ramses Wissa Wassef Art Center, the children who were learning to weave tapestry were also learning how to erect structures built of mud brick, with the aim that one day they might build their own homes. The proof still stands today at the center in the form of the chicken coops that were used to train the children in construction. The theory was that when people participate in this type of activity, they become socially committed and positively empowered.[7] Wissa Wassef knew, understood, and acted on this principle.

More importantly, Wissa Wassef's intention behind the exercise was aimed at the transformation of all these children for the future. His philosophy was crystal clear: he wanted them to be the active participants in their own inclusion in a social group where they would be respected because, in the end, they were going to believe in themselves. He was aiming to empower them; furthermore, he facilitated their economic power to acquire property and make them feel secure by owning a piece of land and a house as adults.[8] Wissa Wassef asked them to model in clay the vision they had for their own houses; in other words, he was putting into practice and encouraging them in the process of participatory design. These participatory houses came into being as the project known as the Seven Weavers' Houses (1970).

One of the main ideas behind Wissa Wassef's efforts was to encourage Egyptians to take control of their decisions and trust themselves. In this case, art was the proper motivational vehicle. He also stressed the necessity of returning to the use of materials that nature offers us in exchange for living harmoniously with the natural environment. In doing so, his goal was to promote widespread pride in the rediscovery and application of the crafts of the past. He managed to put into practice a deep philosophy and created a contemporary Egyptian architectural language. All the while he cultivated a connection with artisans that nobody else ever managed to develop.

All this explains how Wissa Wassef's ideas and practice of how art and architecture could be applied had started to resound internationally. Along with Youssef Chahine, he was invited to talk at the symposium "The Artist in Contemporary Society," hosted by UNESCO on July 15–18, 1974.[9] Unfortunately he passed away mere days before the event.

Ramses Wissa Wassef surrounded by students, c.1940.

Professorship

Wissa Wassef not only has merits as an architect, innovator, and patron of the arts. There are other facets of his life where he excelled in shaping young people's lives. As mentioned previously, he taught crafts at the Ramses Wissa Wassef Art Center and designed other projects that also fulfilled this role. He was a born teacher, but he confronted an inevitable challenge arising from Egypt's sociocultural context during his lifetime. The country had adopted an imported framework of educational practices that largely failed to bridge the gap between the applied methodology and the student. Moreover, Wissa Wassef believed that Egypt's nascent industrialization threatened to kill peoples' sense of wonder and curiosity, the motivating force behind true education. Despite all obstacles, he placed his hope in an optimistic vision of the power of art to enhance the life experience of humans in this world. This could be viewed in his role as a noninstructive teacher at the Ramses Wissa Wassef Art Center, but also as an academic instructor in the university.

Wissa Wassef joined the Faculty of Fine Arts in Zamalek, Helwan University, as a professor in 1938. He taught history of art and history of architecture. In 1957 he became the department chair, a post he held until 1968, when he retired.[1] In 1955 he and Fathy successfully proposed a change to the department's didactic system. The new educational system would be based on a division of the students into three ateliers. This fresh approach was very similar to the system used at the École des Beaux Arts de Paris.[2] The idea behind this new method was to improve the architectural abilities and talents of the students. It is very likely that this move was responding to the two professors' interest in revolutionizing Egyptian public education. The approach was decidedly more participatory than the old traditional method, in which each student had been expected to work individually.

Wissa Wassef himself created many of the visuals and teaching aids he used in his lectures on the history of art and architecture. These varied from examples of prehistoric art to

Sasanian, Assyrian, ancient Egyptian, Roman, and Greek art and architecture—including plans, sections, and elevations of these—and iconic European classical architecture, as well as column bases and capitals. The renderings are exquisitely drawn and demonstrate Wissa Wassef's commitment as a university professor to his students and lectures.[3]

During his three decades as a professor at the Faculty of Fine Arts, Wissa Wassef guided a large number of young people who later on became well-known artists and architects, many of them making their own mark on Egypt's contemporary culture. Among his students were the likes of 'Abd al-Ghani Abul-'Enein, painter and writer; Adam Henein, sculptor and painter; Essam Safey El Din, architect; George Bahgoury, internationally acclaimed French–Egyptian painter and sculptor;[4] Mohie al-Din Hussein, a noted ceramist and artist; Mustafa Gayid, professor of interior design; Nessim Henry Henein, artist and architecture/archaeology writer; Nagi Shaker, artist in cinema and theater and a renowned pioneer in puppet design; and Shadi 'Abd al-Salam, cinema director, script writer, and set designer who, as a second career, decided to study architecture under Wissa Wassef's tutelage, working directly with him as his assistant in 1956.[5]

Among these, a few would follow Wissa Wassef to Harraniya, seeking affordable refuge among the agricultural surroundings. Adam Henein recalls: "Ramses impressed me in such [a] manner that I ended up following him to Harraniya."[6] Wissa Wassef even built the dual houses and studios for 'Abd al-Ghani Abul-'Enein, Adam Henein, and Mohie al-Din Hussein.

It is noteworthy to mention that Essam Safey El Din would go on to convert the House of Ali Labib, Hassan Fathy's formed residence in Darb al-Labbana, into Bayt al-Mi'mar al-Masri (the House of Egyptian Architecture), a museum that among its collection of drawings and models has dedicated exhibitions for Hassan Fathy and Ramses Wissa Wassef.

FROM TOP LEFT, CLOCKWISE:
Teaching material: Iraq, Babylon, ornamentation from the palace of Nebuchadnezzar II.
Teaching material: Rome, bas-relief stone ornamentation, at the Temple of Mars.
Teaching material: Rome, Pantheon.

PART 2

A Descriptive Catalog

This visual and descriptive catalog explores the story behind Ramses Wissa Wassef's projects, accompanied by his drawings as well as archival and new photographs. Despite his large repertoire, much of Wissa Wassef's work is nonextant—whether due to being demolished or remaining unbuilt. Accordingly, this catalog is divided into two sections: extant and nonextant. The latter section includes projects with unknown status due to insufficient information surrounding them that might otherwise lend a clue as to their location and condition. Under these sections, Wissa Wassef's work falls under four main sub-themes—the Ramses Wissa Wassef Art Center, churches, residences, and educational/cultural projects—with "other" added for designs that do not fall into any of these categories. Within these thematic categories, projects are listed chronologically based on the earliest date found for the design. If project drawings are undated, then the construction or inauguration date is used, and if neither apply then it is left undated. Projects not included in this description are those known to have been designed by Wissa Wassef for which there is no visual information available, whether in the form of drawings or photographs.[7]

Projects are named based on how they are labeled in the drawings; if the name appears in French or Arabic then the translation is offered as the title. Alternative names for the projects are provided; these can include transliterated names, variants, or the colloquial name.

The Ramses Wissa Wassef Art Center complex.

Extant

RAMSES WISSA WASSEF ART CENTER

The Ramses Wissa Wassef Art Center is the project for which Wissa Wassef is best known. It is the epitome of his experimentation with traditional construction methods, particularly mud brick, and his belief in the innate creative power and potential of children. It is here that he taught young children to weave and express their creativity, without any formal arts training, in the tapestries that they create, for which the center is internationally acclaimed.

The center occupies an area of approximately 50,000 square meters,[1] with the first plot of land purchased in 1951 occupying 2,200 square meters. The land that is not occupied by buildings is predominantly used as agricultural land, where some of the crops grown generate the dyes used in the cotton and wool yarn for weaving. There is also a garden between the main residential buildings.

The center was built incrementally by Wissa Wassef, who purchased the land over five phases between 1951 and 1969. Most of the construction was carried out after 1962 due to the international success of the tapestry exhibitions, which brought in funds for the center. The center continued to grow even after his death, with interventions by Badie Habib Georgi, his brother-in-law; Ikram Nosshi, his son-in-law; and Ramses Ikram Nosshi, his grandson.

VILLAGE ART STUDIO AND GALLERY—PHASE 1

Date: 1952–53
Location: Ramses Wissa Wassef Art Center, Harraniya, Giza
Alternative names: Berlanty Youssef Wissa Wassef Carpet and Kilim Factory, Dar al-Fann, Rest House

The reception or *madyafa* of the rest house. On the wall are watercolors by Sophie Habib Georgi.

This is the first phase of the Ramses Wissa Wassef Art Center, built between 1952 and 1953. Conceived as an experiment, with the success of the project Wissa Wassef drafted the drawn plans in 1955 when he applied for the licensing of the first two buildings he had built. The first structure to be built was a porter's guardroom, with two rooms built of limestone and clay mortar near the gate. This structure was extended in 1953 into a four-domed room, which is attached to a smaller room that continues as a strip of three additional modules acting as shaded spaces. The linearity of the building is emphasized through the introduction of a trellis partition that creates an exterior corridor, shielding the users from the playground on the rest of the land. About a meter away from the building is a small storage space.

Wissa Wassef experimented with the construction of this building, deviating from typical mud-brick structures. He built the foundations in stone, including the base of the walls up to one meter, and completed the rest of the building in mud brick. He tried to replicate this system in other structures such as Cérés's house, but was unsuccessful. In this project he paired the builders from the Abu Alaa family with local builders so they could learn to work with mud brick.[2] Wissa Wassef involved the children, initiating them in the practice of mud-brick construction through observation. It was this team of builders, who learned from the family of Abu Alaa, who would go on to construct the rest of the buildings at the center.[3]

From 1955 this building was used as Wissa Wassef's personal pottery workshop and had a kiln built next to it. In 1961 it was expanded to include pottery activities for the children. It was further expanded (toward the south) in 1989 by Ikram Nosshi; this intervention included the conversion of the trellis partition into a claustra wall. His daughter Suzanne continued to teach and create pottery there until 2010.

The second building, which is located on the western side of the plot, is the rest house. It consists of a double-height domed room with stained-glass stucco panels by Wissa Wassef, used as a *madyafa* (reception room), which opens onto a larger room with a central column used as a tapestry workshop; the building also contained a clinic where the Harraniya children and villagers could seek treatment, and a restroom. It was in these tapestry workshops that the first generation of Harraniya children learned to weave. The building was expanded by Wissa Wassef to be used as a rest house during his and Sophie's visits to the center, and as a weekend and holiday house.

From 1963 to 1964 Ramses and Sophie, along with their daughters Suzanne and Yoanna, moved into the house as a transition between living at the Giza family residence and the Wissa Wassef Aguza residence (described below), which Wissa Wassef jointly built in 1947 with his brother Oziris, who lived in it until the mid-1960s. In 1977 Sophie and Yoanna—along with Suzanne, Ikram, and their children—moved back to the Harraniya house. In 1978 Badie Habib Georgi expanded the 'first-generation' weaving workshops to the west; this was followed in 1979–80 by the construction of additional floors to the house, which were used by Sophie on top of the 'first-generation' workshops. Sophie was joined by Yoanna and her family in 1981.

The external courtyard of the rest house, which consists of the entrance and open staircase.

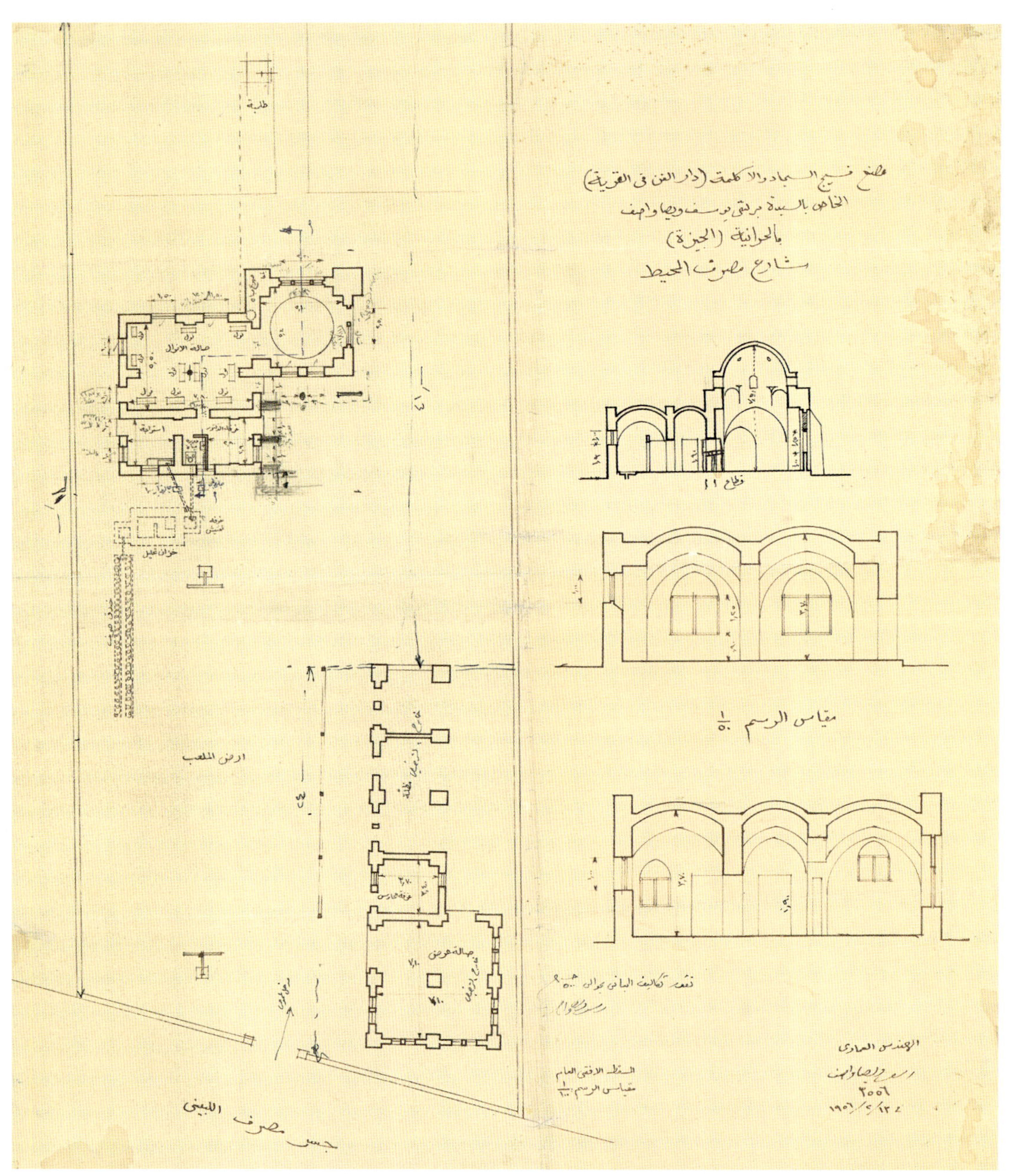

مصنع نسيج السجاد والاكلمة (دار الفن فى القرية)
الخاص بالسيدة برلنتى يوسف ويصا واصف
بالحرانية (الجيزة)
شارع مصرف المحيط
مقياس الرسم ١/٥٠
ارض الملعب
المهندس المعمارى
٢٠٥٦
السقط الافقى العام
مقياس الرسم ١/١٠٠
جسر مصرف اللبينى

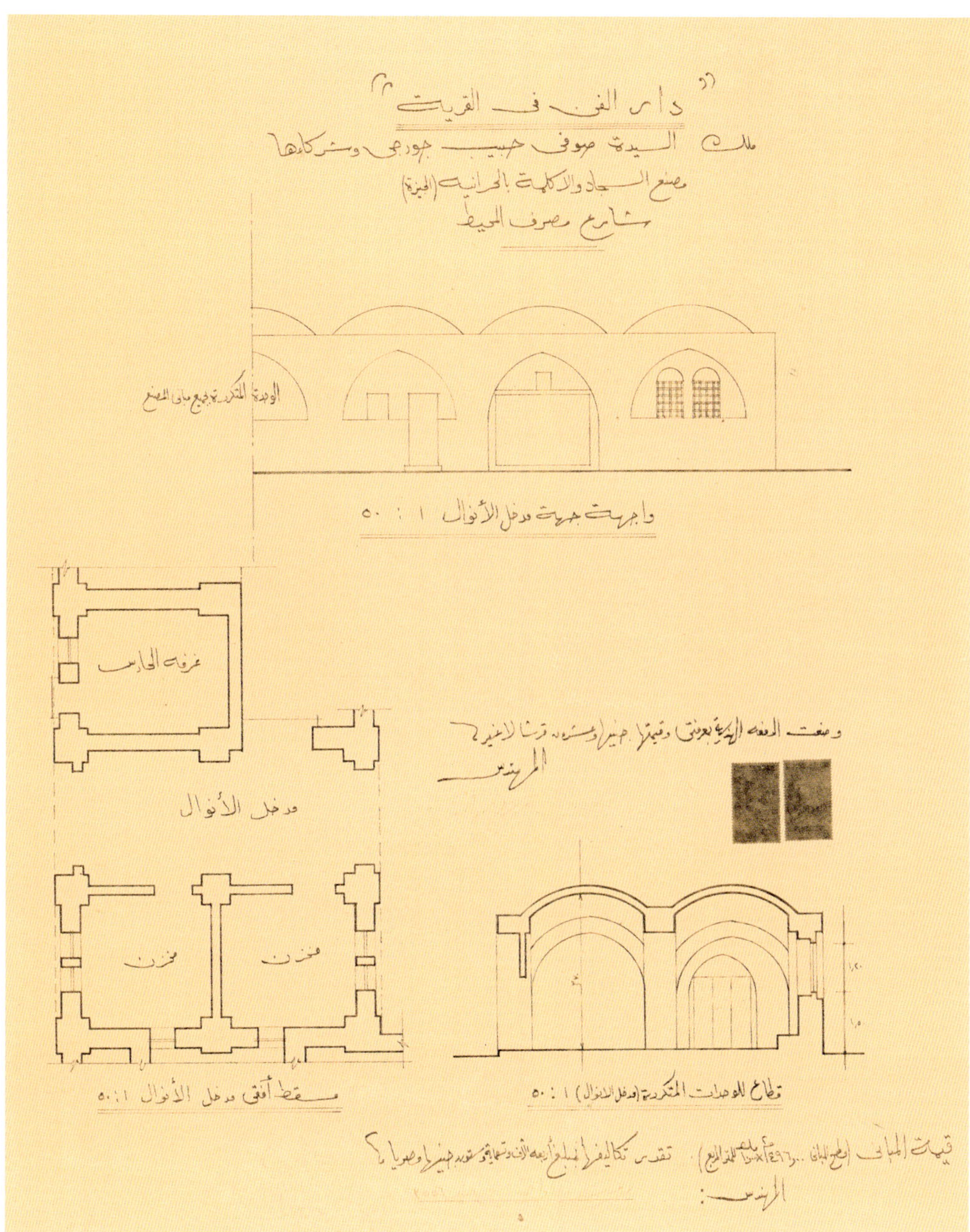

Drawings of the first structure showing Wissa Wassef's 1960s modification including the main elevation (top), section (bottom right), and plan (bottom left).

OPPOSITE PAGE:
Plan of the rest house (top left); sections of the rest house (top right, center right, bottom right); plan of the first structure built after its 1953 extension, which would become Wissa Wassef's personal pottery workshop in 1955 (bottom left).

SOLAR KILN

Date: 1955–56
Location: Ramses Wissa Wassef Art Center, Harraniya, Giza

Since the inception of the art center, Wissa Wassef had wanted children to explore their creativity through different mediums, and that included pottery. He built a solar kiln when he started experimenting with ceramics, including pottery and stoneware, in 1955, which he introduced to the Harraniya children in 1962–63. No drawings or images exist of this kiln, but the family remembers that an elevated solar collector/reflector in the form a plastered dish 3 meters in diameter was lined with mirrors that were focused toward the center of the ground level of the kiln. The solar kiln did not last long and was demolished sometime after. It was replaced with another experimental kiln powered by fuel oil.[4]

The kiln was used to fire porous pottery at 550–600°C, other ceramics with evaporated glazes at 600–1,000°C, and stoneware at 1,000–1,300°C, where the heat enables the clay particles to bind in a nonporous manner. The glazes were made by Wissa Wassef, using a heated stone on which their components were placed; water was poured over to crack the components, allowing them to be ground into a glaze. The heat of the kiln also determined which glazes were used, as some would evaporate while others did not. Achieving the turquoise glaze was the trickiest, as it would require good temperature control to prevent it from turning red, brown, or black. As a result of his research and experimentation with stoneware, Wissa Wassef created different clay mixes and clay glazes.

This kiln was important, not only for educational purposes or the work produced by the center, but also for elements integrated into Wissa Wassef's architectural work—for example, the turquoise hippopotamus and colored tiles in the courtyard of the rest house, or the candlesticks for the Dominican Fathers Priory.

VILLAGE ART STUDIO AND GALLERY—PHASE 2

Date: 1962
Location: Ramses Wissa Wassef Art Center, Harraniya, Giza
Alternative names: Sophie Habib Georgi and Partners Carpet and Kilim Factory, Dar al-Fann

Back of the workshops facing the pottery area and weaving workshops.

After the success of the first international exhibition of the weavers' work in Basel, Switzerland, in 1958, Wissa Wassef expanded the art center with an extension consisting of a gallery and two administration rooms around a courtyard that leads to nine new weaving rooms along the center's iconic curved east–west corridor.

The orientation of this corridor allows for the prevailing wind to enter the workshops, which have brick claustra openings. The gallery is lit via glass oculi inserted in the vaulting and some spotlights; this enables the preservation of the tapestry colors by eradicating direct sunlight. This building was built with rammed earth comprising dry clay mortar, using a mold of 60 × 30 × 30 centimeters.

With the creation of this extension, modifications were made to the buildings of the first phase. The four-domed room adjacent to the new weaving workshops was split in half to create an entrance for the looms, the rest to be used as storage with the addition of another room and the expansion of the original storage space. However, Wissa Wassef added extra weaving studios not long afterward, in 1965–66.

In 1968 Wissa Wassef built a cross-vaulted, two-room apartment above the administration offices. This apartment was used by a weaver who had previously lived in Shubra until her family passed away. Wissa Wassef invited her to come live at the center, as she was unable to live on her own.

The gallery was used as a canteen with a small kitchen until 1970–71, when Wissa Wassef expanded it to be used as a tapestry exhibition space and store. Badie Habib added three small domes on the western side of the tapestry exhibition space in 1978.

Exterior of the gallery extension. Wissa Wassef salvaged an old door from a garbage dump in Historic Cairo and integrated it into the building.

Curved corridor on which weaving workshops are aligned.

Extension to the workshops.

Interior of gallery and store.

Gallery section dedicated to batiks.

Interior of one of the workshops with a window.

Interior of one of the workshops with a claustra.

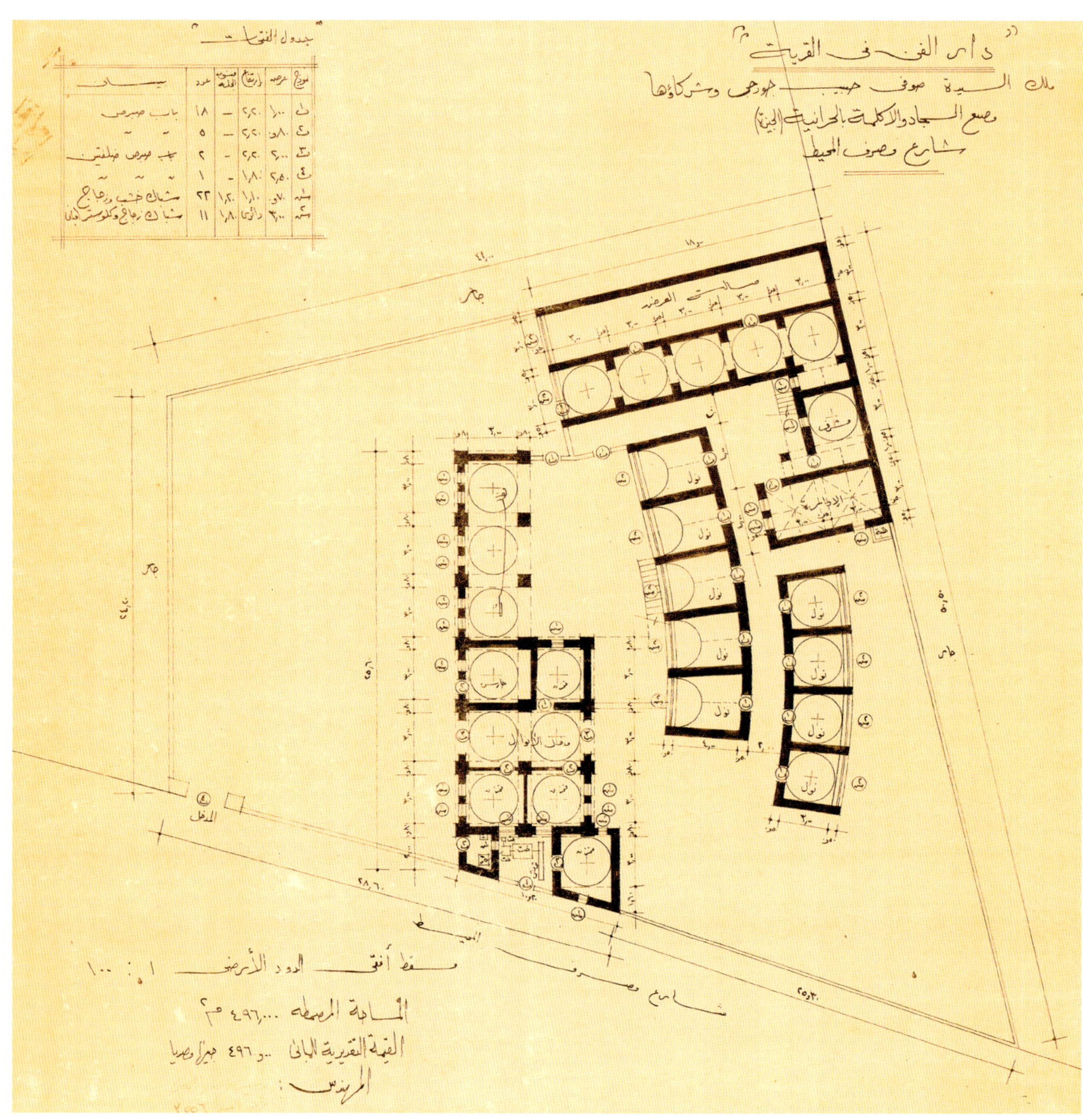

Ground floor plan of the weaving workshops and gallery.

HABIB GEORGI MUSEUM

Date: 1967–70

Location: Ramses Wissa Wassef Art Center, Harraniya, Giza

North elevation.

The museum houses the works produced in the 1940s and 1950s by the students of the sculptor Habib Georgi, as a tribute to his life's work as a sculpting teacher. Habib Georgi was Wissa Wassef's father-in-law and close friend. The museum is designed to showcase the sculptures, and integrates natural-lighting shafts to emphasize these pieces.

This is achieved by the creation of double walls with shafts that have a high opening on the outside and a lower opening on the inside of the building that takes the form of an alcove on which sculptures are exhibited. Depending on the time of the day, this museum and its collection is experienced differently due to the changing light. Wissa Wassef spent six months experimenting with a model of the museum and a table lamp, studying the indirect natural lighting throughout the day and through the seasons while testing and determining the ratios of the shaft openings.

The atmosphere created by the dim rooms, highlighted by the lit alcoves and openings, brings drama to the presentation of the sculptures. The exhibits and the building are in harmony, as the pieces present themselves as part of the building's fabric.

The water table in Maryutiya has been increasing over the years, causing salt and structural damage to the museum. This was so severe that parts of the museum developed severe cracks and collapsed in 2008. One of the walls supporting the main Nubian vault was settling, causing it to lean and the vault to fail. The museum was restored in 2009, under the supervision of Ramses Ikram Nosshi, Wissa Wassef's grandson, with some modifications to the design. The Nubian vault was reconstructed, and the western wall embedded with the lighting shafts and alcoves saved with the addition of stone buttresses. To preserve the main dome, three arches were built as additional support. To prevent future damage of the structure and deterioration of its adobe bricks, an insulation layer that prevents the humidity in the foundations from traveling up the walls was installed throughout the building. Additionally, the museum entrance was modified; previously the building was entered from outside the Ramses Wissa Wassef Art Center or through the porter's house, which was demolished during the restoration. The museum can now be entered via the center's garden.

West elevation, including the buttresses added in the 2009 restoration.

Main dome as viewed from the roof access stairs by the main entrance.

Central hall.

View from central hall toward the vaulted hall.

South end of the vaulted hall.

FROM TOP LEFT, CLOCKWISE:
Exterior corridor.
Combination of alcoves, *mastabas*, and see-through openings for display.
Close-up of an alcove.

Original gate from the street into the museum entrance courtyard, with the porter's house on the right.

View of the museum in its original form.

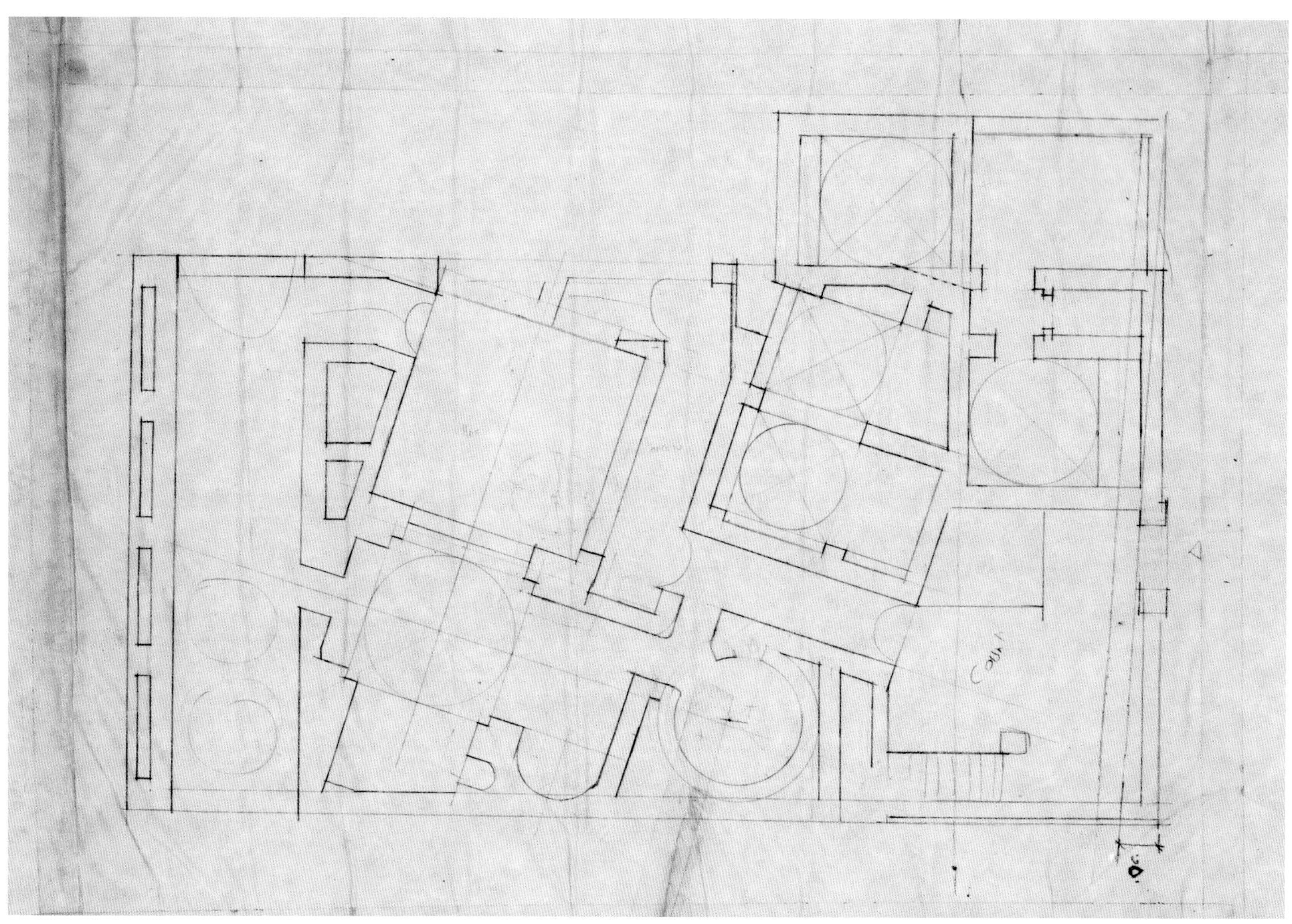

Plan of the museum.

RESTORED
RECONSTRUCTED
NEW CONSTRUCTION
DEMOLISHED PORTER'S HOUSE
CIRCULATION
GROUND DRAINING & WELL SYSTEM

0 2.50 m 5.00 m

Annex Watercolor Gallery
Store
Main Vault Hall 1
Open Court 2
Open Court 1
Central Dome Hall 2
Hall 3
Well Draining

Plan of the museum following the 2009 restoration.

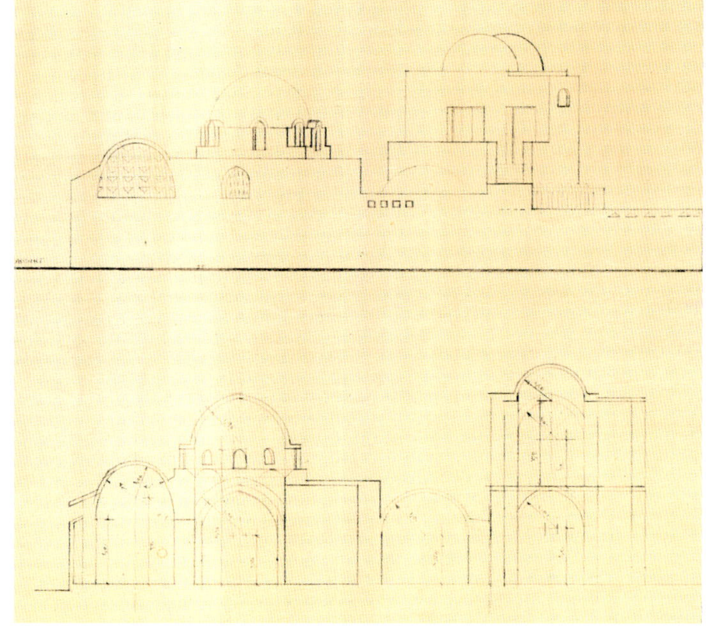

FROM TOP LEFT, CLOCKWISE:
Alternative proposal for the museum.
South elevation of the museum (top), section (bottom).
Sketches of the alcoves and how they introduce light.

CHICKEN COOPS AND TOOLSHED

Date: c.1962–63 and c.1968–69
Location: Ramses Wissa Wassef Art Center, Harraniya, Giza

This was Wissa Wassef's first experiment with teaching the children who attended the weaving school in Harraniya how to build with mud brick. Accommodating to the beginner's skill set and the height of the children, who were aged 14 to 16, Wissa Wassef chose to teach them through the creation of chicken coops. Each coop is approximately 1 meter wide by 2 meters long and roofed with a Nubian vault. Later, around 1968–69, Wissa Wassef built another coop with 3-meter diameter domes. The first set of chicken coops was expanded by Ikram Nosshi in 1974–75. Following on from this exercise, the children built a toolshed comprising a Nubian vault and supported by buttresses.

Chicken coops (left) and toolshed (right).

SILOS

Date: c.1969

Location: Ramses Wissa Wassef Art Center, Harraniya, Giza

Silos.

Back view of silos.

An agglomeration of six grain silos was designed by Wissa Wassef and constructed by the Harraniya children as a learning exercise in building with mud brick. The composition is quite playful, with the varying heights of the silos as well as the curvature of their domes and their varying diameters. The tops are accessible via a spiral staircase that embraces one of the central silos, reaching the leveled area between the domes. The silos are emptied via a metal hatch at the bottom.

CÉRÉS WISSA WASSEF VILLA

Date: 1970
Location: Ramses Wissa Wassef Art Center, Harraniya, Giza

Northwest corner of the house, c.1983/1984, a view that is now blocked with tree canopies.

This house was built for Cérés Wissa Wassef, Ramses's sister, and can be considered a highlight of the architect's residential work. As he confessed to Cérés, he had built her the "house he always wanted for himself."[5] Since Cérés passed away in 2008 at the age of 99, the dwelling has been used as a storage space, which prevents access and the appreciation of its spaces. The house was described quite eloquently by the Aga Khan Award review:

> A bent entrance leads into a domed entrance hall, deliberately lower than and out of alignment with the spaces beyond. The dining and living areas flow into each other and the pivotal position is occupied by the tall dome, which is reflected in the marble fountain set in the floor beneath. An arched aperture between the two flights of stairs draws the eyes upwards and on the first-floor landing the way out on to the southwestern roof terrace cunningly negotiates the shoulder of the dome.[6]

The ground floor was built with limestone and clay mortar, a more budget-friendly alternative than cement mortar, with room corners using cement mortar for its stronger properties. However, the clay mortar does not bind the limestone as well as it does mud brick, and the first floor was continued in limestone and cement mortar. The house is raised 1.20 meters above the ground level to accommodate the garage and pump room underneath.[7] The vaults are constructed from red brick and cement mortar. Initially the building was designed without buttresses but Wissa Wassef added them, worried that the upper story would not support the lateral thrust of the vaults.[8] This unplanned intervention is one of the most emblematic external features of the house accentuating its form, particularly in the north and west elevations with the varying levels, and making it appear as if it has grown from the ground despite its tall height.

FROM LEFT, CLOCKWISE:
East elevation, c.1983/1984.
Hall with stairs leading down to the garage and up to the first floor.
Living space with fountain, c.1983/1984.

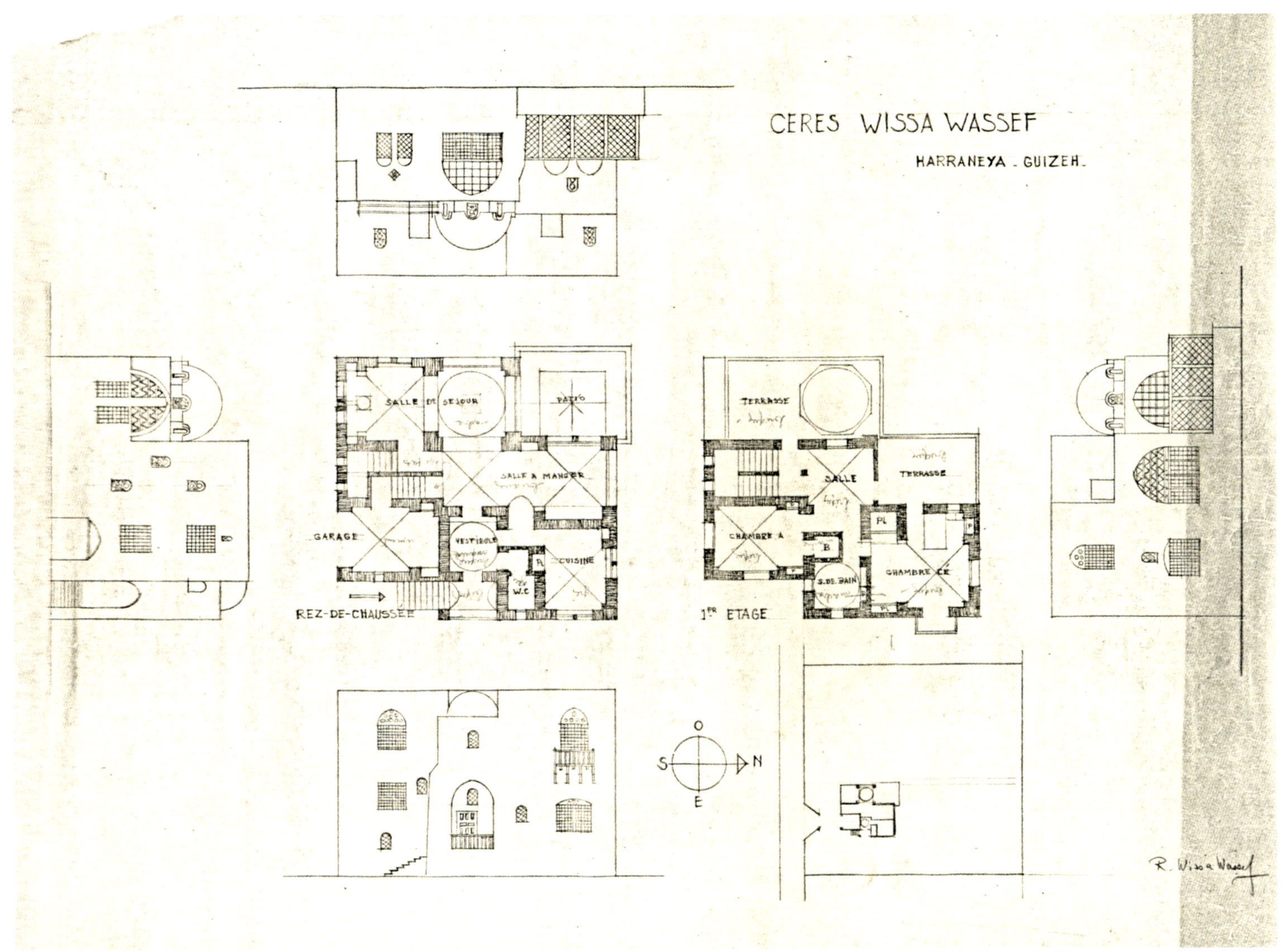

Ground floor plan (center left), first floor plan (center right), west elevation (top), south elevation (left), north elevation (right), east elevation (bottom left), site plan (bottom right).

SEVEN WEAVERS' HOUSES

Date: 1970

Location: Ramses Wissa Wassef Art Center, Harraniya, Giza

Images of the houses after the addition of the upper floor by Badie Habib, showing the house courtyards.

This complex of seven houses located southwest of the Ramses Wissa Wassef Art Center, beyond the fields, was designed for the weavers who worked at the center and did not have their own land or homes. They are arranged in a U shape around a central courtyard, with an alley that leads directly to Harraniya village.

Each dwelling consists of a large vaulted room with an *iwan* (a vaulted recess) and furnished with a *mastaba*, with two smaller detached rooms for the bathroom and kitchen, and a walled courtyard containing a chicken coop and bread oven. An exterior staircase leads to the upstairs room, intended as a vaulted storage and sleeping area. Each house is unique in its arrangement of its rooms and walled garden, with a central garden between the houses, as Wissa Wassef let the weavers discuss the requirements for their homes and gave them clay to model their own distribution of the functions:[9] he was already engaged in participatory design, a method ahead of his time.

Although houses were designed for seven weavers, only six ended up moving in: Karima Ali, Fatma 'Awad, Shehata Hamza, 'Ashur Misilhi, 'Atiyat Selim, and Muhammad Musa. Wissa Wassef passed away before the completion of the houses. At that point in time, only the ground floors had been built, in limestone and mud mortar, to which Badie Habib Georgi added the upper stories in mud brick and mud mortar and roofed them with red-brick groin vaults in 1977, following Wissa Wassef's initial design.[10] Sometime later, the weavers started moving out for varying reasons—choosing financial compensation to purchase houses elsewhere, and returning the dwellings to the Wissa Wassef family. In 1983 Sophie and Badie Habib made alterations and additions to these houses and rented them to teachers at El Alsson School, which had opened the previous year in Harraniya, not far from the art center. In 1994 four of these residences were renovated further by Ikram Nosshi so they could continue to be rented out.

Images of the houses after the addition of the upper floor by Badie Habib, showing the entrance to the courtyards.

Closeup of one of the houses.

One of the houses as seen today after the alterations conducted in the 1980s and 1990s.

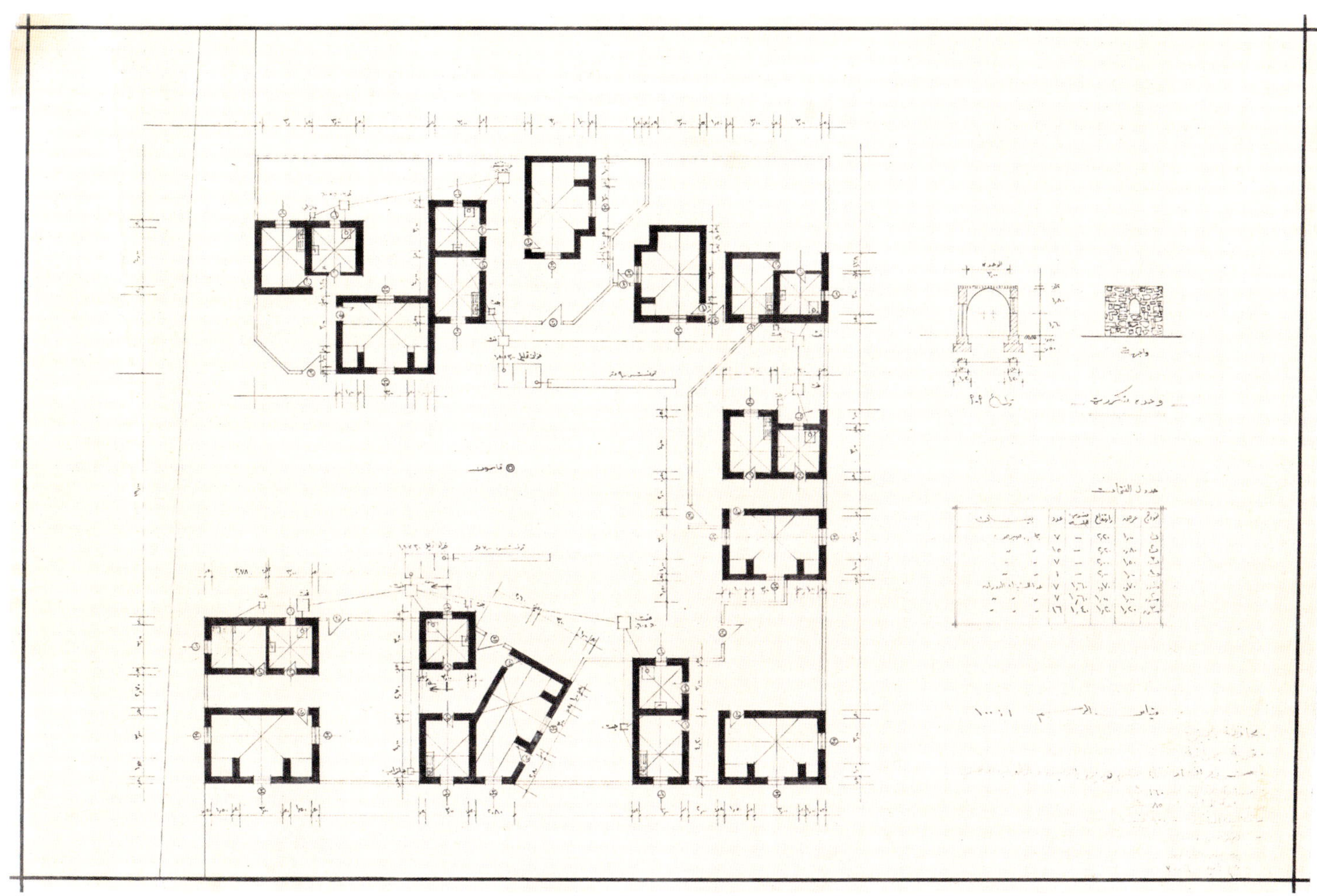

Layout of the seven houses arranged in a U shape.

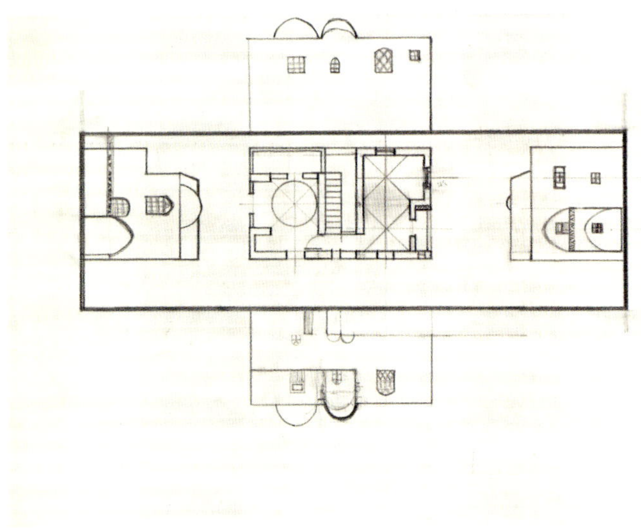

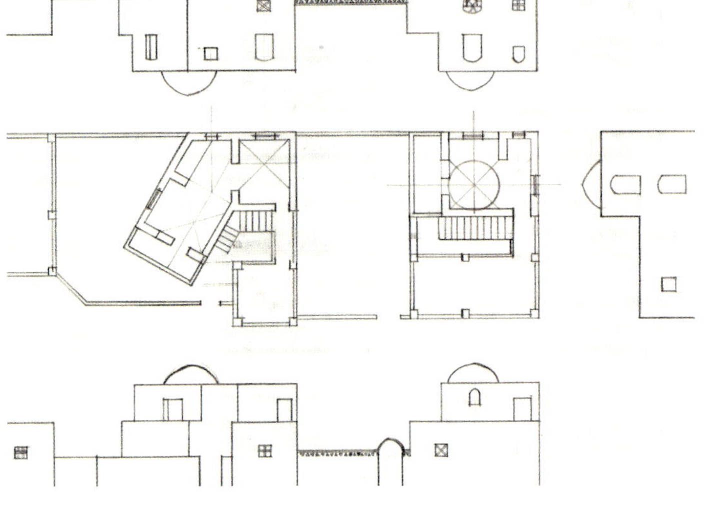

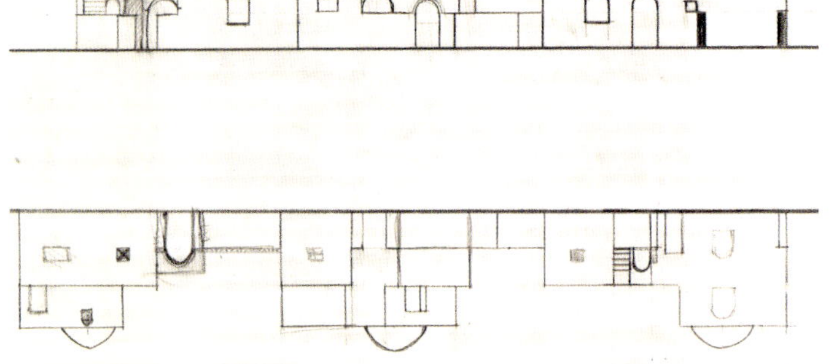

FROM LEFT, CLOCKWISE
Plan and elevations of one of the houses.
Plans and elevations of two houses.
Elevations of three of the houses aligned in a row.

SECOND-GENERATION WEAVING WORKSHOPS

Date: 1971
Location: Ramses Wissa Wassef Art Center, Harraniya, Giza

Wissa Wassef was generous to those around him. The art center's guard did not like living in the village of Harraniya, so Wissa Wassef built him a modest house west of the weaving workshops. A few years later, in 1971, when this building was no longer needed, and Suzanne, his daughter, was preparing to instruct the second generation of weavers, he modified it, retaining some parts of the original structure. Suzanne did not want this second generation of weavers to be close to the existing weavers' workshops so they would not be influenced by their work and would be truly able to harbor their innate creativity, so this relatively remote structure became the studios for the new group of young learners.

Second-generation weaving workshop.

ENGINEER MOUNIR NOSSHI VILLA

Date: 1971
Location: Ramses Wissa Wassef Art Center, Harraniya, Giza

This house was built in 1971 for Mounir Nosshi, Wissa Wassef's friend who would become Suzanne's father-in-law by her marriage to his son Ikram two years later. During construction, the house was modified according to Mounir Nosshi's needs.[11] The ground floor has a small entrance porch leading to a vestibule, from which access may be gained to the living areas—including a terrace, dining room, study, bathroom, stairs, and kitchen. There is also a garage for two cars with direct access to the kitchen. Upstairs there are four bedrooms, two bathrooms, two terraces, and a service room. Groin vaults, adopted for both stories, comprise the main roofing system. The walls are constructed with limestone and cement mortar, while the vaults and domes are of red brick and cement. The exquisite carpentry used in this house sets it apart from the other buildings at the center. An annex was added to the house by Ikram Nosshi in 1994, connected to it by an elevated bridge room.

North view of the house, c.1983/1984.

FROM TOP LEFT, CLOCKWISE:
Living room, c.1983/1984.
Living spaces, c.1983/1984.
South view close up, c.1983/1984.

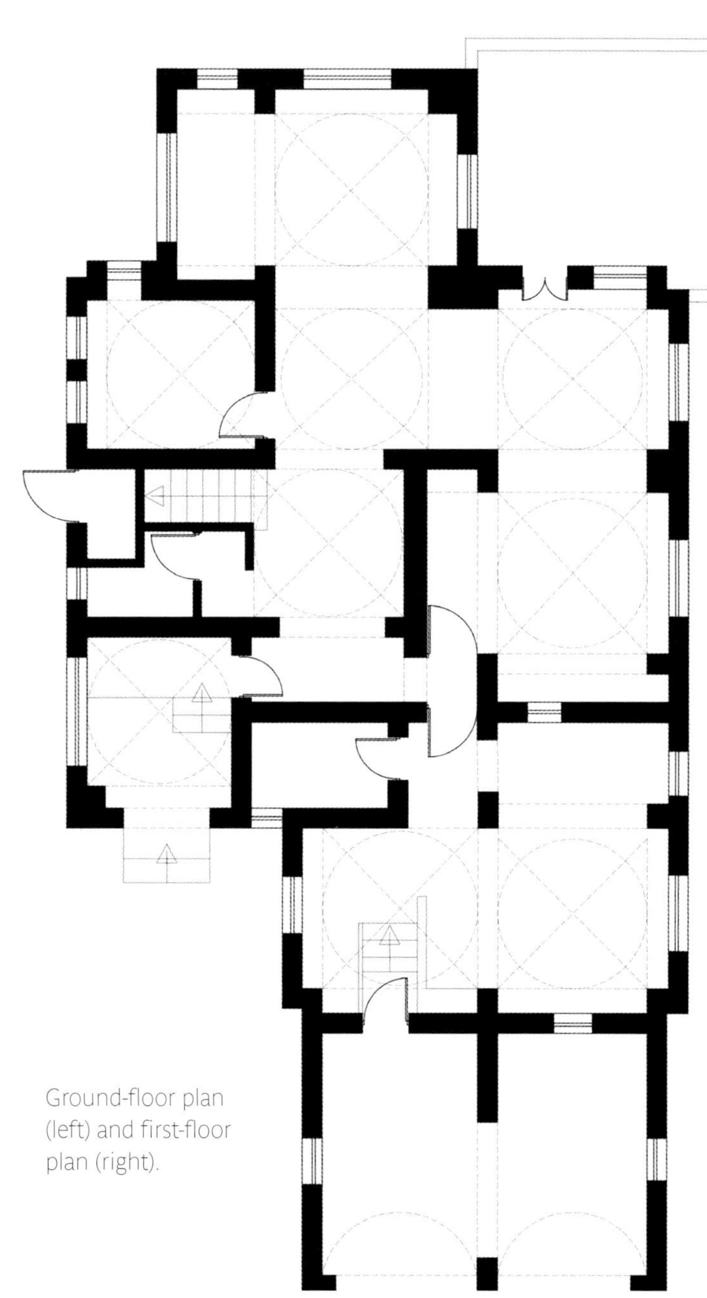

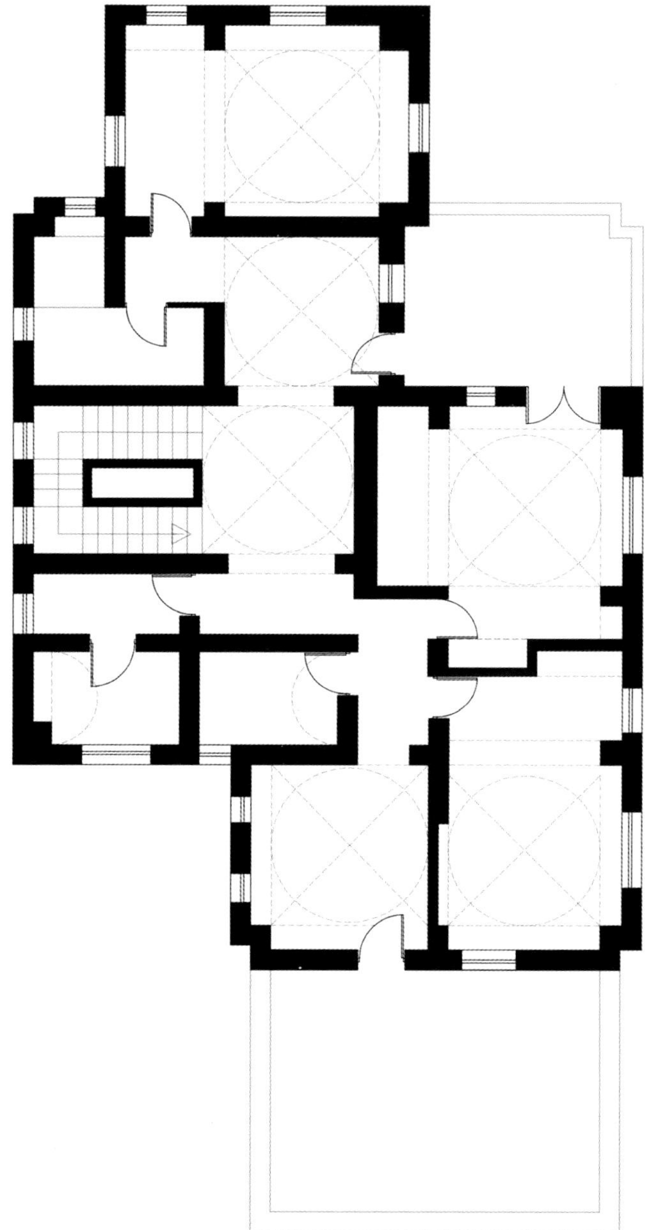

Ground-floor plan (left) and first-floor plan (right).

TEMPORARY CHAPEL

Date: 1972
Location: Ramses Wissa Wassef Art Center, Harraniya, Giza

In 1972, Suzanne Ramses Wissa Wassef became engaged to Ikram Nosshi. For the occasion of the engagement party, Wissa Wassef built a small chapel. It was the first time a priest had come to Harraniya to conduct prayers, making it an important event in the village. Everyone celebrated, as the weavers and villagers were invited to attend. This chapel consisted of a single mud-brick *iwan*. Since this was a temporary structure, made specifically for the event, it was demolished soon afterward.

POSTHUMOUS ADDITIONS

In 1978 Badie Habib Georgi built a northeastern expansion to the tapestry workshops, run by Yoanna Ramses Wissa Wassef, dedicated to fine cotton weaving and batik for the new generation of children. In front of this building is a water basin used to wash the batiks. In 1975 Ikram Nosshi had built a new domed silo with a spiral staircase, adjacent to what would become the Permanent Tapestry Collection Museum. Also known as the Ramses Wissa Wassef Museum, this building with a covered roof terrace was built in 1989 by Badie Habib and his sister Sophie. Ikram Nosshi built a house for himself, Suzanne, and their family next door to his father's house in 1983. The most recent addition to the center was the storage building adjacent to the Permanent Tapestry Collection Museum, built by Ikram Nosshi in 2012.

Given the changing conditions of Harraniya in recent years—making the center prone to rising damp, which causes structural damage—many of the buildings were insulated by Ramses Ikram Nosshi as a preventative measure to avoid the damage suffered by the Habib Georgi Museum occurring in other buildings. This was done by cutting a 1-meter-long horizontal strip at a height of about 30 centimeters above the ground and with a depth of half the wall thickness, in which to insert insulation sheets. This repair niche was then sealed with brick. This process was repeated along the full length of the wall in 1-meter sections, and then replicated on the other side of the wall so the insulation is placed underneath the whole wall without having to dismantle it.

This group of newer buildings is located west of the main weaving studios. This image shows Ikram Nosshi's 1975 silo (front left); Badie Habib Georgi's 1989 Permanent Tapestry Collection Museum, also known as the Ramses Wissa Wassef Museum (back); and Nosshi's 2012 storage building (front right).

CHURCHES

CHURCH OF THE ARCHANGEL MICHAEL IN SHUBRA

Date: 1952
Location: Yusuf ibn Ayyub Street, Tusun, Shubra, Cairo
Alternative names: Kanisat al-Malak Mikha'il, Kanisat ra'is al-mala'ika al-jalil Mikha'il bi-Tusun

Interior shot of church.

Wissa Wassef's role in the creation of this church is something of a mystery. The church was established in 1937 in a temporary structure; the current building, following a basilica plan, was built in 1952 and is the same as the one in Wissa Wassef's archive drawings. The church's own historical narrative credits Engineer Fawzi Mansur with the design of the church, also naming the site supervisors and the contractor, with no mention of Wissa Wassef.[26] The paintings and mosaics were added to the church incrementally, predominantly between the 1970s and the 1990s, and are mostly signed by artists Galal Ramzy and Isaac Fawzy. The plan in Wissa Wassef's archive is annotated in pencil, proposing changes in dimensions, steel reinforcement, and the design of the stairs and dome over the altar—suggesting that Wissa Wassef might have been a consultant on this project, even if unofficially.

Interior side shot of church.

Interior shot of church from gallery.

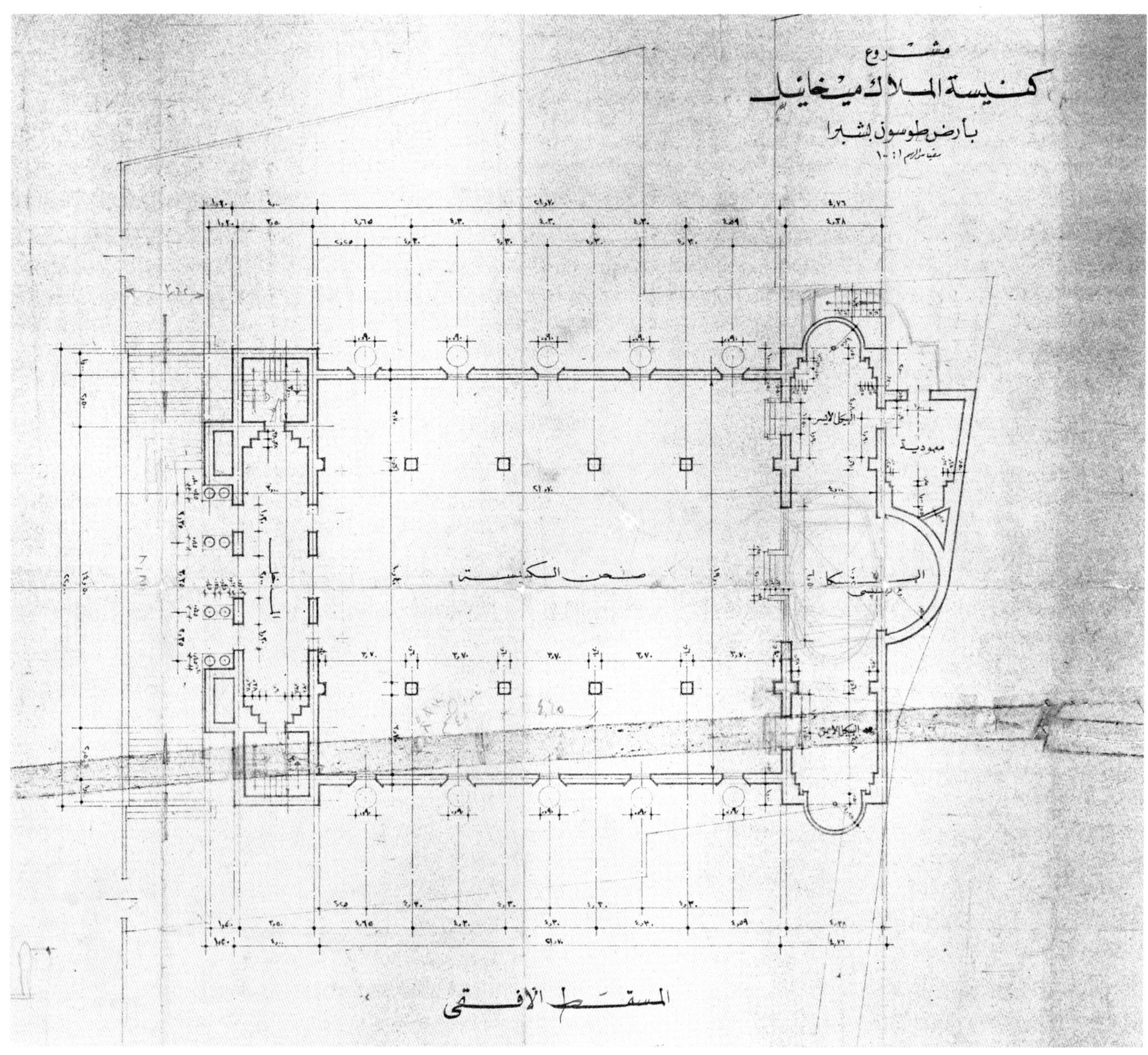

Annotated photocopy of plan.

DOMINICAN FATHERS PRIORY CHAPEL RENOVATION

Date: 1953, chapel renovation (extant); 1959, roof extension (nonextant)
Location: al-Tarabishi Street, Abbasiya, Cairo
Alternative names: Dominican Institute for Oriental Studies, Institut dominicain d'études orientales (IDEO)

General view of chapel facing the sanctuary. In the right niche, a nativity scene is being set up in anticipation of Christmas.

Built in 1931, the priory was designed by Auguste Perret. The complex was originally envisioned to have three buildings, of which one would have been a nunnery, but only one structure was ever built.[23] The chapel followed a plain monastic style. In the 1950s the priory wanted to renovate the chapel, with the aim of adopting a focus on enculturation, and commissioned Wissa Wassef to implement a more Coptic style.[24]

The south-facing sanctuary initially comprised a recessed niche into which the altar was embedded; the niche was flanked by two smaller altars. Wissa Wassef added depth to the sanctuary, effectively turning it into a room rather than a niche, and recessed the two side altars.

He created a new marble altar with a mosaic Coptic cross, gifted by Fawzy Sebeh, and framed by a *mashrabiya* iconostasis with icons reproduced from a Coptic monastery.[25] He also designed mosaic panels depicting the Stations of the Cross aligned along the east wall. The windows are topped with stained-glass stucco panels depicting Biblical scenes such as those from the stories of Noah's Ark and Jonah and the Whale. Wissa Wassef designed a false ceiling with recessed lateral lines forming a cross over the space. The middle of the cross is emphasized with cross-shaped stained-glass stucco panels inserted into the ceiling.

A smaller side-chapel altar was also designed by Wissa Wassef, for which he created a mosaic background and glazed pottery candlesticks. In another room, used as a receiving office, he designed stucco ceiling-lighting units in the form of plates with a cross.

In 2010 the chapel underwent another renovation led by Frère Jocelyn Dorvault, in which the Stations of the Cross were collected and arrayed in a grid on the northern end of the east wall. The apse was painted blue, and copper lighting pendants were installed.

The existing plans by Wissa Wassef show a 1959 proposal for the addition of some rooms on the roof, which was never implemented.

General view of chapel with garden entrance on the right.

OPPOSITE, FROM TOP LEFT CLOCKWISE:
Marble altar with mosaic cross.
Mosaic panels depicting the Stations of the Cross. Previously these were arrayed through the room but in 2010 were relocated and displayed in this grid formation.
Stained-glass and stucco windows depicting biblical scenes.

IC XC
YC ΘY

Chapel entrance from within the priory. The door is topped with a stained-glass and stucco panel.

The marble altar at the side chapel, framed with mosaic. The candlesticks were also made by Wissa Wassef.

Stucco ceiling lighting unit in the priory's receiving office.

Stucco ceiling of the chapel with stained-glass panels forming a cross and providing indirect lighting.

Exterior view of the garden entrance to the chapel.

Chapel interior prior to Wissa Wassef's redesign.

Chapel interior sometime after Wissa Wassef's redesign.

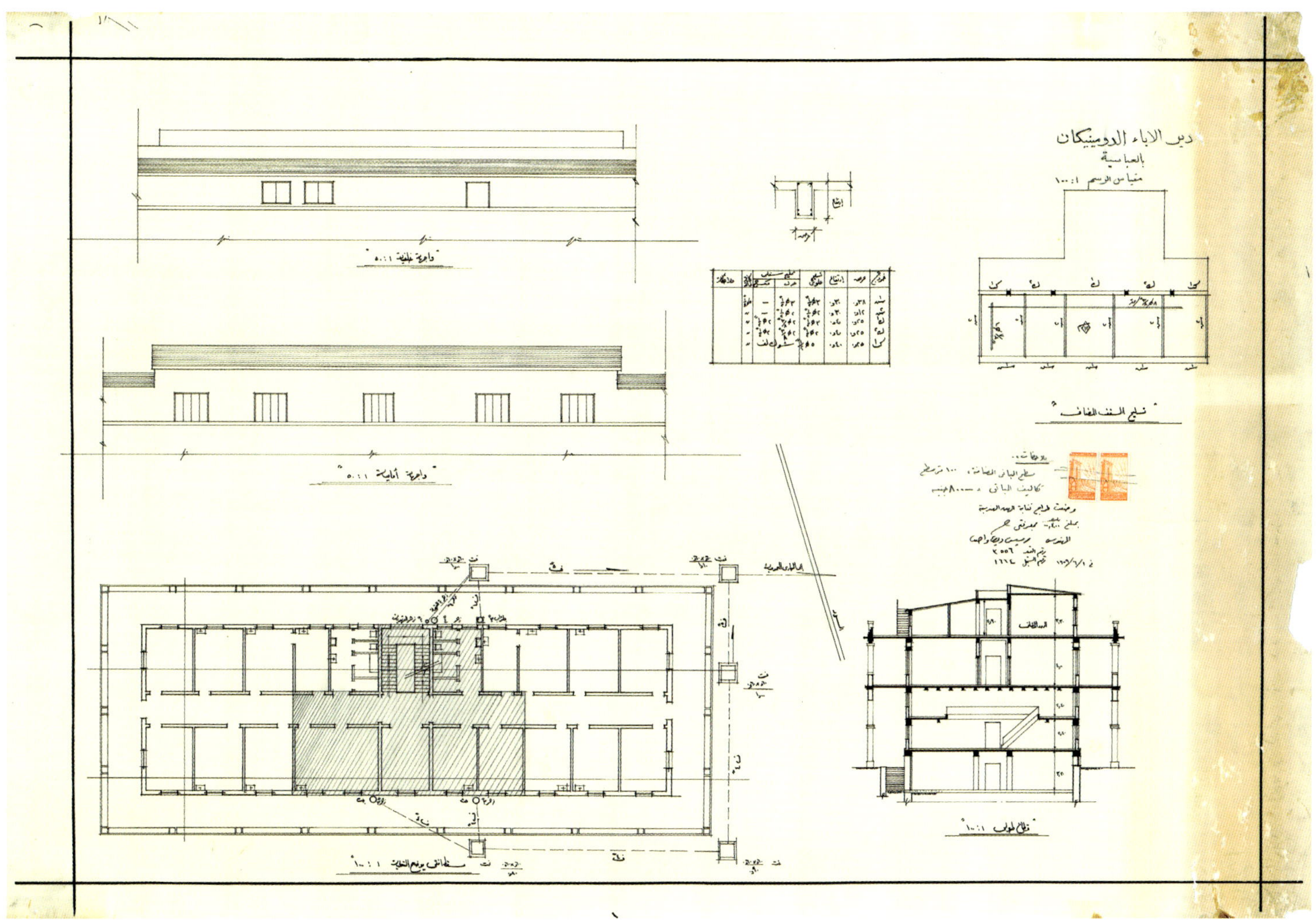

Elevation of extension (top left), section of priory including roof extension (bottom right), plan for the roof extension (bottom left).

ST. GEORGE AND ST. ABRAM CHURCH IN HELIOPOLIS

Date: 1954
Location: Heliopolis Square, Heliopolis, Cairo
Alternative names: Mar Girgis Coptic Orthodox Church in Heliopolis, Great Martyr Mar Girgis and Bishop Abram Church, Kanisat al-shahid al-'azim Mar Girgis wa-l-Anba Abram

This church takes a prominent position on Heliopolis Square. The plan follows a cruciform shape with a large Byzantine dome at its intersection, and half domes on the sides.[12] One enters the church enclosure from the square to find oneself in front of a *doksar*, or domed entrance canopy, the bottom of which is clad in stone to set it in contrast against the rest of the plastered elevation.

On the plane behind and above is a stained-glass stucco panel in the form of a cross depicting St. George. The *doksar* leads to the narthex, which adopts a U shape to envelop the western side of the cruciform plan; at its ends are the stairs that lead to the gallery. In an earlier proposal the narthex was open to the exterior, forming an arcade. The nave is emphasized by its large span uninterrupted by aisles.

The *haykal* (sanctuary) is a hybrid of the building's three apse and triconch forms—in other words, there are three domed spaces from which apses extend to the east, south, and north. The sanctuary is framed and accentuated by a triumphal arch, which in recent years has been clad with wood paneling to create an archivolt for additional contrast.

Side shot of exterior showing the belfry.

Adam Henein was selected to paint the frescoes on the dome of the church. He adopted traditional techniques and pigments, like those used in the historic monasteries of Egypt. At some point halfway through the painting process, the church administration changed its mind and they were painted over.[13] The stained-glass stucco panels in the sanctuary, Byzantine dome, and transept half domes are Wissa Wassef's, while the panels in the nave are the work of another artist. However, at least two of the panels on the Byzantine dome appear to have been replaced, following a style more similar to the ones in the nave rather than the rest of the dome.

There have been some minor modifications to the interior. For example, the iconostasis is not original; the wooden cladding of the triumphal arch was added; and the tall stained-glass panels inside the transept were added in 2015, covering the original window grilles, which would have had an impactful silhouette seen through plain glass. The design of these window grilles starts with a minimalist Coptic cross that has its outline offset radially, creating a visual representation of emitting light rays. Outside, offices and service buildings have been added at the sides of the plot as well as to the east of the church, following the procurement of more land.

Main elevation of church.

Transept window grille.

Gallery window grille.

FROM LEFT, CLOCKWISE:
Main view of church interior.
View of church nave facing the entrance.
Upper transept stained-glass stucco panel by Wissa Wassef.

FROM LEFT, CLOCKWISE:
One of three stucco and stained-glass panels inside the sanctuary.
Byzantine dome stucco and stained-glass panel, number two of twelve.
Byzantine dome stucco and stained-glass panel, number eight of twelve.

كنيسة مارجرجس
للاقباط الارثوذكس
بمصر الجديدة

Plan of the church.

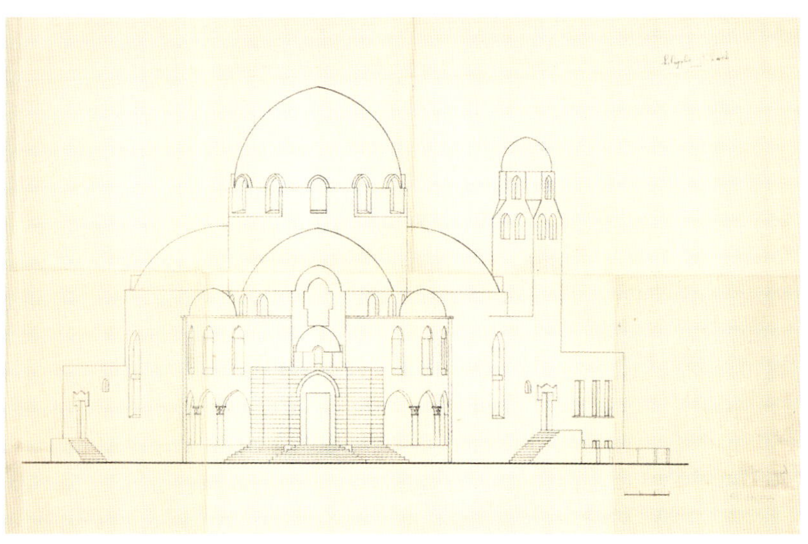

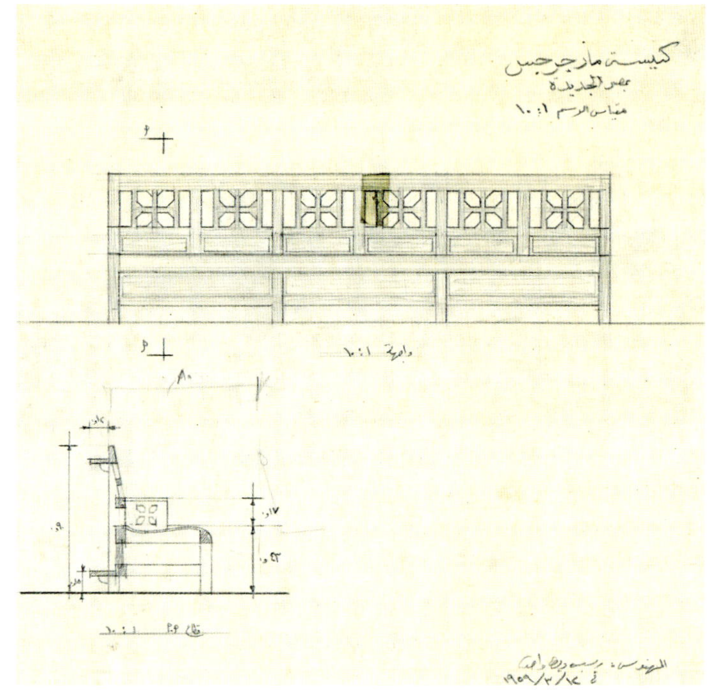

FROM TOP LEFT, CLOCKWISE:
Main elevation of the church, showing a previous proposal for an exonarthex which is open to the exterior as an arcade.
Detailed drawing of the wooden pews.
Section through church.

CHURCH OF THE VIRGIN MARY IN ZAMALEK

Date: 1957
Location: Mar'ashli Street, Zamalek, Cairo
Alternative names: Mar'ashli Church, Kanisat al-Mar'ashli, Kanisat al-qiddisa Maryam al-'adhra' al-qibtiya al-urthudhuksiya bi-l-Zamalik

Church entrance consisting of a large portico embracing a *duksar*. The portico niche is clad in mosaic including a Coptic inscription around the rim.

This outstanding church has become an icon of contemporary Coptic sacred spaces in Egypt, as well as an important landmark within the residential island of Zamalek. Wissa Wassef designed this structure drawing inspiration from pharaonic and traditional Coptic art. The exterior is imposing in scale, with its great height emphasized by vertical elements like the stucco louvered windows, buttresses, portal opening with blue mosaic niche embracing the *doksar*, and telescopic stand-alone belfry.

This 'traditionalist' church[14] follows a boat-shape morphology emphasized by its buttresses and ribs, and a modified Byzantine plan, with the aisle columns removed. It integrates traditional features such as a ciborium over the altar and a triumphal arch over the sanctuary, accentuated through the contrast between the increased natural lighting of the sanctuary and the dimmer choir and nave.

The iconostasis appears to embrace the hall, as the wooden paneling continues along the internal walls as a dado.[15] A door on the right near the iconostasis leads to the baptistery, which used to have a blue mosaic niche designed by Wissa Wassef, replaced in 2009.[16]

A low budget had been set for the project during its initial visualization, so Wissa Wassef initially designed a stouter version of the current church. When the budget was raised, he increased the height—and thus its monumentality. William Selim Hanna was the structural consultant on the project.[17]

The first painted icons were made by Adam Henein, but these were replaced. The existing icons are the works of Margaret Nakhla, Isaac Fanous, Ragheb Ayad, and Emma Kaly Ayad. The church's western wall is adorned with twin vertical tapestries of the Tree of Life woven by Mariam Hermina at the Ramses Wissa Wassef Art Center.[18] The stained-glass stucco windows were designed by Wissa Wassef. At the time, there were limitations on imports into Egypt, due to President Gamal Abd al-Nasser's policies, and Egypt did not manufacture colored glass, and so these windows were made from recycled glass.[19]

Exterior side elevation showing the window grilles.

General view of the church.

Lighting unit and column capital designed by Ramses Wissa Wassef.

TOP LEFT:
Stained-glass and stucco panels over altar and ciborium.

Stained-glass and stucco panels on the interior walls.

FROM TOP LEFT, CLOCKWISE:
Interior view of the church.
Interior northern elevation.
Lectern.
Door and chair designed
by Wissa Wassef.

Church entrance door.

St. George shrine near the entrance.

Perspective of
the church.

Original proposal,
with a stouter design.

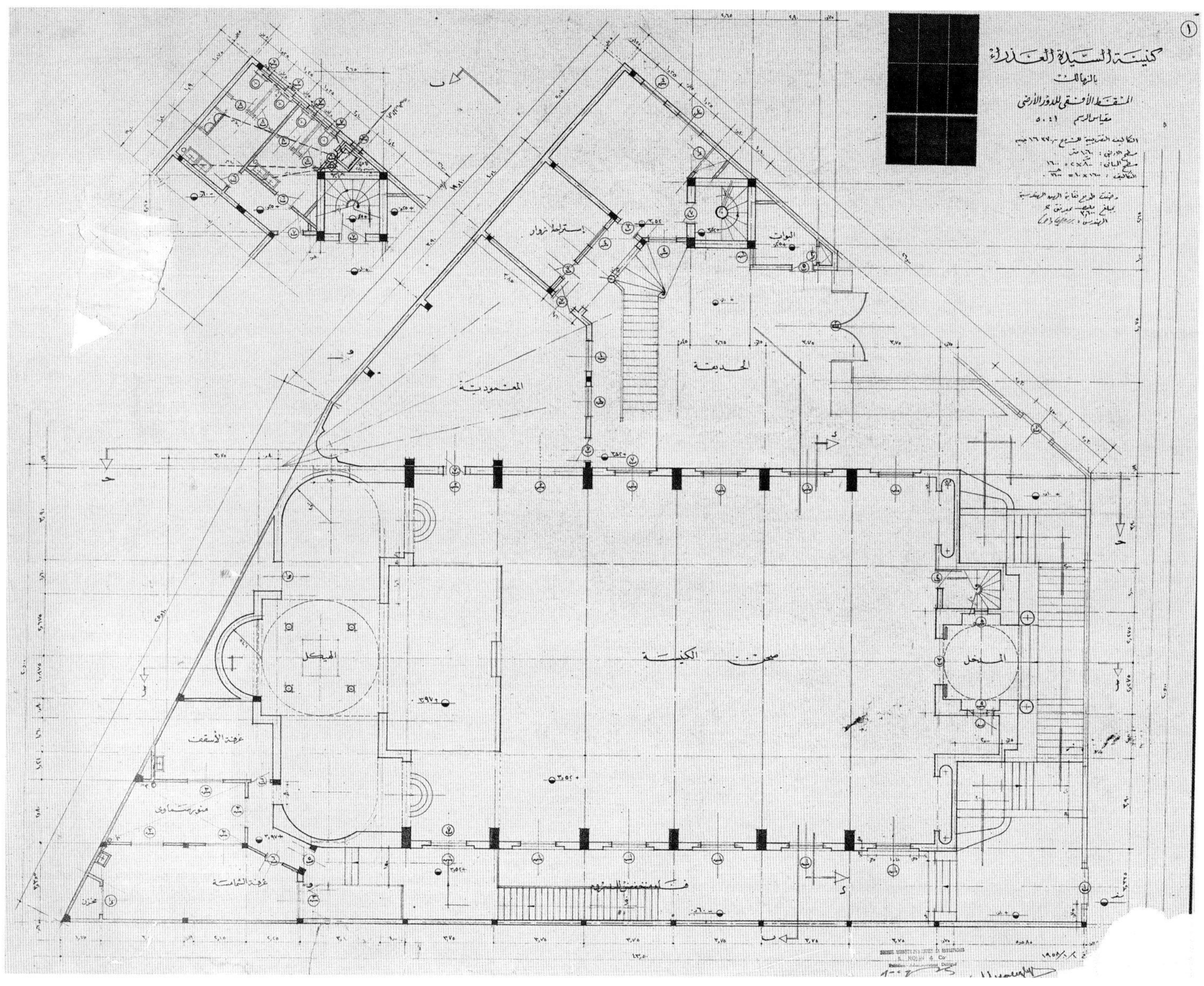

Plan of the church.

Main elevation.

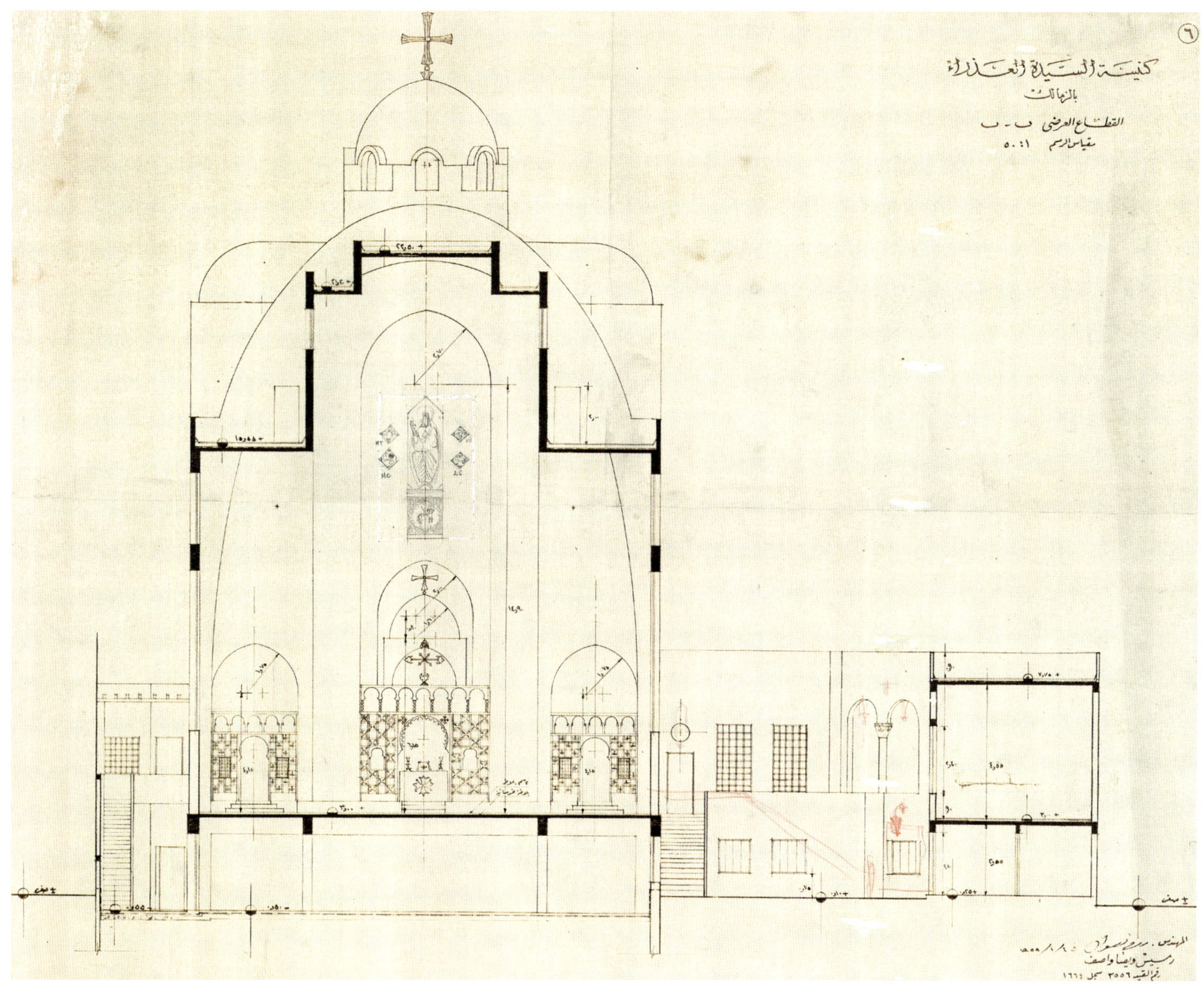

Transverse section showing sanctuary.

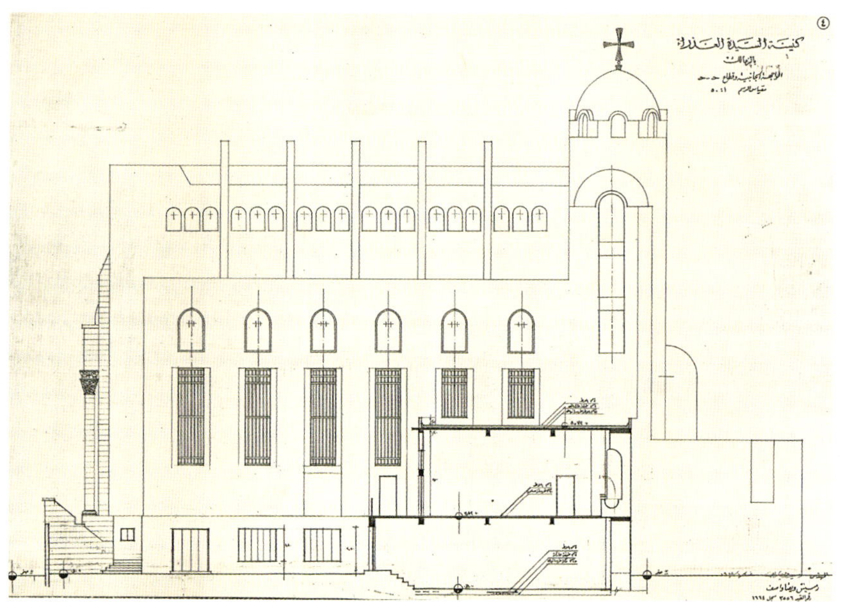

Side elevation including section through annex building.

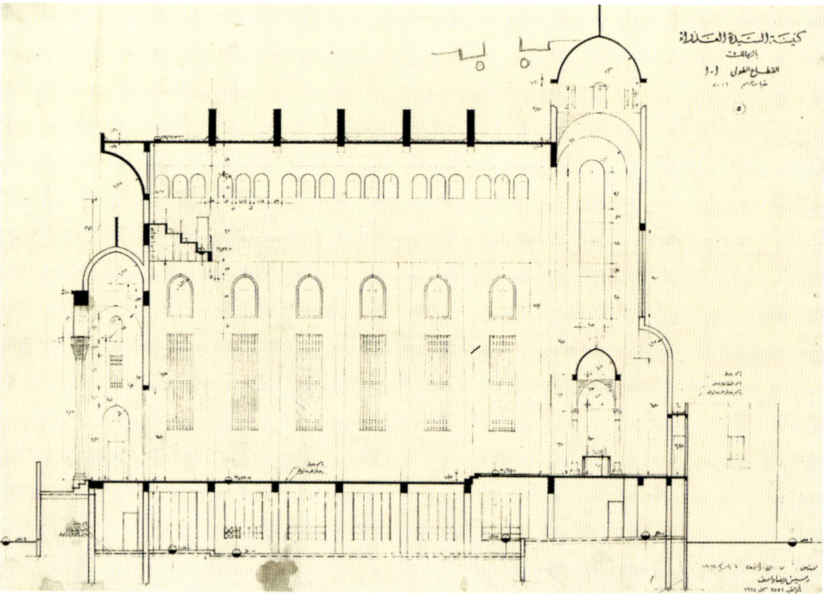

Longitudinal section.

SANCTUARY OF ARCHANGEL MICHAEL COPTIC ORTHODOX CHURCH IN DAMANHUR

Date: 1958
Location: Mahmud al-Habashi Street, Damanhur
Alternative names: Kanisat ra'is al-mala'ika al-jalil Mikha'il al-qibtiya al-urthudhuksiya, Kanisat al-Malak Mikha'il

Sanctuary, showing the triniches and stained-glass and stucco windows designed by Wissa Wassef. The church archive has the watercolor proposals for these four windows. The ciborium is a later addition.

The earliest reference of the Church of the Archangel Michael in Damanhur dates to between the end of the sixteenth and the start of the seventeenth centuries, but it is unknown if the building that existed up to the 1950s was from that time period or later. At the start of the 1950s, work was being conducted on the existing church building to change the *haykal*, or sanctuary, which led to the accidental collapse of the church's roof.[20] The church administration commissioned an architect (whose signature is illegible) and the contractors "Entreprise Ch. & F. Akladious" for its restoration in January 1953.[21] The 1953 design proposed the preservation of the existing walls and columns while introducing a new narthex, sanctuary, gallery, bell towers, and roof. In 1958 Wissa Wassef was commissioned to design the sanctuary, which he drew within the existing 1953 proposal for the church. Moheb Stino was the structural engineer for the new construction, including the main oval dome of the roof. The following year, Wissa Wassef designed the carpentry works for the iconostasis, the windows, the doors, and the *mangiliya* (lectern). It is unclear if these were implemented and changed in recent years, or never actually implemented. Later, in 1994, the community services building was added to the church enclosure, with Kamal Nassif Ghali as the structural engineer.[22]

Wissa Wassef designed two proposals for the triple-apse sanctuary. In one proposal, each apse contains a niche framed by columns and topped with a pediment, following a Western style. In the other, the profile of the arched niche is offset and a plaster cornice connects the three offset outlines, emphasizing their arches. The latter proposal was implemented. The three original altars of each apse predating the 1950s were preserved; they follow the older tradition of altar design, with four marble columns carrying a slab. The dome over the main altar contains clerestory windows; the three eastern ones were designed by Wissa Wassef as stained-glass stucco panels while the rest are plain glass. Below them on the apse wall is an oculus, also containing one of Wissa Wassef's designs. The main, central dome also contains stained-glass stucco panels, but there is no record of who made them.

Church interior. The designers of the iconostasis and stained-glass windows in the elliptical central dome are unknown.

OPPOSITE PAGE:
Close-up of the lateral sanctuary niche designs made by Wissa Wassef.

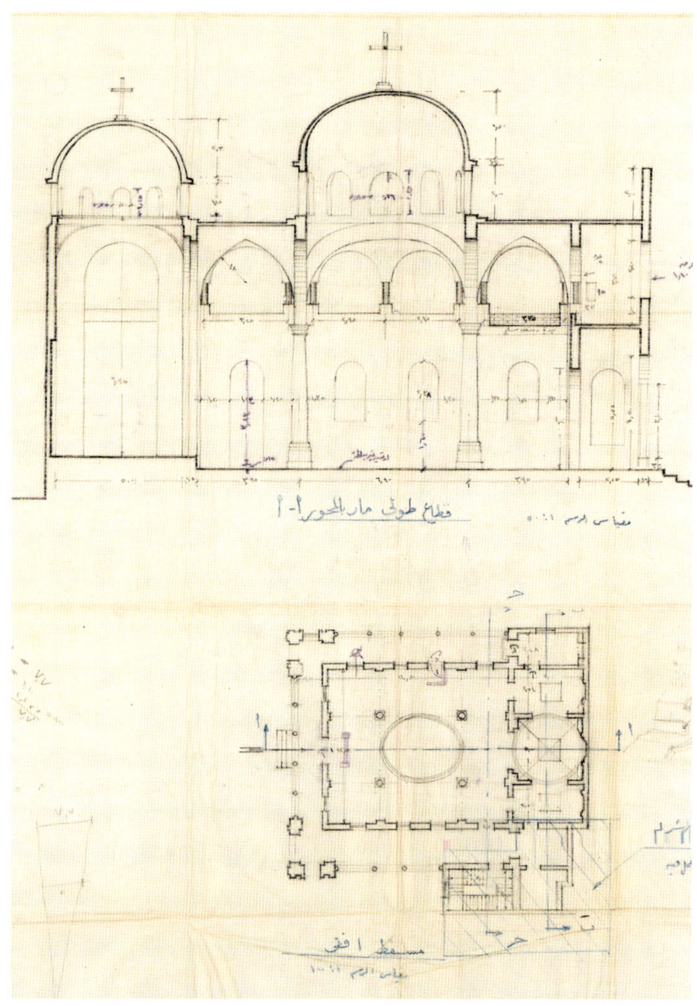

Longitudinal section (top); plan of the church (bottom), which includes a sketch of the sanctuary niches.

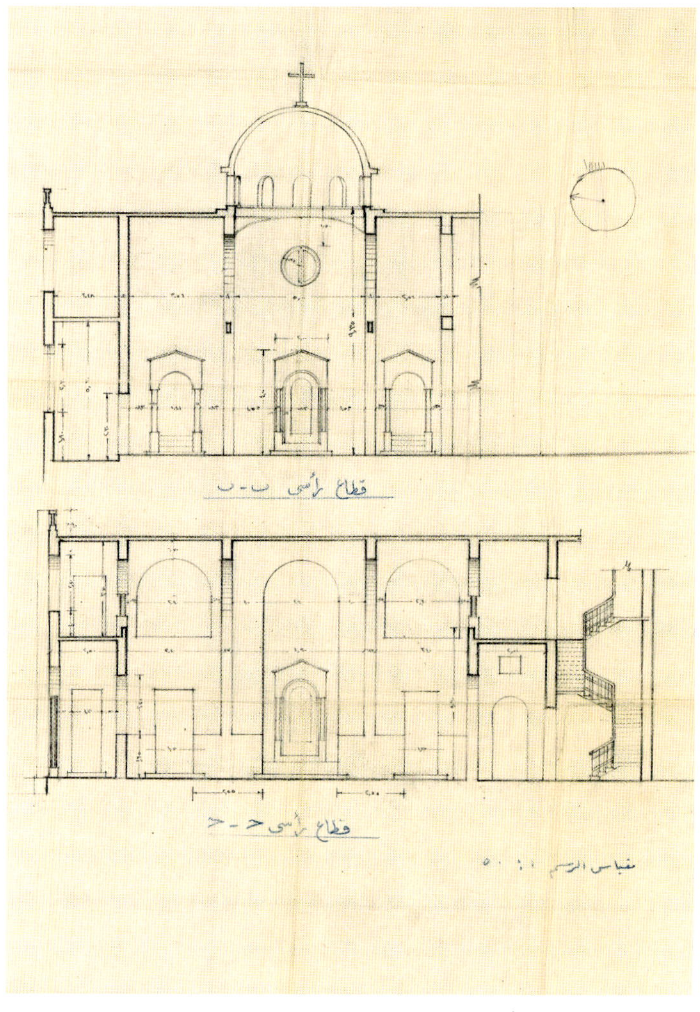

Transverse section through the sanctuary showing an initial proposal for the niches (top). Transversal section at the location of the iconostasis, which is not drawn (bottom). It is unclear if this original proposal was done by the architect who designed the church or by Wissa Wassef.

Sketch of sanctuary niche (top left), door (top right), and iconostasis proposal by Wissa Wassef (bottom).

Sketch of the scene for the central stained-glass and stucco medallion located in the sanctuary.

STAINED-GLASS STUCCO WINDOWS AT ST. MINA COPTIC ORTHODOX CHURCH

Date: Unknown

Location: Abu Qir Street, Fleming, Alexandria

Alternative names: Mar Mina the Martyr Coptic Orthodox Church, Kanisat Mar Mina al-Shahid bi Fleming

General view of church interior from gallery.

Construction started on the St. Mina Coptic Orthodox Church in 1946, and it was inaugurated in 1948. The church has two sets of stained-glass windows: the lead and stained-glass ones along the aisles, created by Isaac Fanous and Sawsan (a devotee of St. Demiana Monastery), and the stained-glass stucco ones mainly located in the clerestory of the barrel vault, which were created by Wissa Wassef.[27] The windows along the nave consist of sets of pairs centered over the arches that support the vault, making up a total of twenty panels. They are crowned with a cornice following the shape of crenellations.

At the rear of the church is a staircase leading up to the gallery. The stairwell contains two more panels, one of which is signed "Ramses Wissa Wassef." The gallery overlooks the nave; at either side of the gallery is a ledge-type balcony with a door and a stained-glass stucco panel. It is unclear if Wissa Wassef's stained-glass stucco panels were added during the construction of the church or at a later stage.

Interior elevation, showing stucco and stained-glass windows by Wissa Wassef in the clerestory, and lead and stained-glass windows by Isaac Fanous and Sawsan in the side aisle.

PAGES 104–107:
Stucco and stained-glass windows
by Wissa Wassef.

RESIDENTIAL

WISSA WASSEF AGUZA RESIDENCE

Date: 1947

Location: 13 al-Fardus Street (formerly al-Durri Street), Aguza, Giza

Alternative name: House of Suzanne and Yoanna Wissa Wassef

Inspired by traditional residences, one of the main features of this house is the *qa'a* with its two main *iwans* (here, the *iwans* have groin vaults) and a smaller side *iwan* that acts as an alcove. The central sunken *durqa'a* area contains a marble fountain, and this double-height space is topped by a dome that does not act as a *shukhshikha* despite its location and form, as its openings are sealed with stained-glass stucco panels. The *qa'a* has been adapted, for a contemporary lifestyle, to accommodate a Western-style dining room in addition to the reception space.

The lower section of the main façade is clad in *hashmi* stone, which includes two decorative relief panels at the entrance that were designed by Wissa Wassef and carved by Sayyida Misak and Yahya Abu Siri'a, students of Habib Georgi.[28] The entrance is accentuated by being recessed in a portal that integrates a balcony on the first floor. Fenestration is provided by *mashrabiyas*, stained-glass stucco windows, and arabesque wooden shutters following folkloric designs.

Ramses Wissa Wassef bought this plot of land with his brother Oziris and they jointly built this house. Oziris was the first to marry and move into the residence, leaving it in the mid-1960s when he emigrated with his family. When Oziris moved out, Ramses and his family were still living at the Giza family house but moved into this building in

Main elevation of the house.

1964–65. When Suzanne and Ikram Nosshi married in 1973 they moved in with the family, and in 1976 Yoanna married and moved out. Simultaneously Suzanne and Ikram moved to Harraniya, together with Sophie, into the rest house. During this time Badie Habib Georgi designed an extension to the house consisting of two floors, and Yoanna moved back in from 1977 until 1981, when she moved to Harraniya. In the mid-1980s the house was rented out as the residence for the French cultural attaché. Then, from 2008 to 2012, it was used by the Turkish Cultural Center. Due to the later interventions, and the urbanization of the surrounding area, the house today appears quite different from the original design and much of its exterior dynamism has been lost.

Entrance window composed of a geometric stucco grille at the top and a metal grille at the bottom, separated by a carved stone lintel depicting flora and fauna.

Carved stone panel with gazelles, above the front door.

Qa'a, facing the dining room.

Qa'a, as viewed from the upstairs gallery.

Pierced dome of one of the bathrooms.

Door leading to the garden.

Geometric stained-glass and stucco panel.

FROM LEFT, CLOCKWISE:
Stucco claustra opening.
Fauna stucco panels.
Wooden cupboard following the traditional style.

Marble mantel following the traditional style.

Fireplace in one of the *iwans* of the *qa'a*.

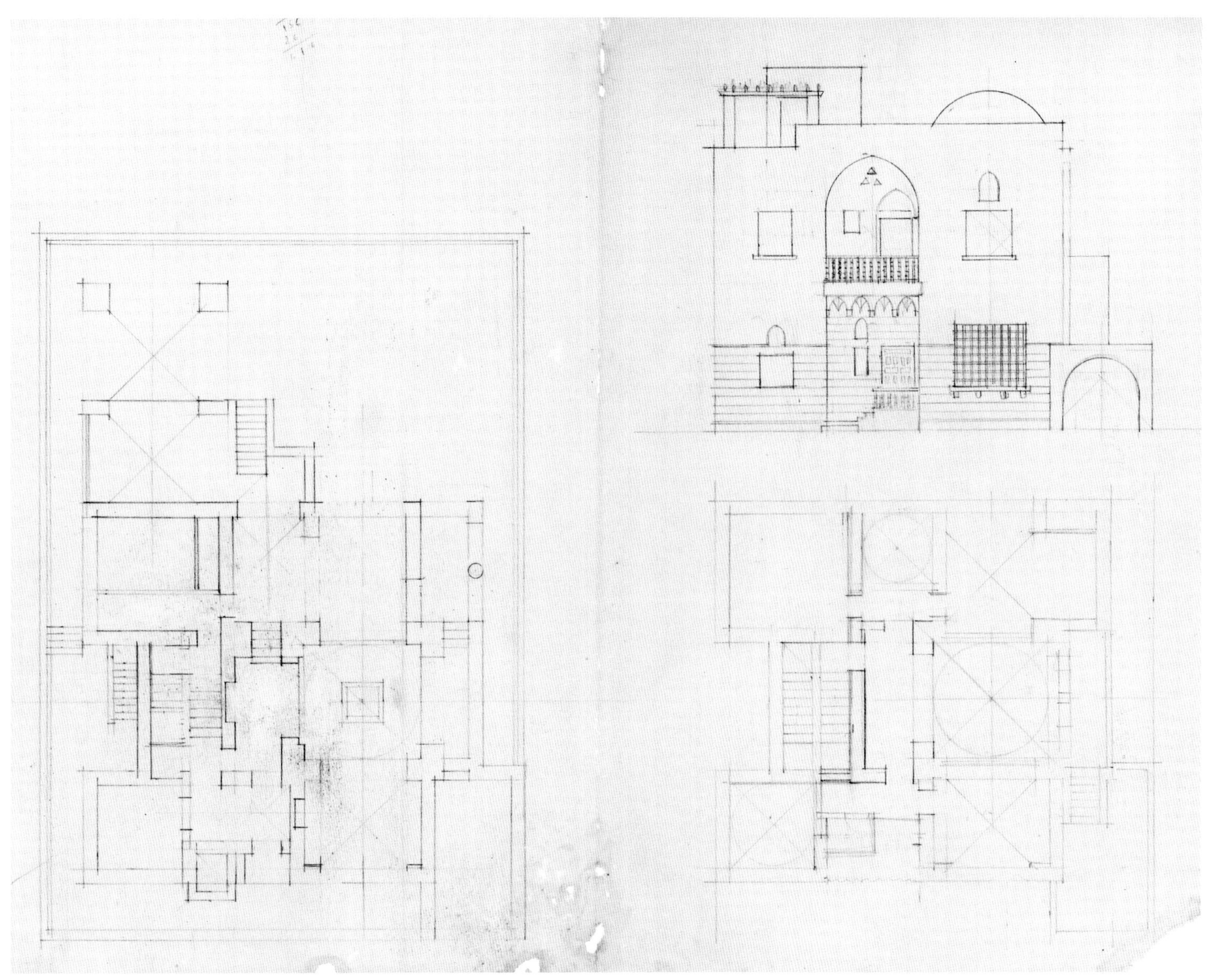

Ground-floor plan (left), main elevation (top right), upper floor (bottom right).

INA MAKKAR HOUSE

Date: 1967
Location: Maryutiya Road, Harraniya, Giza
Alternative names: Ina Maggar House, Ina Magar House, Enna Makkar House

This modern villa in Harraniya has a plan split along two intersecting axes at an obtuse angle. It was built for Ina Makkar, the wife of the architect's cousin George Wassef. The ground-floor plan consists of an entrance vestibule; a triple-space living area, including the dining room, which opens onto a large terrace that dominates the exterior view of the house; a kitchen; storeroom; vestibule; guest washroom; two bedrooms; and a bathroom. The two bedrooms can access an external court, located behind the entrance, via a hall. The living room is equipped with a fireplace and niche. The stairwell leading to the roof was positioned in such a way as to allow future construction on the roof. This would happen in 1982–83, when Ikram Nosshi added two rooms upstairs, creating the first floor.

The modernist Ina Makkar House follows clean lines throughout, accentuated by the minimalist fenestration treatment with large sliding louver shutters. The exterior elevations consist of regular, clear, marked rows of irregular rough-hewn stone, highlighting the clean lines and the façades' modern appearance despite the use of a rustic material. Terraced planters surround the elevated large terrace, creating the perfect transition between the natural and human-made domains.

General view of the house, 1983/1984.
OPPOSITE: General view of the northwest elevation of the house, 1983/1984.

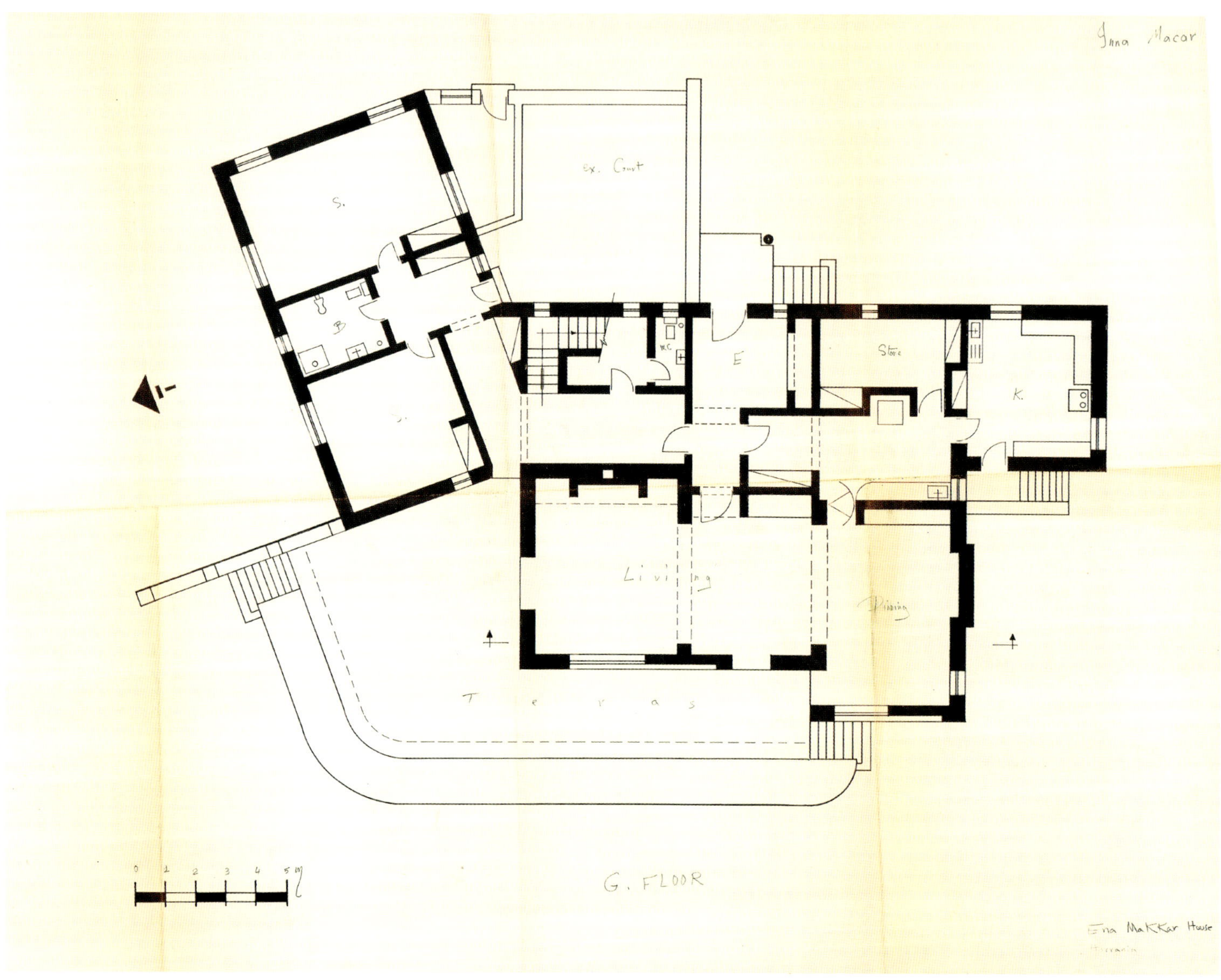

Ground-floor plan.

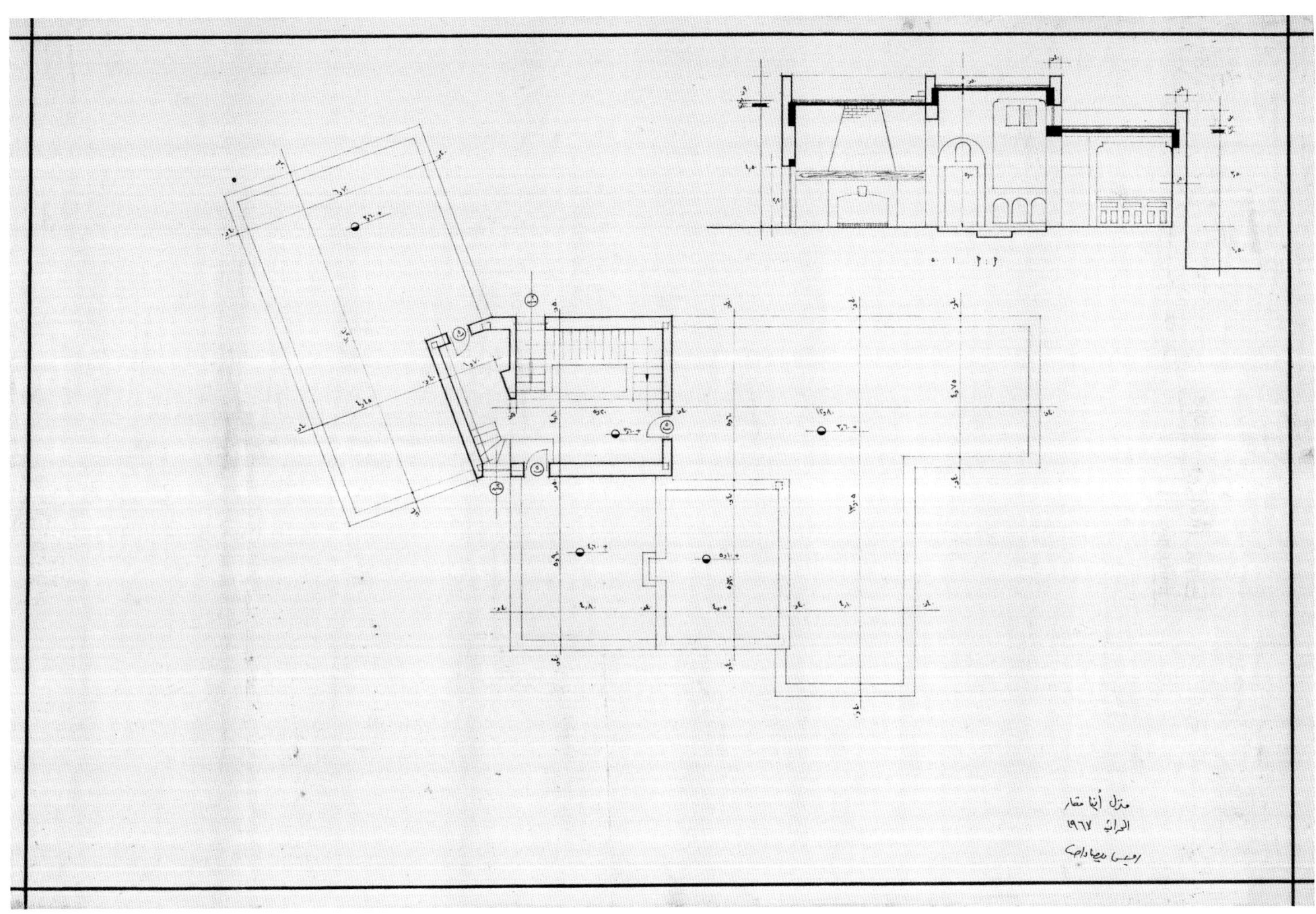

Section through living spaces (top right) and first-floor plan (bottom).

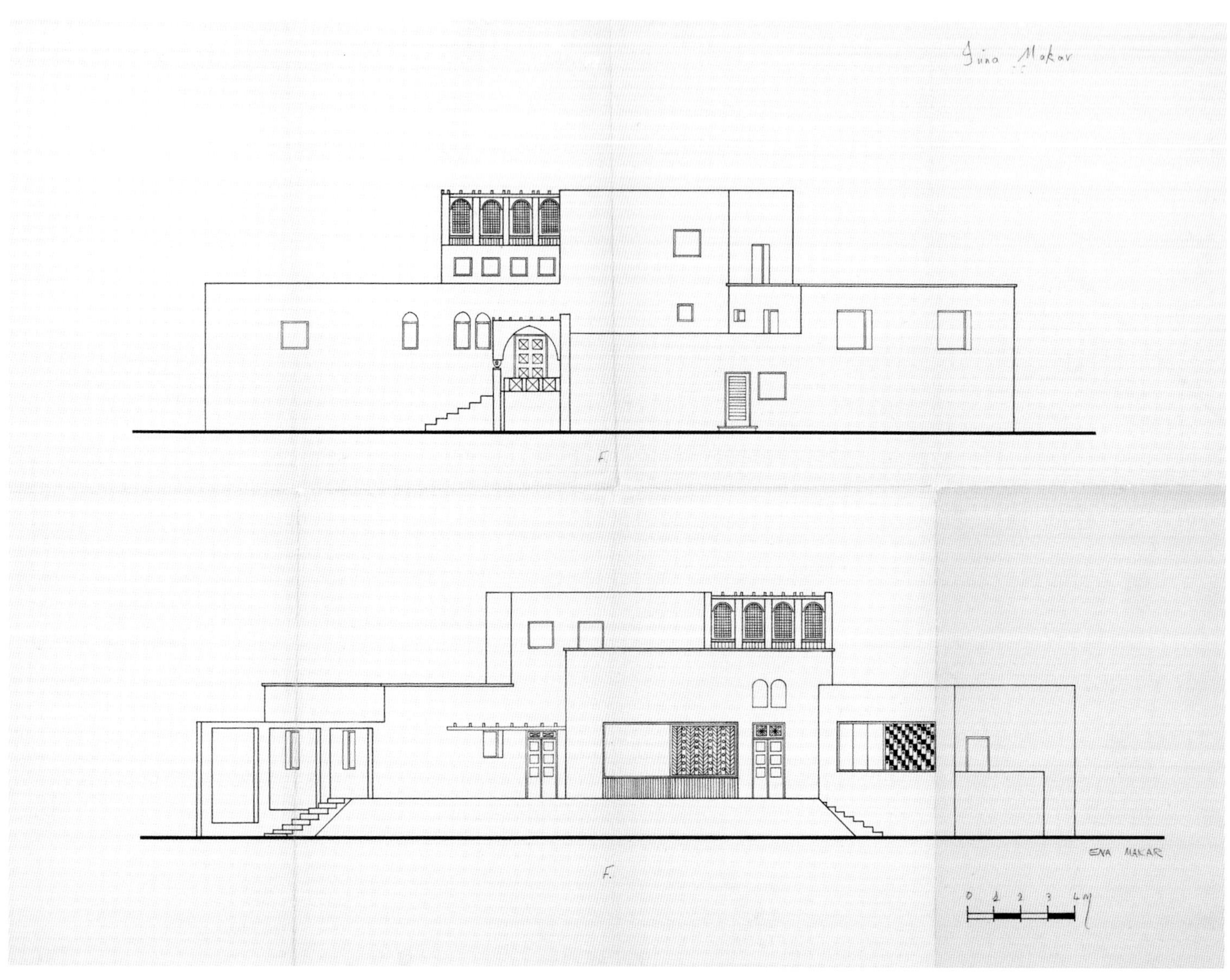

Southeast elevation (top) and northwest elevation (bottom).

MOHIE AL-DIN HUSSEIN HOUSE AND STUDIO

Date: 1968

Location: Maryutiya Road, Harraniya, Giza

General view of the house from the garden in 1983, prior to the plastering of the façades.

This residence was built by Wissa Wassef for his student Mohie al-Din Hussein, who would become a renowned ceramics artist. The house has a domed entrance porch that leads to an almost ambulatory corridor, part of which continues as an exterior walled patio. It surrounds an open courtyard, which was used in a variety of ways—acting as an extension to Hussein's workshop on some occasions or, alternatively, as an open exhibition space or sitting area.[29] The northern side of the house contains two bedrooms and a bathroom, with a staircase leading upstairs to a third bedroom. Adjacent to the entrance on the east side are the main living areas, consisting of a series of spaces aligned linearly, which have been extended over time.[30] The southern part of the dwelling contains three workshop rooms, one of which is a linear space roofed with a Nubian vault.

The floors are all of ceramic tiles that were made by Hussein himself. He also made the colored tiles decorating the main gate. The walls are made from limestone, while the vaults and domes are in mud brick.[31] Initially the limestone was exposed on the exterior but at some point after the mid-1980s the house's exterior was plastered and painted in terracotta-red.

The building was opened as a gallery in 1980.[32] In recent years, with the rising water level, the plot has become flooded and substantial damage has been caused to the house, including large cracks owing to settlement. Its condition prevents the accessibility and usability of the house and its garden. At an advanced age, Hussein moved to Alexandria and sold the property.

FROM LEFT, CLOCKWISE:
Main elevation of the house, in its flooded and dilapidated state in 2017.
Ground-floor plan.
Main elevation.

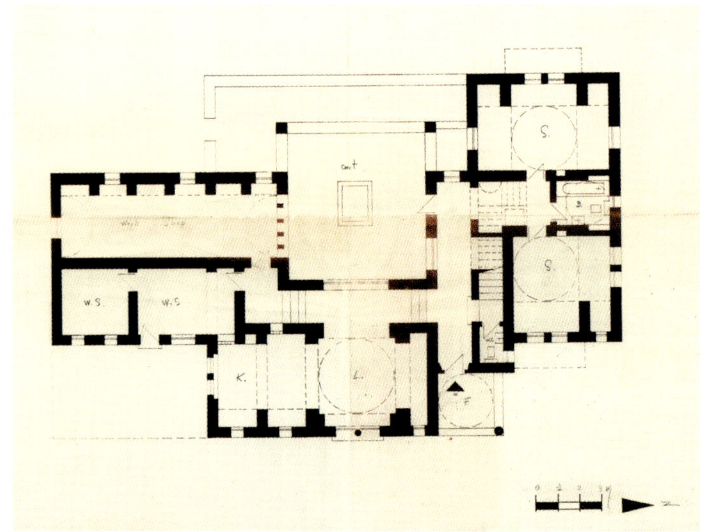

EDUCATIONAL AND CULTURAL

JARDIN D'ENFANTS AT THE LYCÉE FRANÇAIS DU CAIRE

Date: 1936
Location: Intersection of Muhammad Mahmud Street (formerly el-Kassed/al-Qasid Street) and Yusuf al-Gindi Street (formerly al-Huwayati Street),[33] Bab al-Luq, Cairo
Alternative names: Lycée Français du Caire de la Mission Laïque Française de Bab el-Louk, Lycée El-Horreya de Bab el-Louk

General view of the kindergarten.

The main school building was originally designed by V. Erlanger in a neo-Islamic revival style and inaugurated in 1931;[34] five years later, in 1936, Wissa Wassef designed the kindergarten, or Jardin d'Enfants, and implemented some minor modifications to the original building. The school had originally been established in 1909 at the Mazlum Pasha Palace[35] and was relocated to its current location, where it was called the Lycée Français du Caire until 1957 following the Suez Canal war, when it was renamed the Lycée El-Horreya de Bab el-Louk.[36]

The surviving plans resemble the overall layout of the existing building, but follow a modernist style with clean lines and minimalist façades instead of the vernacular style that was implemented. Plans showing the final design do not survive. The layout follows an angular U shape. Classrooms overlook a playground surrounded by a shaded arcade (or colonnade in the existing plans). The whole nursery is fenced off from the rest of the school and has its own access from Muhammad Mahmud Street.

The kindergarten was built on part of the playground of the lycée and was Wissa Wassef's first domed building. The walls are composed of limestone bound with cement, lime, and sand mortar, while the domes and vaults are constructed from red brick. Most rooms initially had a stained-glass stucco window, but most of these were destroyed during the 2011 revolution as a result of clashes on Muhammad Mahmud Street and in a fire that broke out in 2012.[37]

Wide cross-vault arcade dividing the courtyard from the playground.

One of the larger classrooms in the kindergarten.

FROM LEFT, CLOCKWISE:
Detail of vaulting merging with the window niche.
Claustra opening.
Window carpentry patterns.

General view of the kindergarten.

General view showing the classroom domes.

Interior view of a classroom.

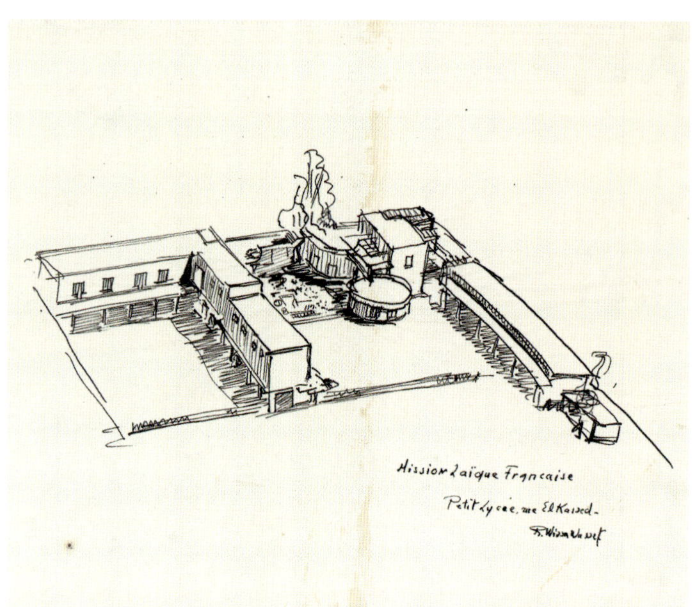
Mission Laïque Francaise
Petit Lycée, rue El Kassed

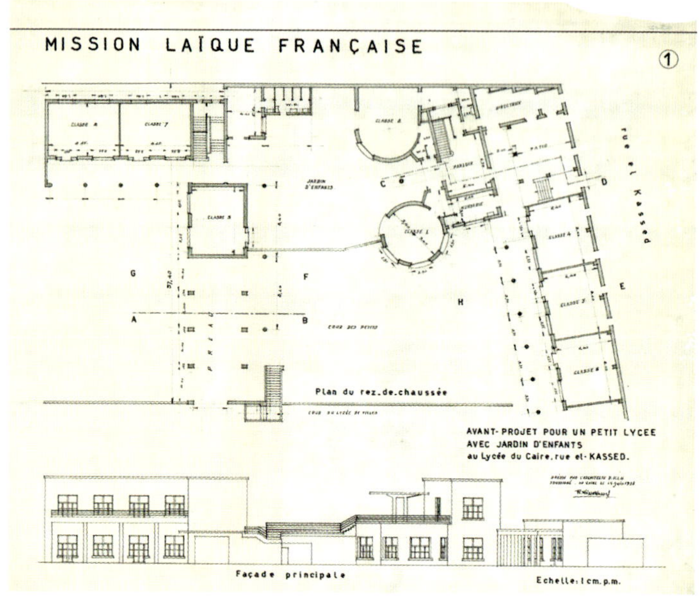
MISSION LAÏQUE FRANÇAISE
①
rue el Kassed
Plan du rez.de.chaussée
AVANT-PROJET POUR UN PETIT LYCEE
AVEC JARDIN D'ENFANTS
au Lycée du Caire, rue el-KASSED.
Façade principale
Echelle: 1 cm. p.m.

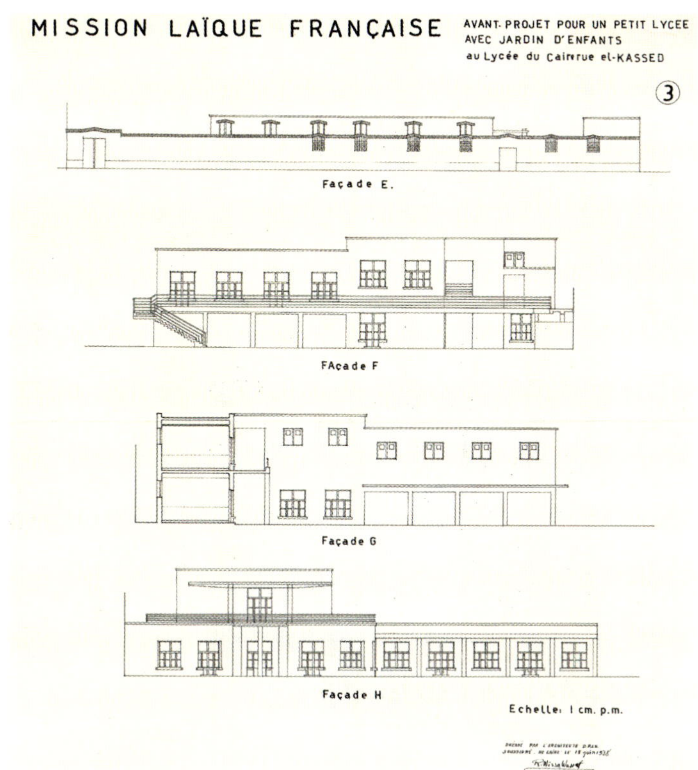

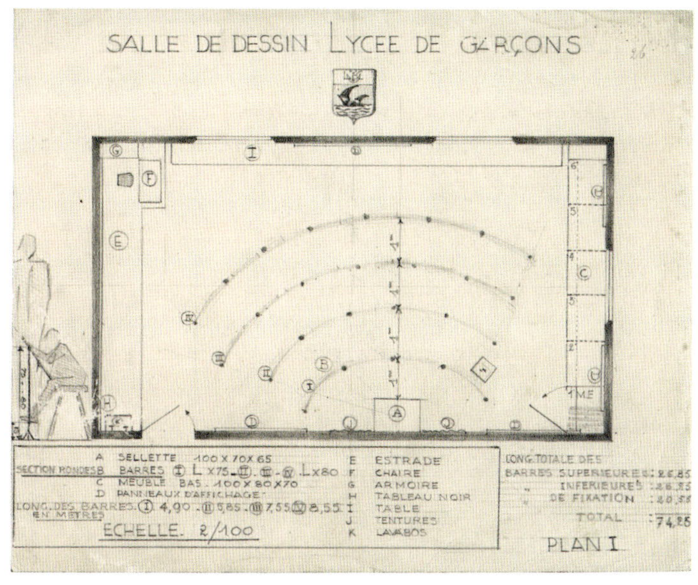

FROM LEFT, CLOCKWISE:
Modernist elevations, from the unimplemented proposal.
Plan of the boys' design classroom at the lycée. The girls' classroom is essentially the same except that the room is less oblong and more square in shape.

OPPOSITE, FROM TOP LEFT, CLOCKWISE:
Axonometry of the kindergarten in the original modernist style.
Plan of the kindergarten, modernist proposal. The final design follows a similar layout.
Render of the design classroom at the lycée.

LYCÉE FRANCO-ÉGYPTIEN D'HÉLIOPOLIS

Date: 1936
Location: Intersection of al-Nuzha Street and Uruba Street (formerly Fuad I Avenue), Heliopolis, Cairo
Alternative names: Lycée de la Mission Laïque Française à Héliopolis, Lycée El-Horreya Héliopolis

General overview of the school, c.2013.

The school was designed by Jacques Hardy and Ramses Wissa Wassef. Collectively they created several master-plan proposals for the campus, which was inaugurated in 1937.[38] However, construction was phased, as Hardy and Wissa Wassef continued to contribute to the development of the school even after it had started operating. Their drawings ranged over an eight-year span, from 1936 to 1944.

As in the Lycée El-Horreya de Bab el-Louk, the Jardin d'Enfants stood out from the rest of the school. In this case, there are three round classrooms arrayed radially. The design of the campus placed great emphasis on sports. It contained football and handball pitches, a swimming pool, and an equestrian track that was later used as a car drop-off point following the termination of the school's equestrian program some years later.[39]

During the Second World War the large campus grounds were considered a suitable location for bomb and air-raid shelters. In 1961, the school was nationalized, changing its name to Lycée El-Horreya Héliopolis and introducing the Egyptian curriculum. It had initially been a boarding establishment, which contained separate sections for the female and male students; after its nationalization, the boarding system was removed and dormitory spaces were converted into regular classrooms. Later, in the 1980s, the tip of the school grounds at the intersection of Uruba and al-Nuzha streets was turned into the El-Horreya Post Office and Yahya al-Refai Experimental Language School. This resulted in the demolition of the general culture and events hall building, as well as the swimming pool.[40]

General shot of one of the school buildings and playgrounds, c.2013.

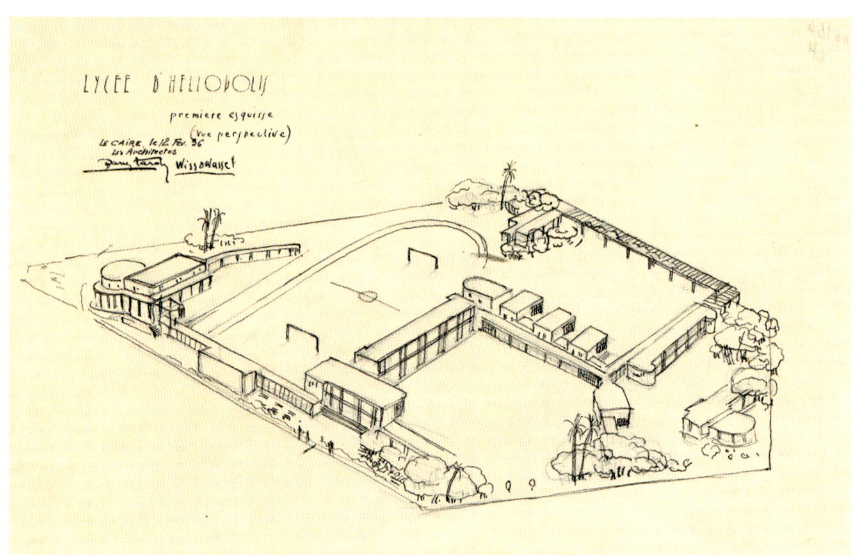

Masterplan proposal 1.

Masterplan proposal 2.

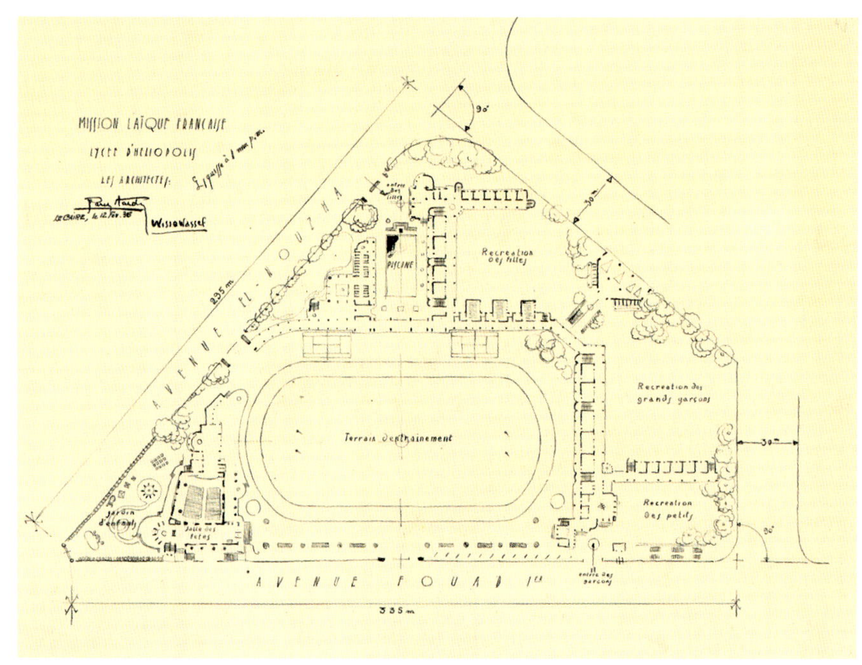

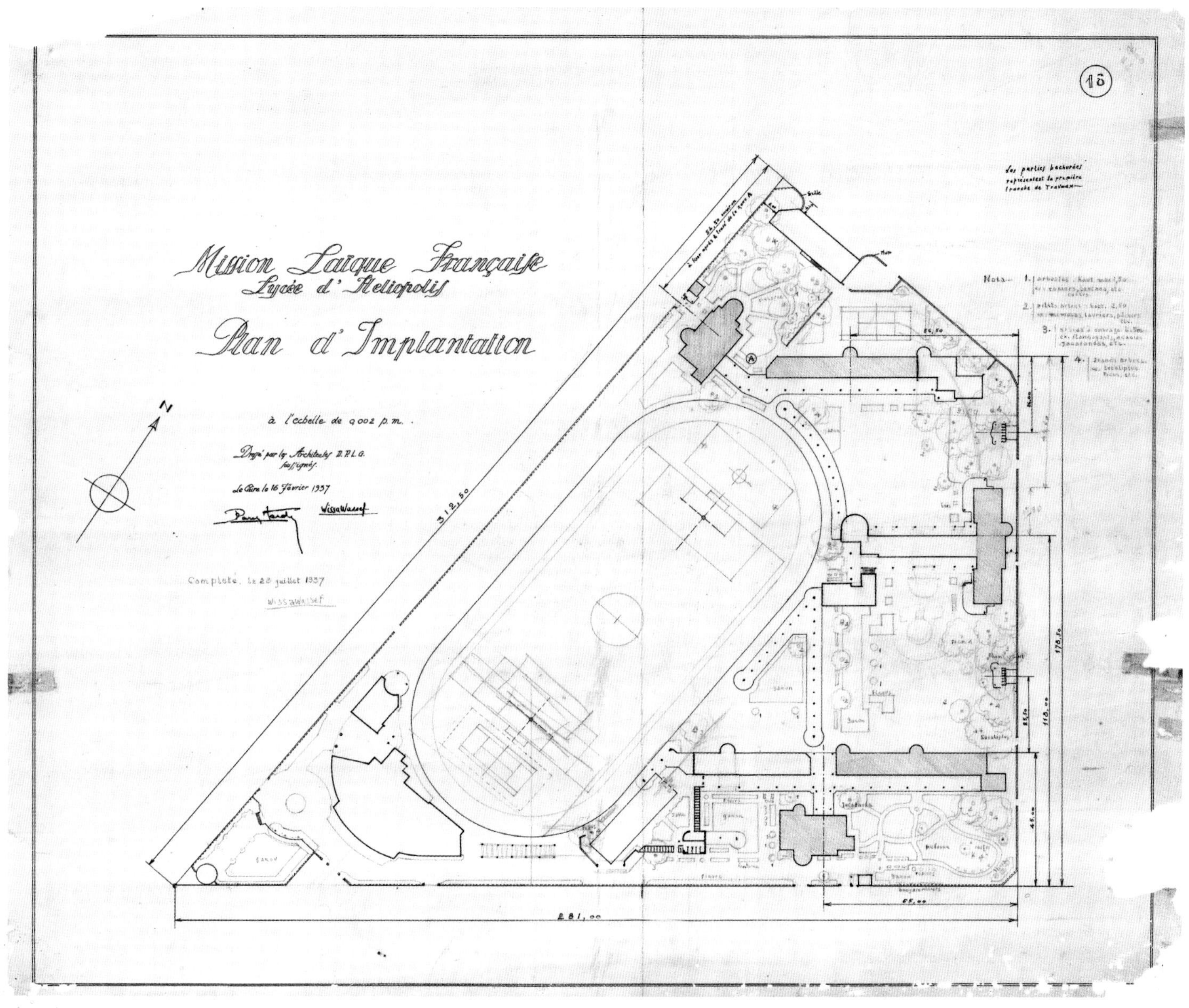

Masterplan proposal 3.

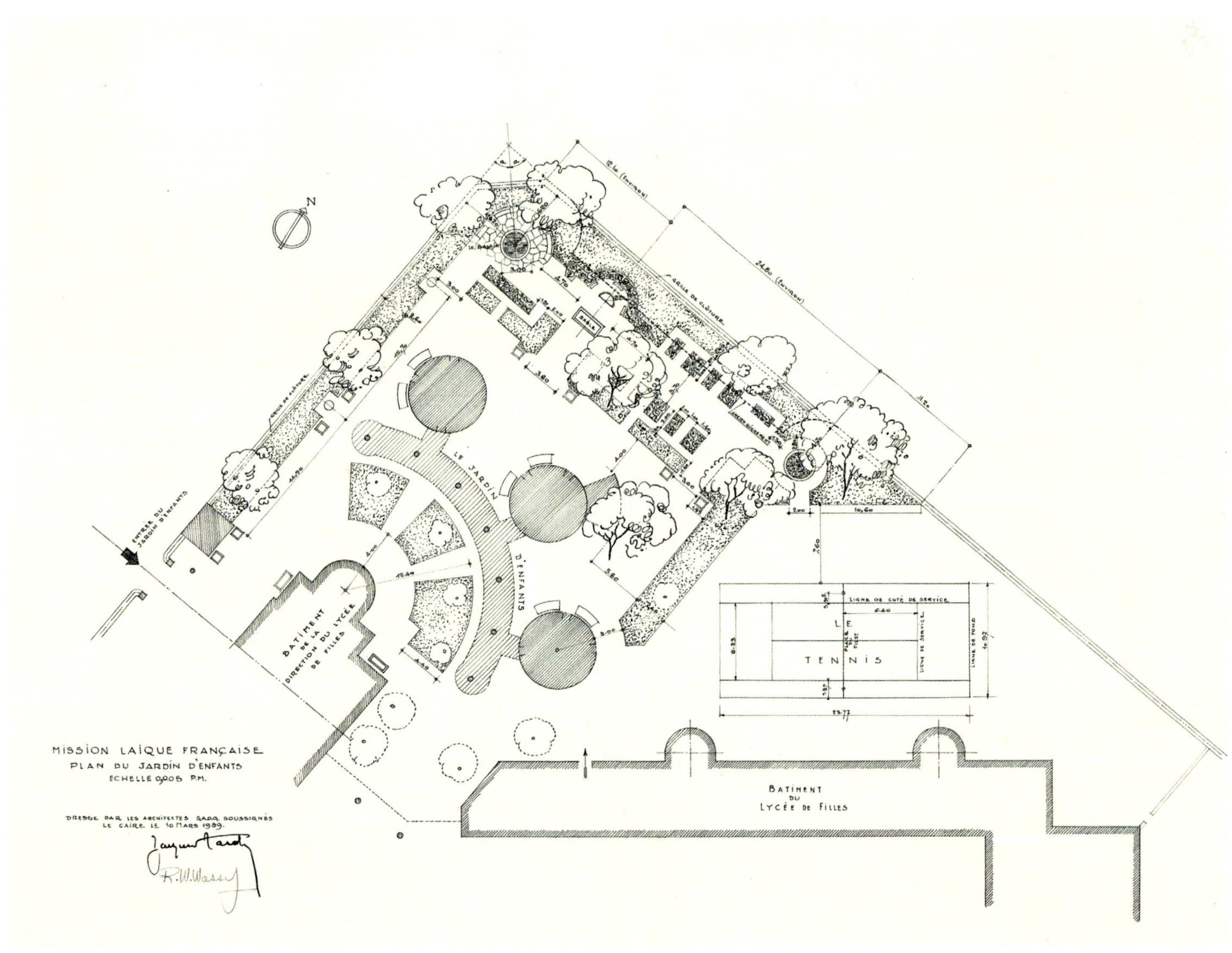

Site plan of the kindergarten.

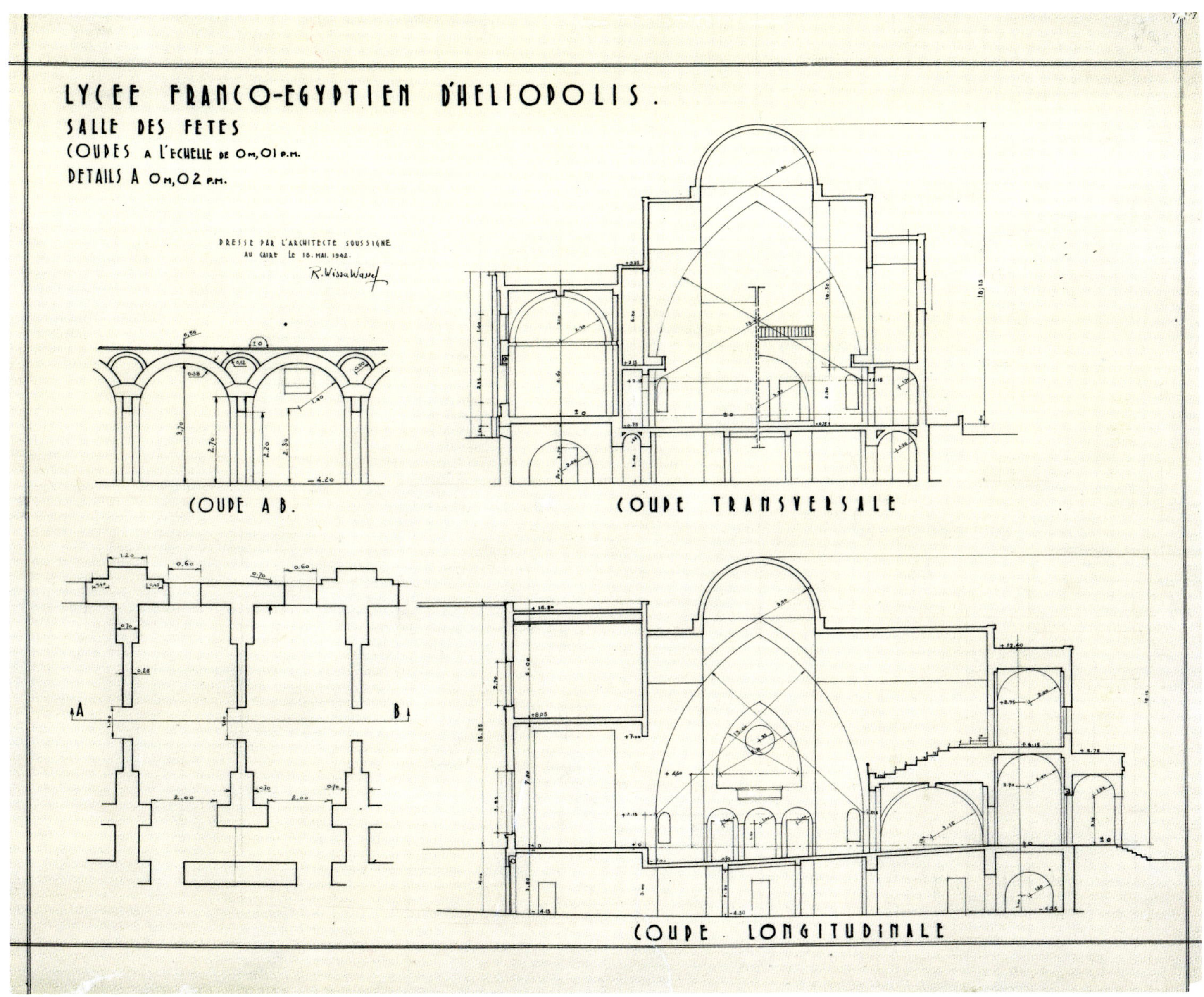

Sections of the now demolished events hall.

SCHOOL IN OLD CAIRO

Date: 1941
Location: Religious Complex, Old Cairo, Cairo

Side shot of the school.

This modest school was built by Wissa Wassef at Qasr al-Shama', in what is known as Mugamma' al-Adyan (the Religious Complex) in Old Cairo. It is located at the rear of the complex, in a walled compound that appears unoccupied in cadastral maps of the time. The main gate into the compound was on its northeastern wall between the Qasriyat al-Rihan ('Basil Pot') Church—also called the Church of the Blessed Virgin Mary, founded in the fifth century and rebuilt in the ninth[41]—and the Church of the Great Martyr St. George. The site has undergone many changes since the school was built, most notably when the Qasriyat al-Rihan Church was destroyed during a fire that broke out in 1979 (it was eventually renovated in 2002). Other changes included the removal of the stone gate leading to the walled compound located between the two churches, the addition of other buildings, and the transformation of the open square once used to play impromptu football games into an official football pitch around 2009.

The school started off as a community primary school *(madrasa ibtida'iya ahliya)*, where as an extracurricular activity Wissa Wassef first introduced weaving to children and started developing his philosophy on creativity. One individual remembers a sign over the compound gate naming the institution "School of Saint Isithorus" and it being called the Ladies Association.[42] The school was built by the same family of builders as those responsible for Hassan Fathy's school in New Gourna: the Abu Alaa family from Kafr al-Naggar and Kafr al-Mahamid in Aswan. In recent years, the school was renovated and given stone cladding and new doors. It has also ceased functioning as a regular school, and now serves as a center for courses and activities.

Main elevation of the school, May 1988.

Main elevation of the school after the renovation.

Interior shot of classrooms, prior to renovation and change of function.

Clay model showing the school and its enclosure, including the three domes of the sanctuary of the Church of the Great Martyr St. George, and an unidentified nonextant structure with a larger dome, perhaps part of a larger proposal by Wissa Wassef.

MAHMOUD MOKHTAR MUSEUM

Date: 1960
Location: Tahrir Street, al-Gazira, Cairo

General view from the museum grounds.

The Mahmoud Mokhtar Museum was built at the pinnacle of Wissa Wassef's career to commemorate the famous sculptor, a pioneer of modern Egyptian art. This modernist building, with its bold reinterpretation of ancient Egyptian architecture, is true to Wissa Wassef's efforts at creating contemporary architecture with a strong Egyptian identity.

The museum is a freestanding structure, rising from its garden setting like an island and drawing on one of the ancient Egyptian creation myths, in which an island arises from Nun, the primeval ocean. The ground floor of the building takes on the shape of a *mastaba*, like the tombs of the pharaonic Old Kingdom. On top of the *mastaba* is the first floor of the museum, and part of the *mastaba* roof acts as a terrace serving its main entrance. This terrace is connected to the street via a pedestrian bridge. The main entrance consists of a portico supported by five pillars reminiscent of temple architecture. This comprehensive symbology is used to immortalize Mahmoud Mokhtar's work while also functioning as his tomb; a room on the ground floor at the rear of the *mastaba* form serves as his mausoleum.

The interior of the building is cleverly designed to integrate curving walls, which sensually guide the visitor through the museum. This contrasts with the predominantly rectilinear exterior, yet both have been masterfully designed in harmony. One of the more architecturally prominent spaces is the Seasons Hall, which is cylindrical in shape and has four semicircular niches. The dark marble flooring rises up to take the form of pedestals on which the sculptures are displayed. A thin glass perimeter separates the floor from the wall, creating an ethereal effect when the floor lighting is turned on. The building was designed with a high level of consideration for the curating of the sculptural pieces: a variety of niches embraces and accentuates the specific artworks. Clerestory slit windows were also strategically placed to provide lighting, but many of these have been blocked by the addition of service and administration rooms behind the museum in later years. Sometime over the last few decades, the rooms were painted in bright hues, such as orange and blue, but they have now been restored to a lighter, neutral color. Under the *mastaba* terrace is a large hall for temporary exhibitions.

View of the portico and main entrance to the museum.

The seasons circular hall, with the sculpture of the *Khamasin* (Sandstorm Season) at the center.

View upon entering the museum from the main entrance.

One of the major curves of the museum, containing two columns tied with a bench that act as a viewing frame.

Different angled shot, showing the curvature of the museum interior, the architectural viewing frame, and recessed niches to emphasize displayed sculptures.

Continuation of the museum curvature ending in a semicircular niche.

Sketches showing the development of the design concept.

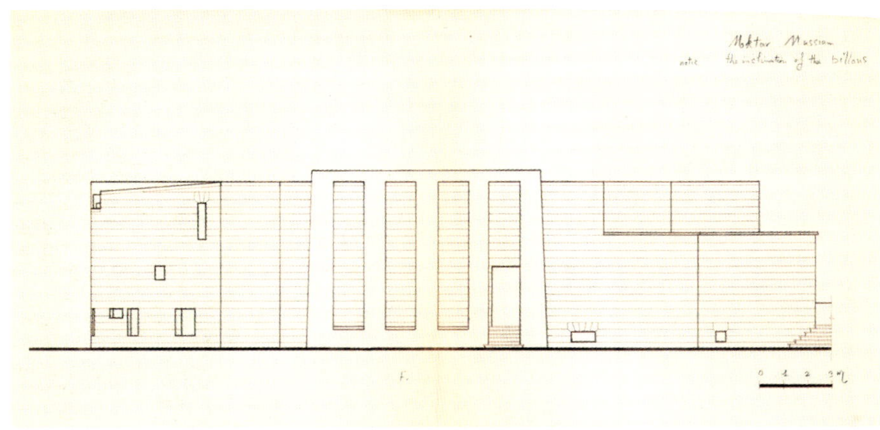

Main elevation.

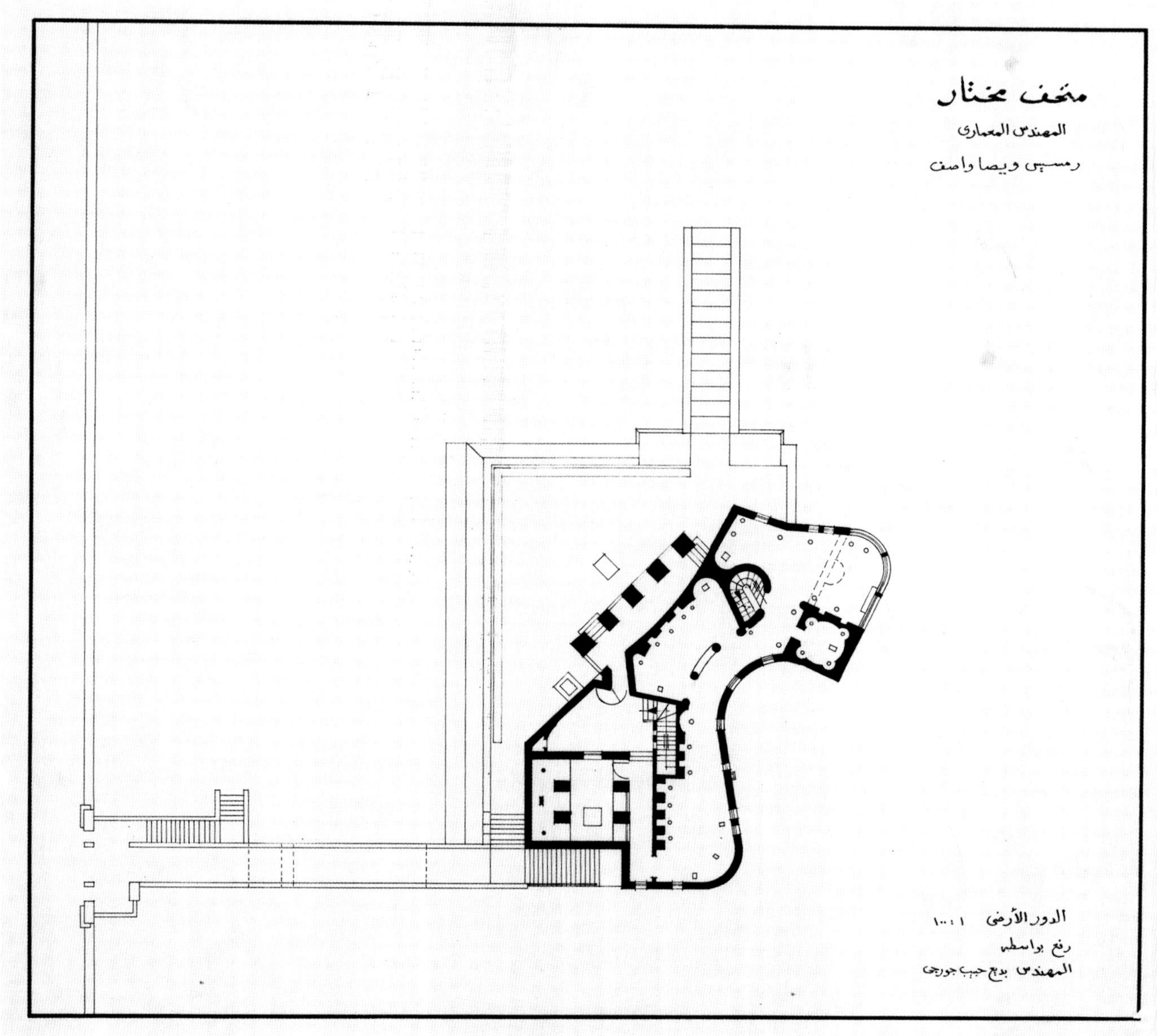

Main-floor plan, consisting of the upper level.

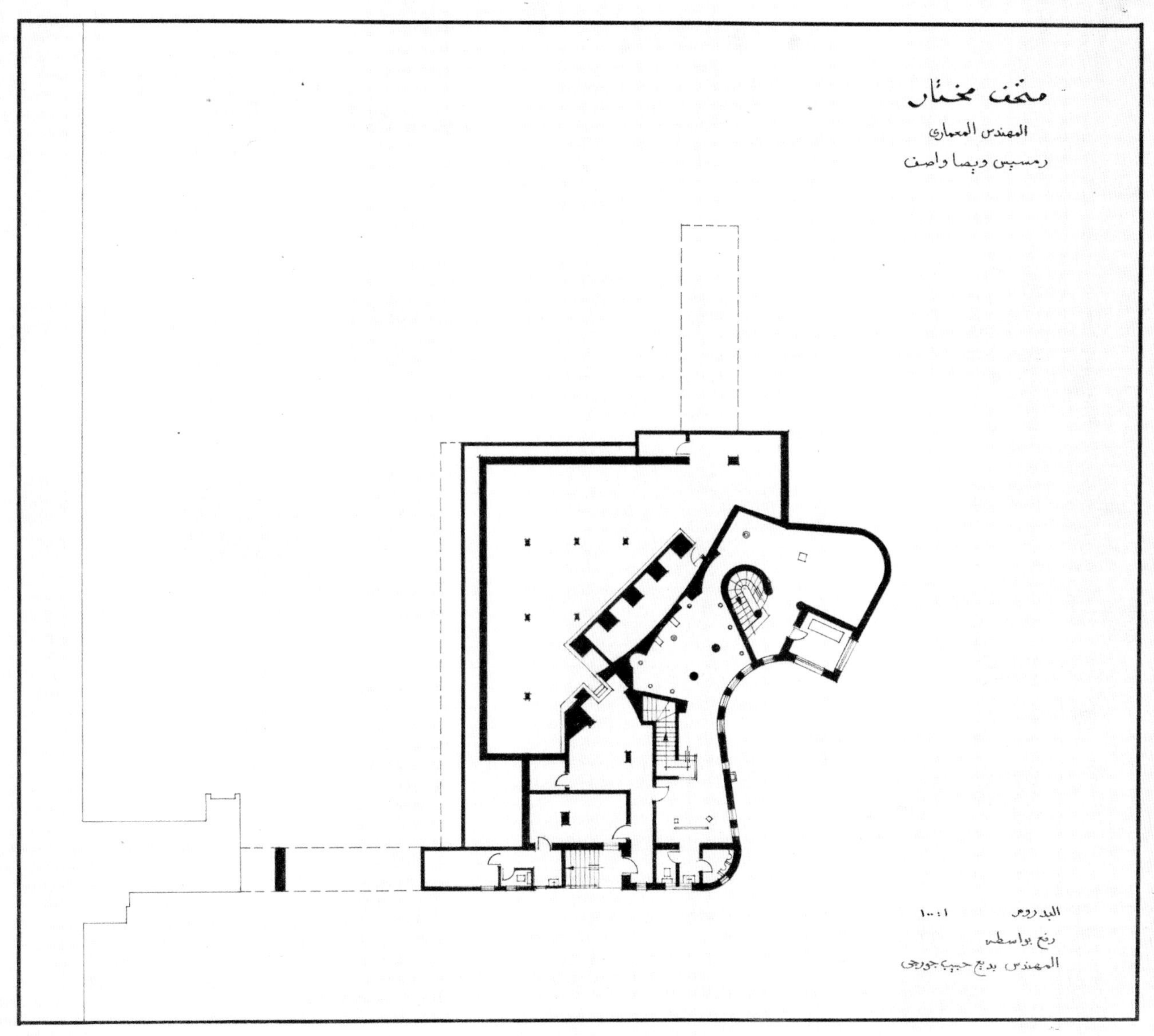

The lower-floor plan.

OTHER

AL-CHARK INSURANCE COMPANY BUILDING RENOVATION

Date: 1944
Location: Talaat Harb Square (formerly Sulayman Pasha Square), Downtown, Cairo
Alternative names: Immeuble al-Chark, Al-Sharq Insurance Company Building

Building as viewed from Talaat Harb Square, c.1950s/60s.

Built between the late nineteenth and early twentieth centuries, this edifice was subsequently remodeled in 1937 by Jacques Hardy—who removed the dome at the top to add an extra floor, added plaster strips with vegetal decoration on the elevations, and modified the ground-floor extension.

In 1944 Wissa Wassef drew up plans for a further remodeling; project-meeting minutes suggest that work did not start until 1946, and that the architect and musician Abu Bakr Khayrat was also involved.[43] The plans in Wissa Wassef's archive confirm that each of the architects submitted a proposal. In Wissa Wassef's proposal the ground-floor layout was modified to create stores with street access, including a redesign of the corner store unit. The first floor, which initially was a series of small offices overlooking a corridor circulating through the building's core, was split into two sections. The first, overlooking Talaat Harb Street (formerly Sulayman Pasha Street), was turned into one large office with smaller office rooms. The other half, overlooking Qasr al-Nil Street, was converted into small duplex apartments.

Wissa Wassef and Khayrat also embraced the role of graphic designers, jointly designing the emblematic logo of Al-Chark Insurance Company (spelled al-Sharq in Archives) that was installed on the building.[44] The decorative elements on the elevations were simplified into the fluted strips recognizable today. Eventually the company logo was replaced with that of Misr Life Insurance, and in 2016 the corner elevation overlooking the square was covered with composite-aluminum cladding, which was removed not long afterward. For the past few years, the building has been in quite a poor state.

Perspective of the building as per Ramses Wissa Wassef's renovation.

Original appearance of the building prior to Jacques Hardy's renovation in 1937.

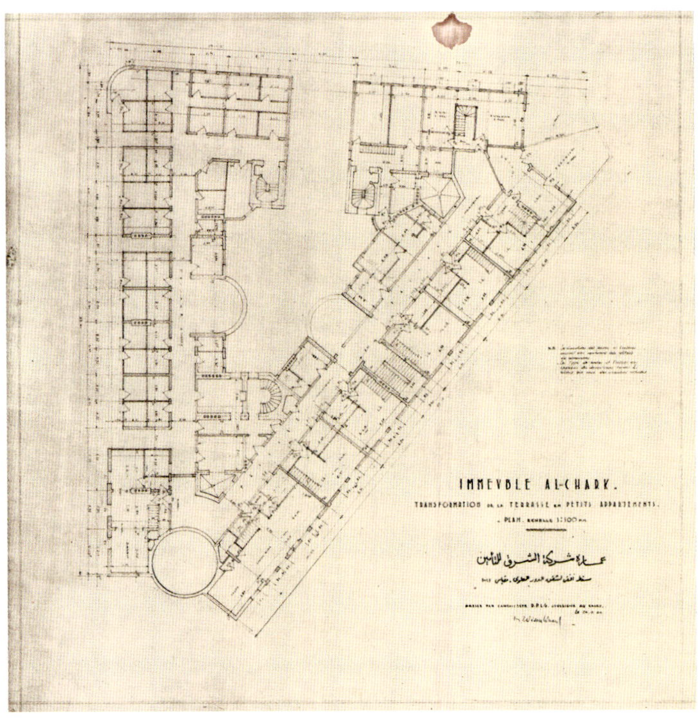

Renovated floor plan by Ramses Wissa Wassef.

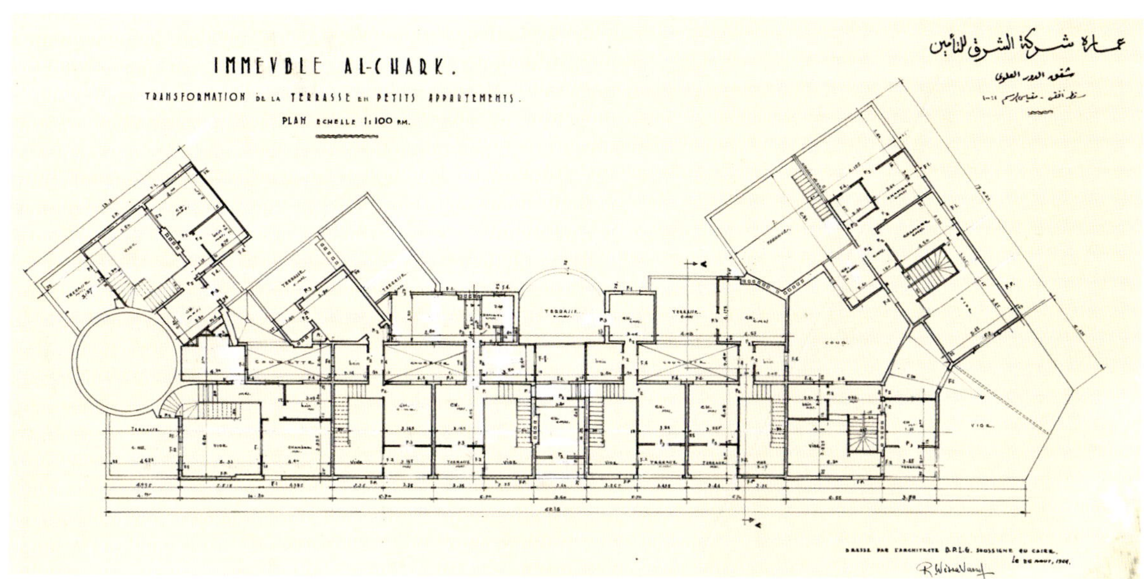

Upper-floor plan of the duplexes level.

1944 elevation by Wissa Wassef.

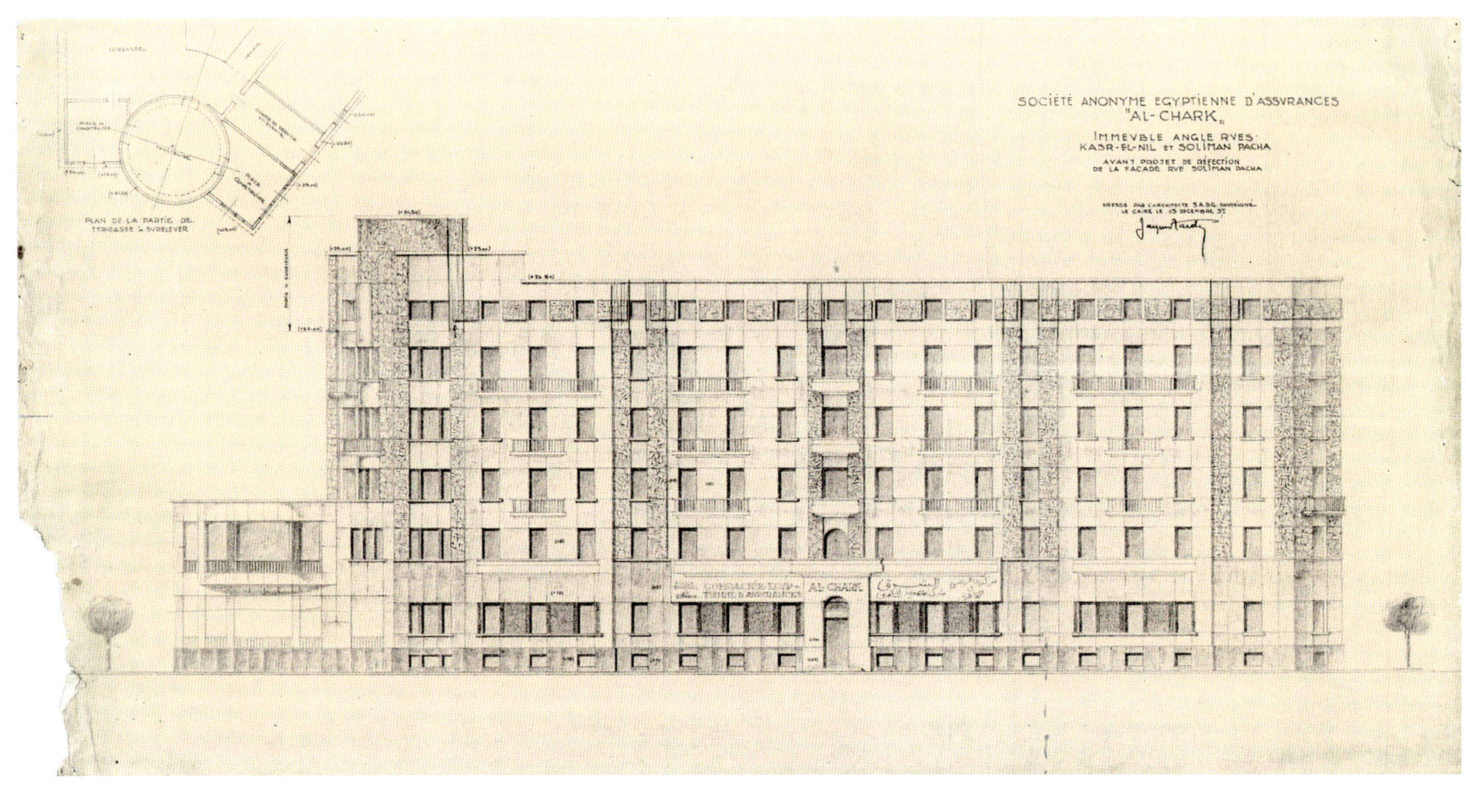

1937 elevation by Jacques Hardy, preceding Wissa Wassef's renovation.

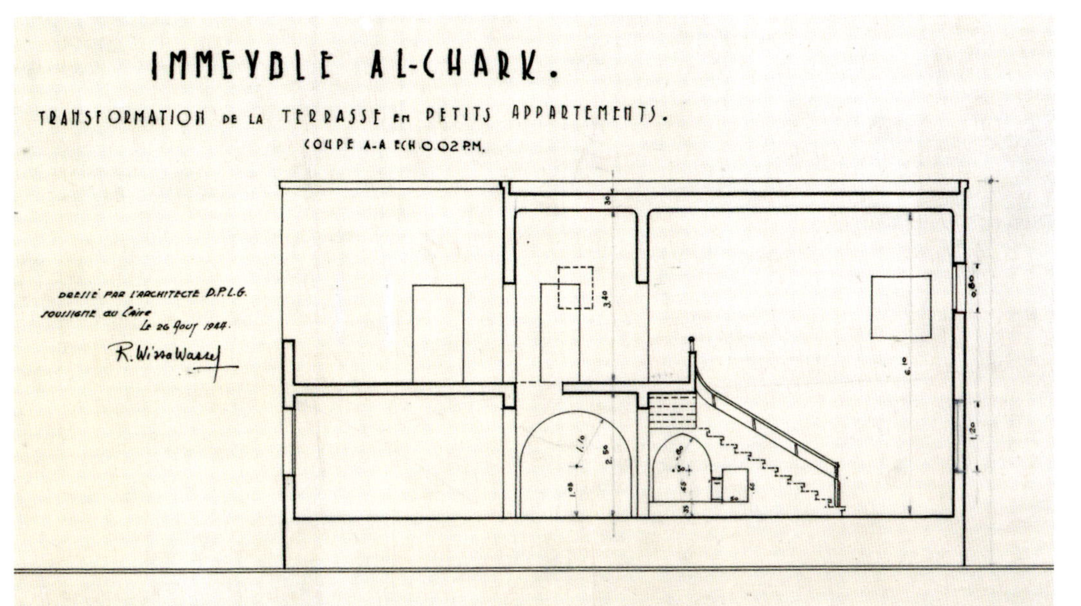

Section of one of the duplexes.

Al-Chark Insurance Company logo by Ramses Wissa Wassef and Abu Bakr Khayrat.

STAINED-GLASS STUCCO WINDOWS AT THE SOCIAL BUILDING, EGYPTIAN SHOOTING CLUB

Date: 1949–52
Location: Nadi al-Sayd Street, Dokki, Giza

General shot of the lantern.

Built between 1949 and 1952, the Social Building at the Egyptian Shooting Club is the work of renowned architect Antoine Selim Nahas.[45] The club itself was established in 1939, prior to the construction of the Social Building. The elegant building and its interior are enhanced by stained-glass stucco windows and panels designed by Wissa Wassef. The building's main entrance is crowned with a stained-glass stucco medallion or *qamariya* inscribed with the name of the club atop a hunting bird, and the club's former blazon—both of which are surrounded by small icons of fish, gazelles, ducks, and birds as well as the initials C.R.E.C.P. (Cercle Royal Égyptien de Chasse et de Pêche).

In the main lounge, the stained-glass stucco windows are arrayed around the drum of the lantern *(shukhshikha)*, which is topped with a shallow octagonal roof. The stained glass colorfully depicts a plethora of fauna or hunting game.[46] In the side rooms off the main lounge, there are also blind-niche stained-glass stucco windows with artificial backlighting, of which a set of two is definitely by the architect, with one signed "RW.Wassef." However, there are two sets of three panels that are uncharacteristic of Wissa Wassef's work, putting into question whether they are by his hand, primarily because of the compositional symmetry and the framing of the scenes.

Main entrance to social club.

One of the sides of the lantern transition zone.

Side lounge panels.

Another side of the lantern transition zone.

NEMATALLA LOUIS MAUSOLEUM

Date: 1960
Location: Heliopolis Cemetery, Ard al-Gulf, Heliopolis, Cairo
Alternative name: Bulus Farag Allah Mausoleum

This mausoleum was commissioned by Nematalla Louis for his father.[47] Although the surviving plans demonstrate a design inspired by traditional Coptic architecture and do not match the constructed modernist mausoleum, its design is nevertheless attributed to Wissa Wassef.[48] The dates of the construction correspond to those of the design. The mausoleum consists of a small chapel with a crypt underneath it.

In the surrounding cemetery, mausoleum designs are replicated. These duplicate designs may be located in the same or different areas of the cemetery. Wissa Wassef's design was repeated a further two times—for different families, but both dating to 1961.

Perspective shot.

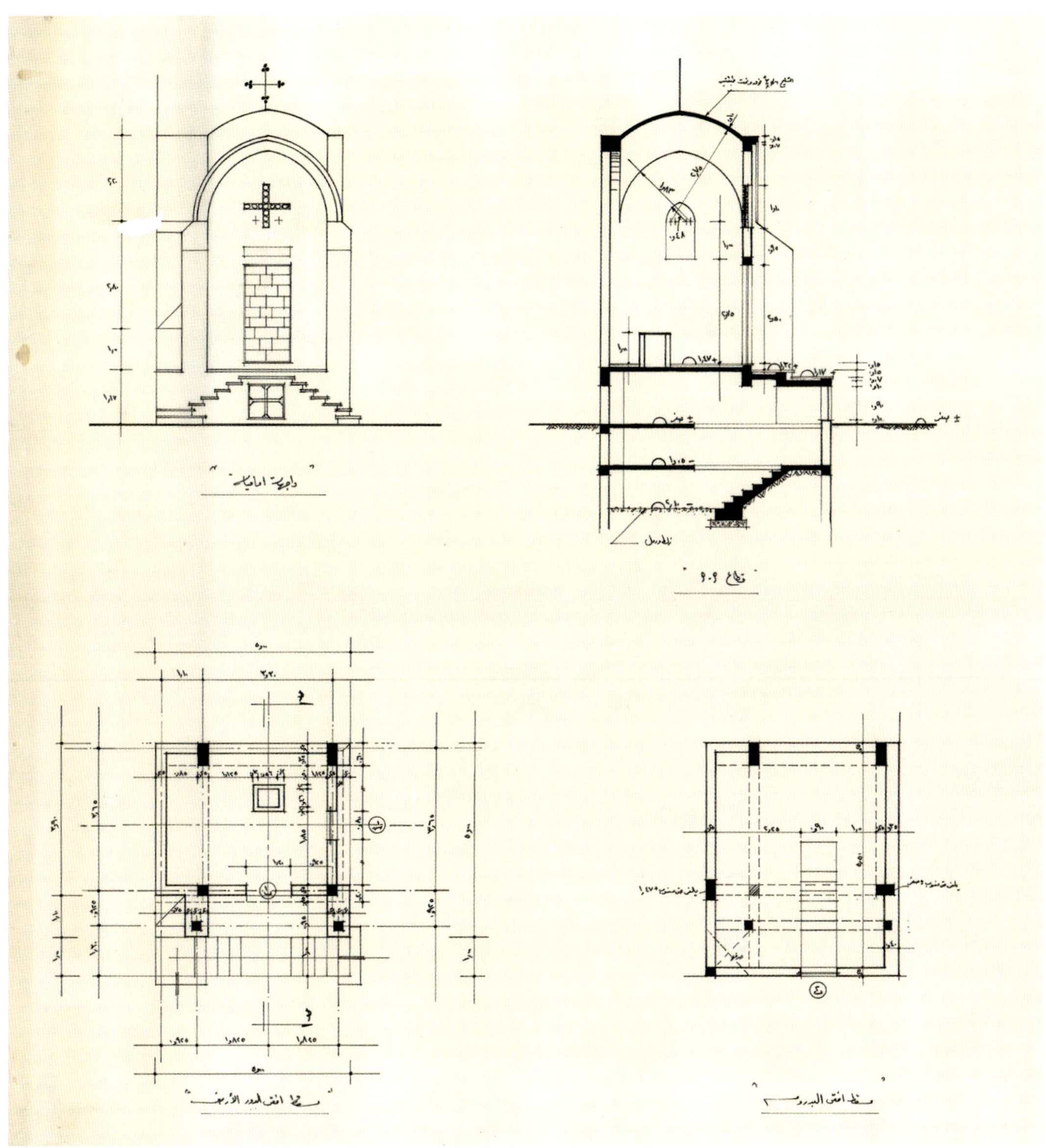

Original proposal: main elevation (top left), section (top right), chapel plan (bottom left), crypt plan (bottom right).

AL-DAR RESTAURANT

Date: 1968
Location: Maryutiya Road, Harraniya, Giza

Main entrance, 1983/1984.

Ismail Nafa'i originally came to Wissa Wassef requesting a house, but later changed his mind and converted the building into a restaurant. Only one plan of the building has been found, along with one rudimentary sketch. From the car drop-off area, one enters the restaurant into a two-bay corridor that overlooks a courtyard. At the end of this corridor is a doorway, over which is a glazed tile with a relief inscription,[49] which leads to the restaurant vestibule and stairs with decorative tiles embedded in the risers.

The vestibule is a domed double-height space with stained-glass stucco panels, a trio of glass piercings in the dome above each of its corners, a *mashrabiya* looking from the first-floor room into the vestibule, a four-panel door framed with decorative tiles and a wooden canopy, a side vestibule with a *mashrabiya* looking out and a door leading to the outdoor dining area, and an arched way with an arabesque door leading to the restaurant dining hall. The dining hall roof is made up of six pendentive domes pierced with eight glass oculi. Upstairs is what would have been the main bedroom in the original dwelling but was used as an office, with another *mashrabiya* looking outward (as well as the one looking into the vestibule), a wooden-beamed ceiling, and a balcony. The peculiar setup is a testament to the design of the building as a house prior to its final designated function.

In 1982–83 Ikram Nosshi made some renovations and expansions to the kitchen, as well as adding a new dining hall. Around the mid-1980s Essam Safey El Din added a store in the courtyard of the restaurant. At some point between this latter addition and the early 1990s, the restaurant Andrea was added in the rear yard of al-Dar, both restaurants operating side by side until they closed at some point in the 2000s. Since then the buildings have been abandoned.

FROM TOP LEFT, CLOCKWISE:
Two-bay corridor overlooking courtyard, 1983/1984.
Restaurant vestibule, 1983/1984.
Restaurant dining hall, 1983/1984.

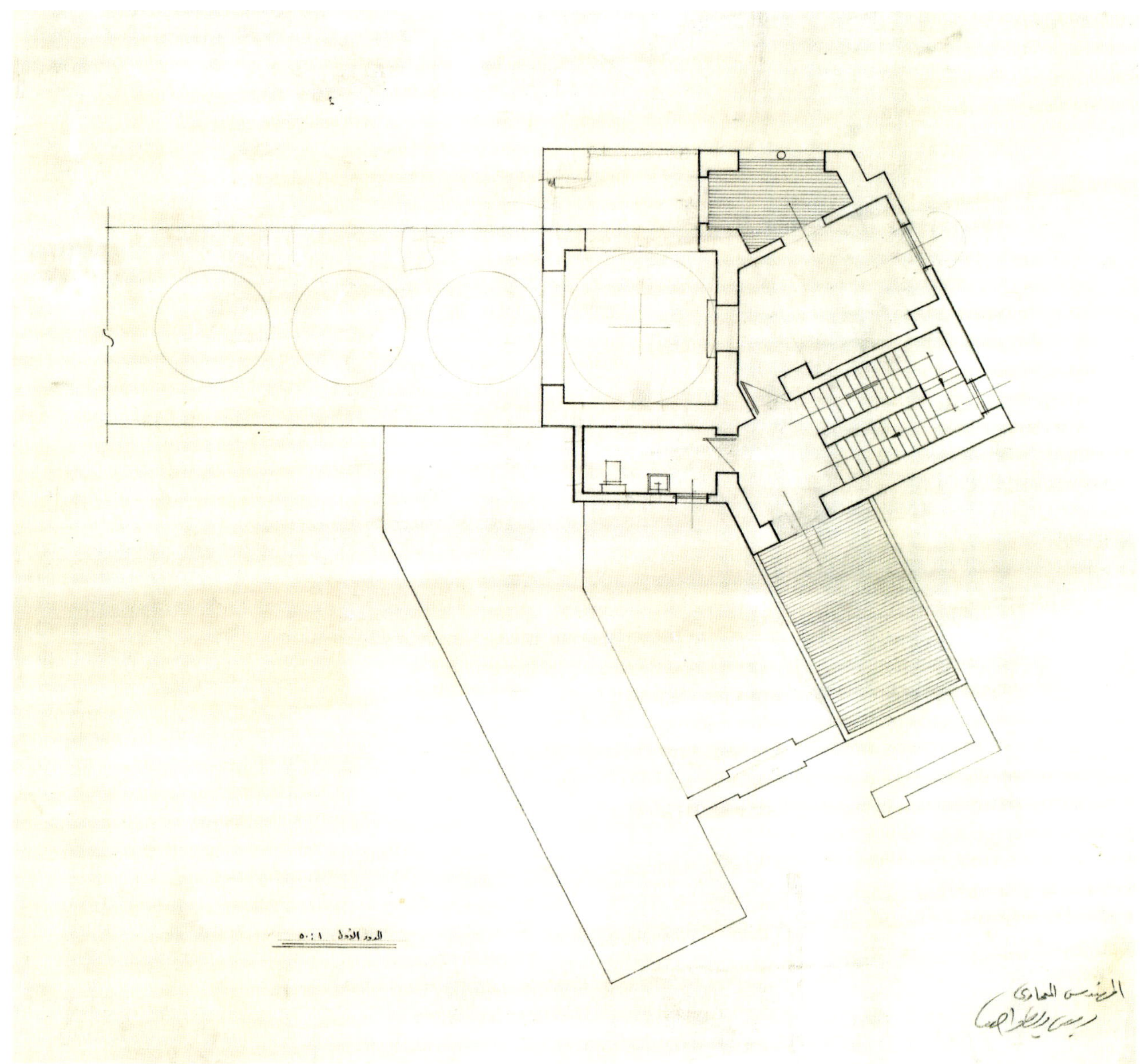

First-floor plan.

LOUNGE CEILING AT THE PALESTINE HOTEL

Date: 1964
Location: Montazah Palace, Alexandria
Alternative name: Helnan Palestine Hotel

The hotel was built to host the attendees, mostly kings and heads of state, of the Arab Summit held in Alexandria on 5 September 1964. Commissioned in February 1964 by Gamal Abd al-Nasser to occupy part of the gardens of the Montazah Palace, which had become state property following the revolution of 1952, the hotel was completed in six months.[50] Most likely the hotel was named "Palestine" due to the creation of the Palestine Liberation Organization (PLO), which was backed by Nasser, during the same year in which it was built and inaugurated.[51] Since its opening, the building has undergone renovations and expansions, but Wissa Wassef's work remains intact despite little to no maintenance of the lighting system.

The hotel lobby includes a stone relief depicting underwater scenes of Poseidon and mermaids by the Egyptian sculptor May 'Abd al-Karim. The lounge is decorated with a pierced stucco-and-glass shallow domed ceiling designed by Wissa Wassef. It depicts a central circle filled with ancient Egyptian stars and surrounded by female figures and sets of two kneeling Horus figures facing each other—all of whom have their arms raised as if they are the air lifting the sky disk, like the god Shu. They are surrounded by the twelve signs of the zodiac and five-pointed stars.

This composition is embraced by a crescent shape formed by sea waves and filled with fish. Below this sea is a map of the Arab world commemorating the Arab Summit for which the hotel was built, with the attendant countries represented by their flags. At the center is Egypt (or the United Arab Republic, as it was then called) represented by the 1958 flag along the Nile; to its south is Sudan, and to the west are Libya, Tunisia, Algeria, and Morocco followed by a strip of sea. To the east of Egypt is the Red Sea, including the Sinai Peninsula, and the countries of the Levant and the Gulf countries with the Gulf of Aden to their south: Jordan, Lebanon, Syria, Kuwait, Saudi Arabia, and Yemen.[52] To the far east is Iraq, depicted with two unidentified rivers. South of Iraq is a displaced larger flag that dominates the rest without having a correct geographical location; presumably, it is the flag of Palestine[53]—a symbol of the Palestinian plight, and the namesake of the hotel. The space between the countries depicted contains representations of local flora and fauna.

Central shot of the dome focusing on the map of the Arab Summit countries.
OPPOSITE: General view of the lounge.

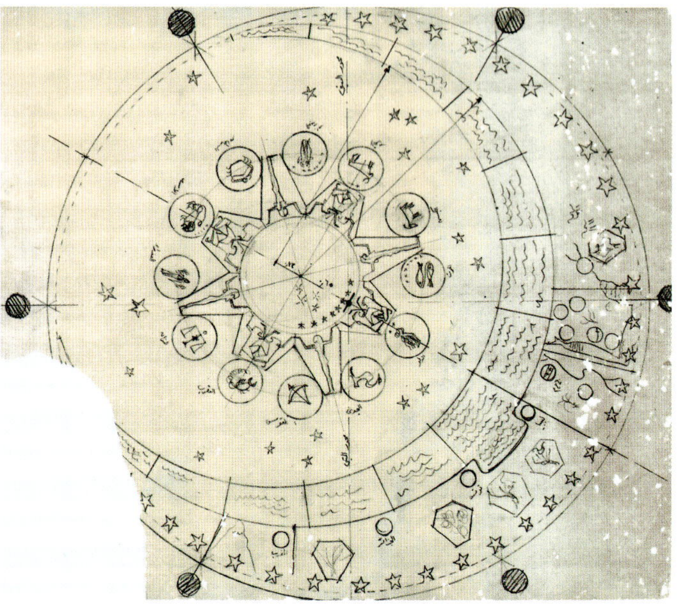

Preliminary sketch of the zodiac that appears on the dome.

Nonextant

CHURCHES

EVANGELICAL PRESBYTERIAN CHURCH

Date: 1940
Location: Off Ramses Street (previously al-Malika Nazli Street), Cairo
Alternative name: Église Presbytérienne Évangélique

This contemporary church was Wissa Wassef's first ecclesiastical design. Tasked with accommodating 1,550 people in its ground floor and gallery spaces, Wissa Wassef experimented extensively with the configuration of spaces and their form. The design predominantly followed an auditorium-type shape with a telescopic section, creating a staggered exterior. The ribs of the telescopic interior frame the sanctuary and create a triumphal arch. The church complex includes secondary services such as an events hall and street-front stores. A proposal exists for a small apartment above the events hall.

The elevation trials vary from enforcing a linear accent on the entrance to incorporating a loftier narthex. The latter option—although contemporary, with an Art Deco influence, particularly in the pediment—also integrates classical elements with the relief carvings on either side of the entrance. A perfect balance is struck between the minimalism of the form and the complexity of the ornamentation.

TOP:
Main elevation.
BOTTOM:
Main elevation alternative.

OPPOSITE, FROM TOP LEFT, CLOCKWISE:
Main elevation alternative.
Section showing telescopic ribs of nave and sanctuary.
Alternative design for the sanctuary.
First-floor proposal.

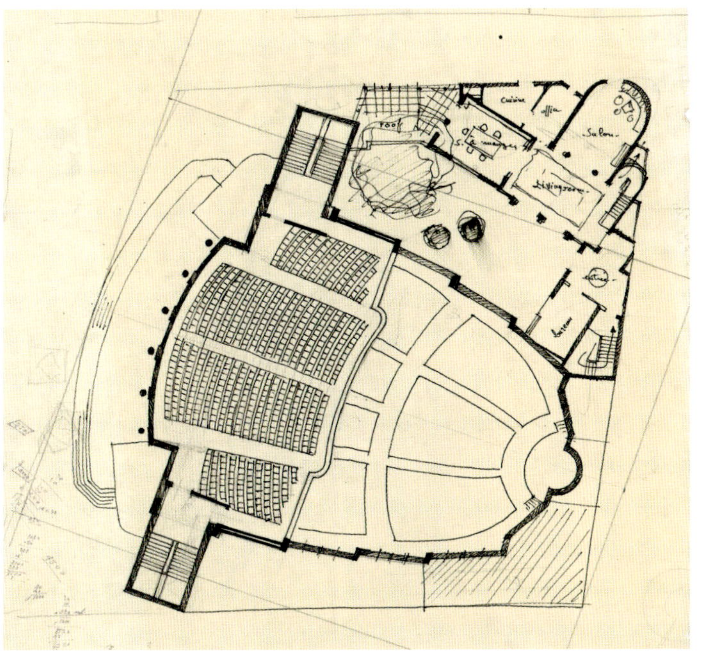

ST. GEORGE THE MARTYR COPTIC ORTHODOX CHURCH, GIZA DIOCESE

Date: 1947
Location: Murad Street, Giza
Alternative names: Kanisat Mar Girgis al-Shahid al-qibtiya al-urthudhuksiya, Matraniyat al-Giza

Wissa Wassef's involvement in the design of this church is uncertain, as the clergy attributes its design to Mourad Bakhoum.[1] Additionally, there is doubt over who designed the original stained-glass stucco windows, which were changed in the first decade of the twenty-first century. The front elevation of the church is adorned with a dominant stained-glass stucco window depicting St. George slaying the dragon.

Wissa Wassef proposed five unique compositions for the layout of this church, some of which had several versions with variations for the narthex, community services buildings, or location on the site. He also sketched out four elevation proposals. In some of these, the church faced east, while in the others it is oriented southeast so the building is perpendicular to the main street. The existing building follows the second orientation and has a barrel vault covering its nave, which was not in any of Wissa Wassef's proposals.

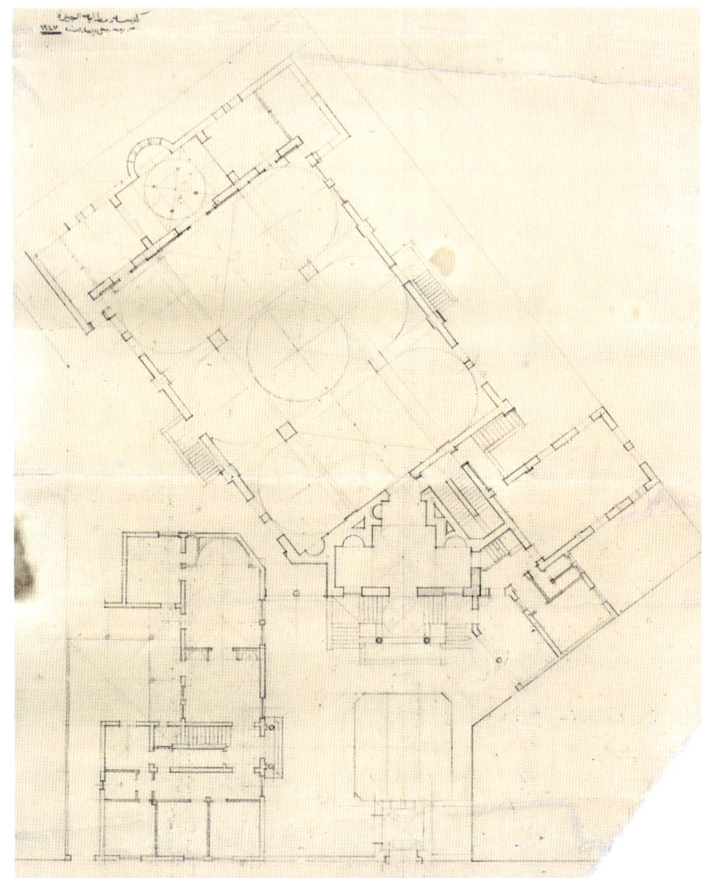

Proposal 1 plan.

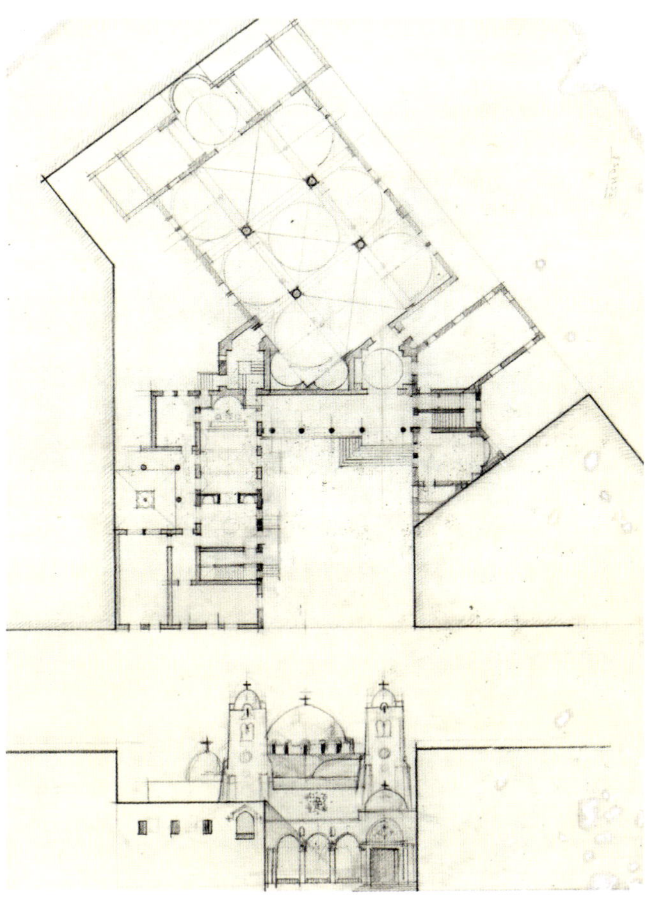

Proposal 2 plan (top), and main elevation (bottom).

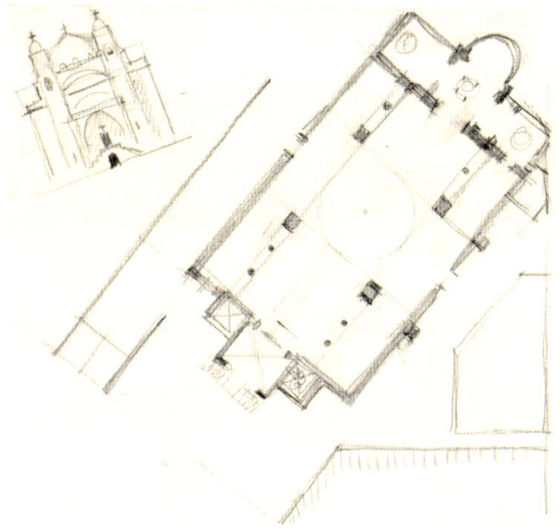

Proposal 3 plan (bottom), and main elevation (top).

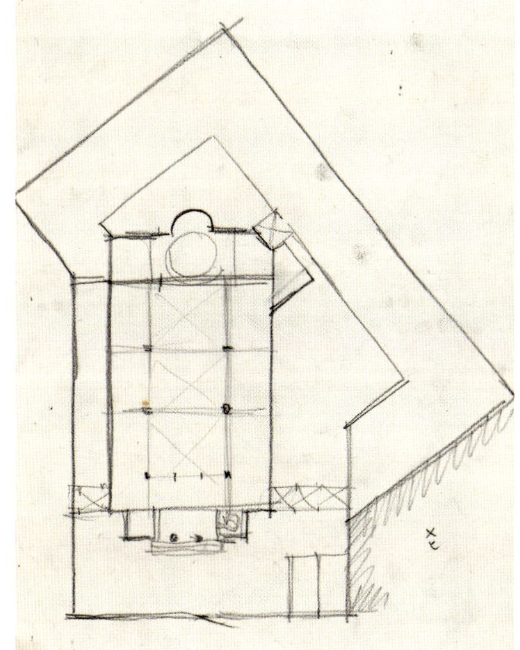

Proposal 4 plan.

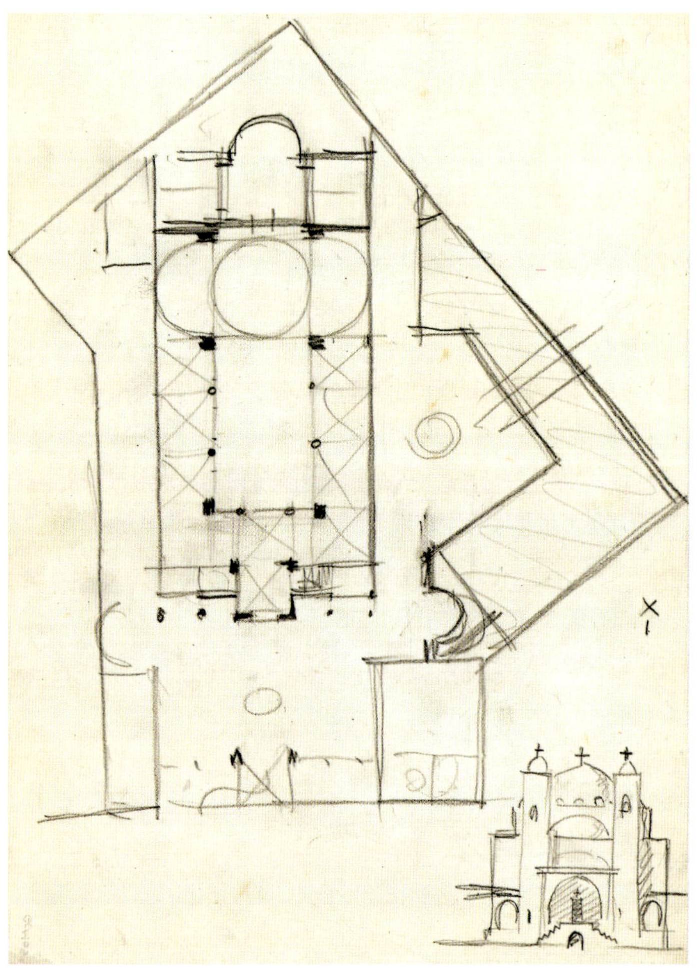

Proposal 5 plan (top) and main elevation (bottom).

Proposal 1 main elevation alternative.

TWO MARTYRS CYRUS AND JOHN COPTIC ORTHODOX CHURCH

Date: c.1947
Location: al-Anba Kirullus Street, Abu Qir
Alternative names: St. Cyrus and St. John Coptic Orthodox Church, Two Great Martyrs Abakir and Yuhanna Coptic Orthodox Church, Kanisat al-shahidayn Abakir wa Yuhanna al-qibtiya al-urthudhuksiya

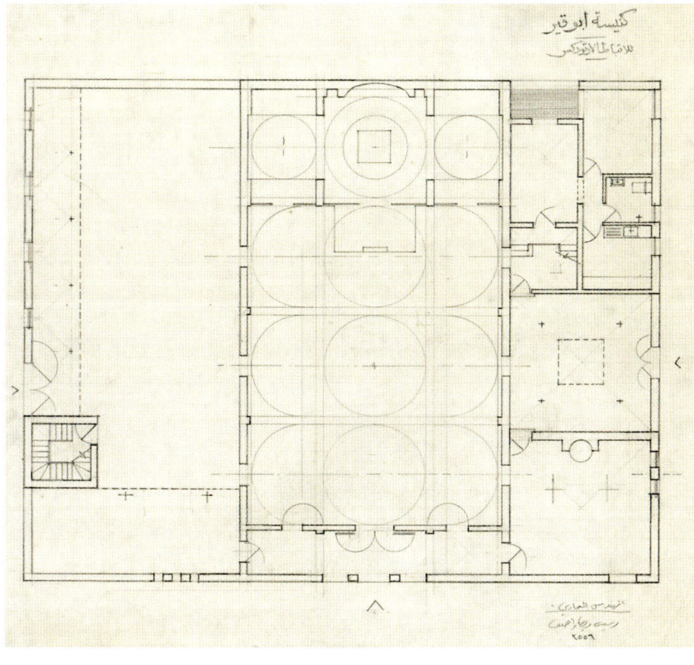

Proposal 1, alternative 1, ground-floor plan.

Wissa Wassef experimented with various designs for this church. The first proposal consists of a building oriented southwest and placed centrally on the plot. It has a large nave, without aisles, and is roofed with three central domes—each supported by two half domes. There are also some side rooms and courtyards for the congregation. This design has an alternative configuration with the church on the side of the plot, leaving a larger open space onto which the other rooms open. This alternative was developed further to include guesthouse apartments on part of the open space.

The other proposals vary from having a square nave with one large central dome to the same configuration but with the large central dome flanked by a half dome between the nave and the narthex. The *haykal* also varies between a tri-apse and a triconch.

Ultimately, in 1947, the contractors Sharubim and Farag Akladious built a church that does not follow any of Wissa Wassef's designs.[2] The existing church is aligned with the street, with a southeast orientation. It has a barrel-vaulted nave and a belfry to the side of the church door rather than on the corner of the building as in Wissa Wassef's proposals.

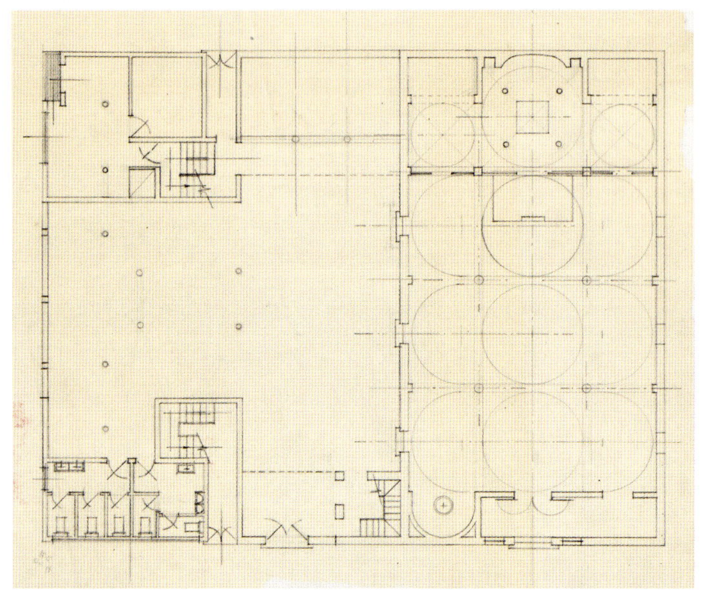

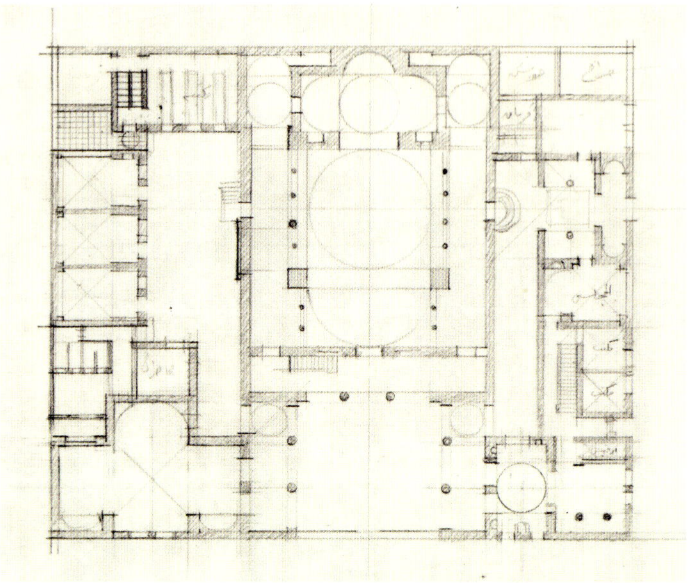

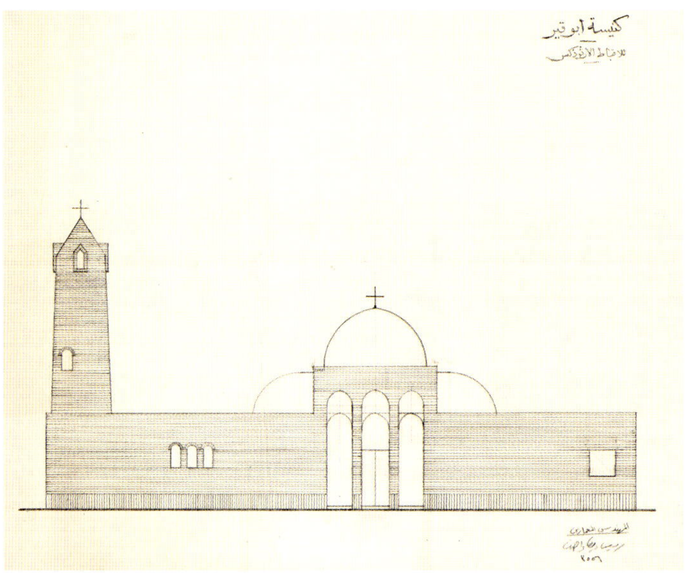

FROM TOP LEFT, CLOCKWISE:
Proposal 1, alternative 2, ground-floor plan.
Proposal 2, ground-floor plan.
Main elevation of proposal 1, alternative 1.

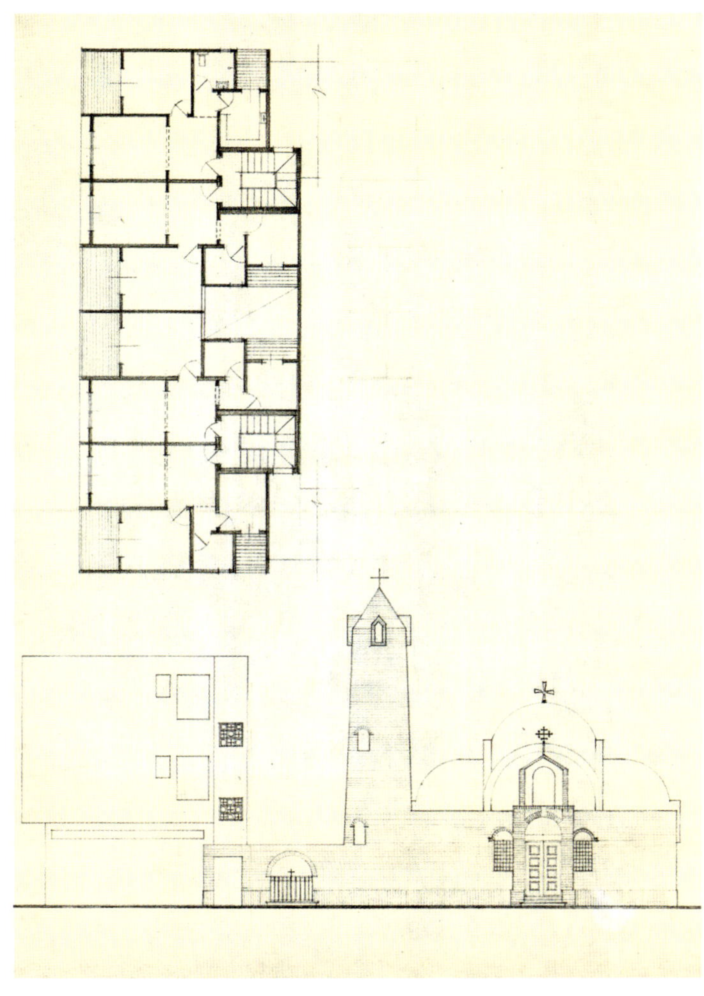

Main elevation of proposal 1, alternative 2 (bottom), plan of guesthouse apartments (top).

Side elevation sketch.

ST. JOSEPH CHURCH

Date: 1952
Location: Alexandria

Most likely this church was never built; its exact proposed location is unknown. Its design follows a boat-shaped morphology like that of the Church of the Virgin Mary in Zamalek, but its manifestation is quite different. In the Zamalek church the ribs run along the inside, pierce the protrusion that contains the clerestory, and run along the outside of the church to pierce back in and run along the flat ceiling. Here the church has concrete arches appearing as ribs supporting the nave's barrel vault. It follows a basilica plan, with a gallery over the side aisles.

One of the most prominent features of the building is the way in which its belfry breaks the symmetry of the elevation, being attached to the side of the church on the eastern end. Having it separated rather than embedded in the bulk of the building gives it and the sanctuary dome prominence without competition between them.

Great attention is paid to the sections. In the longitudinal section, columns are topped with two types of capitals and the arches that support the barrel vault end with a Coptic cross. The sanctuary dome transitions from a square space with the use of squinches, and a vegetal band decorates the edge of the gallery's floor slab. In the transversal section, the iconostasis consists of wall paneling while the central part is a wooden screen, behind which is the altar and ciborium. The apse is topped by the sketch of a central figure with four medallions around it.

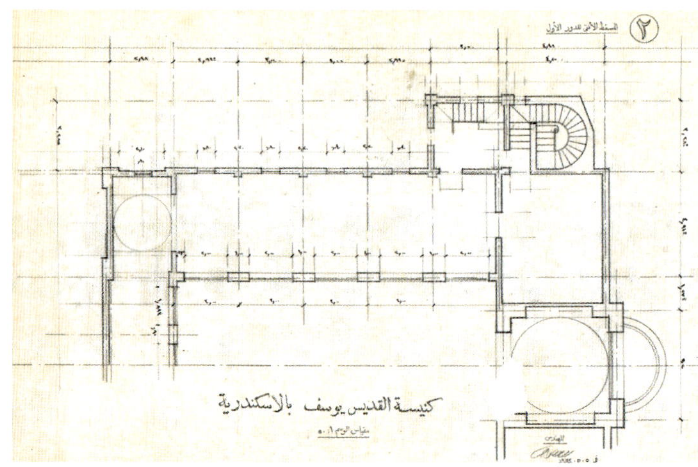

Partial ground-floor plan.

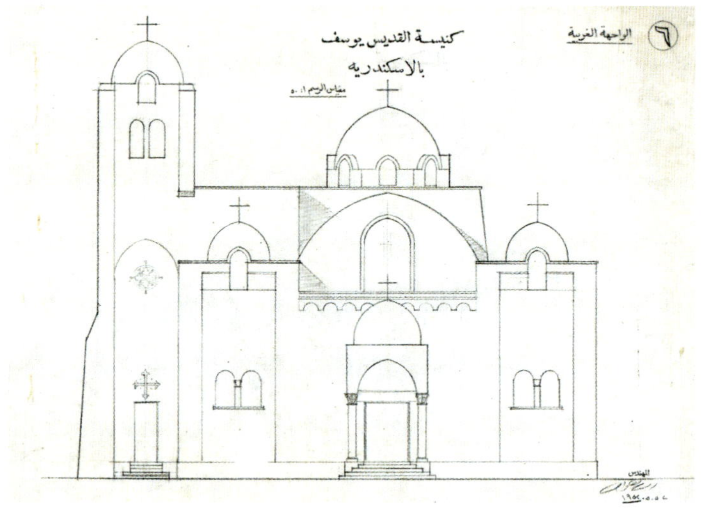

Main elevation.

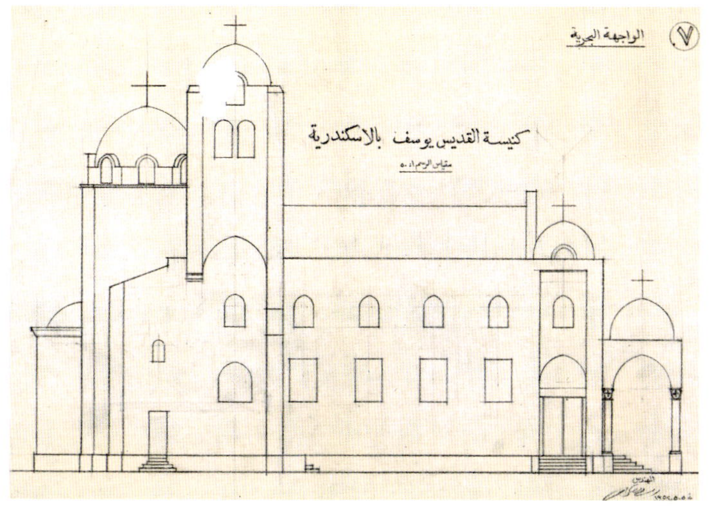

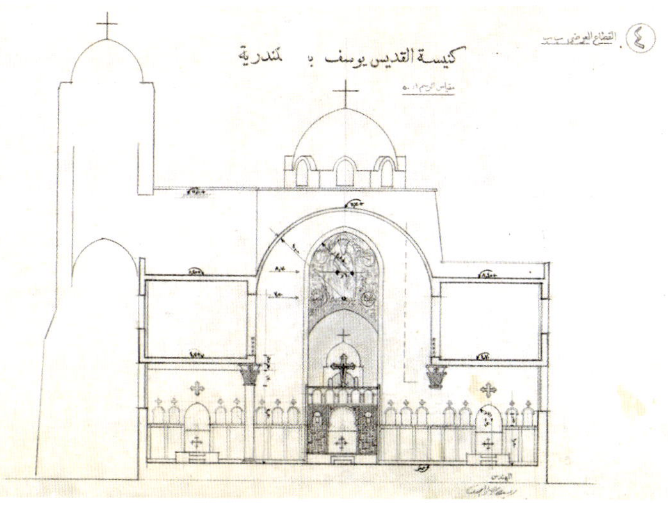

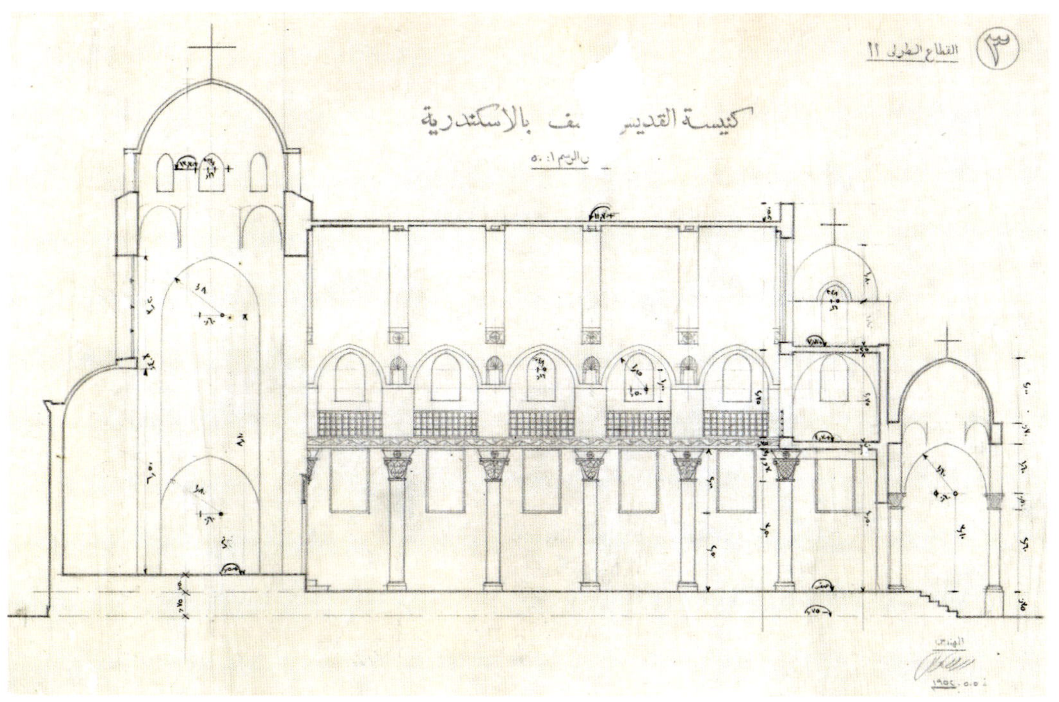

FROM TOP LEFT, CLOCKWISE:
Side elevation.
Transverse section.
Longitudinal section.

ST. GEORGE MONASTERY ON THE NILE BANK

Date: 1956

Location: Nile Corniche, Kozzika, Tora, Cairo

Alternative names: Mar Girgis Monastery in Tora, Mar Girgis Church in Kozzika, Dayr Mar Girgis bi-Tura 'ala shati' al-Nil

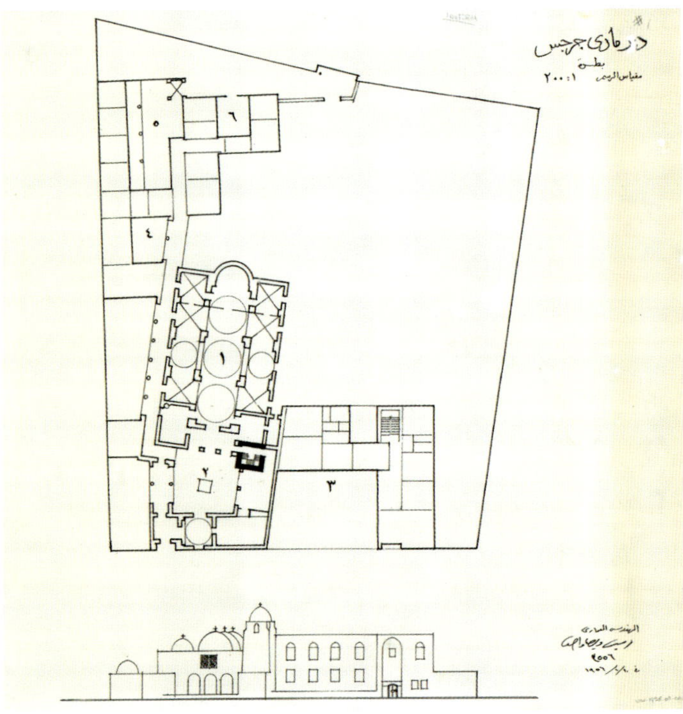

Site plan for the monastery, including the ground floor of the church (top) and the main elevation (bottom).

The monastery of St. George in Tora had been in existence since at least the eleventh century, when it was known as Dayr al-Fukhar, and later as Dayr al-Arman. During a large part of its history, it had an important connection with the monastery on top of Gabal Tura, Dayr al-Qasir. In 1956 the monastery was demolished to make way for the construction of the Nile Corniche road. The building was not documented prior to its demolition, and historical sources provide little information on its architecture and modifications over the centuries. However, it did contain a large *hawsh* (courtyard), a Roman well, the old church, a series of buildings, and a large garden with fruit-bearing trees.[3]

The Coptic Church was compensated financially for the destruction of its monastery and was granted permits to build a new church, although this is now disconnected from the Nile by the Corniche road. Wissa Wassef drew up a proposal for the new building. It seems to have been aimed at preserving the memory of old Coptic churches and monasteries, introducing small courtyards throughout the complex, a larger courtyard, a church following a plan that builds on the typologies of old churches with a mix of vaults and domes (the latter aligned in a cruciform formation), a minimalist belfry, and variation in fenestration.

However, in the end the replacement church complex was built in 1958 following the design of Naguib Stino.[4] Its ground-floor chapel contains the wooden elements and icons that were salvaged from the monastery.

EVANGELICAL CHURCH, COMMUNITY CENTER AND OFFICES

Date: 1958
Location: 39 Kamel Sedky Street (formerly, and more commonly, known as al-Faggala Street), al-Daher, Cairo

It seems that the Evangelical Church wanted to develop this plot of land on Faggala Street, approaching its development from different perspectives. The plot used to contain the Evangelical Primary School for Girls in Faggala, designed by a different architect whose signature is too faint to decipher,[5] which appeared in the 1933 Map of Cairo by Alexander Nicohosoff as the American Mission Girls School.[6]

One of the options for the development was to include the construction of the Evangelical Church's community center and offices. Wissa Wassef designed two schemes for this project. A third scheme exists among his collection but it is unlikely to be his, as it follows a different style in terms of inking, architectural concept, and layout. (It might have been given to him along with the school drawing to use as a reference.)

One of his designs introduces a sizable atrium, which leads to a large hall and side offices and community rooms. Despite integrating the atrium, which is a classical feature, the building is quite modern in its façade treatment. The other design proposes a large hall roofed with a shallow vault, with an adjoining L-shaped building containing the offices. One of the main features of this proposal is the entrance to the hall, which plays on a straight skin of glass and columns—behind which is a solid convex wall.

The other known option for the development of the land was the construction of a new church. In one of the designs, the main body of the church is square, with a large central dome supported by half domes on each side and small domes on the corners, and the sanctuary on the north. A courtyard lies to the west and has a needle-like belfry. The other design consists of a sketch proposing a square plan with two chamfered corners to create a corridor north of the church leading to the next-door plot. However, none of the proposals were built. The Evangelical Church maintained its offices in an apartment in the area until recently relocating to Heliopolis.

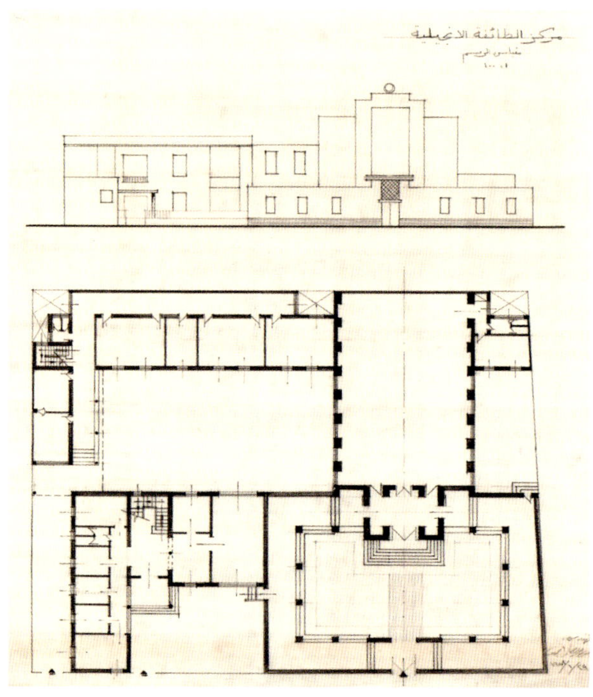

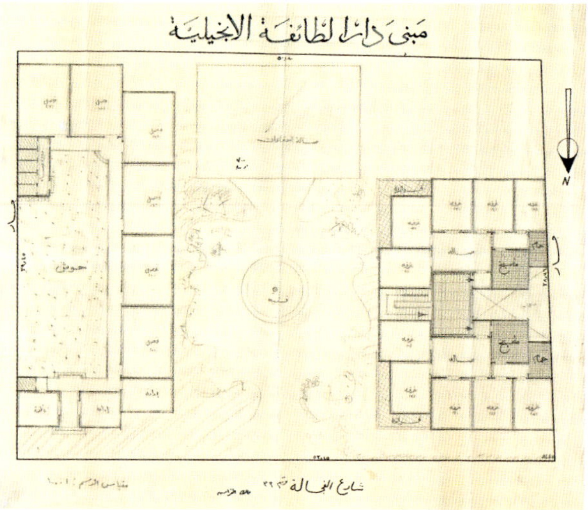

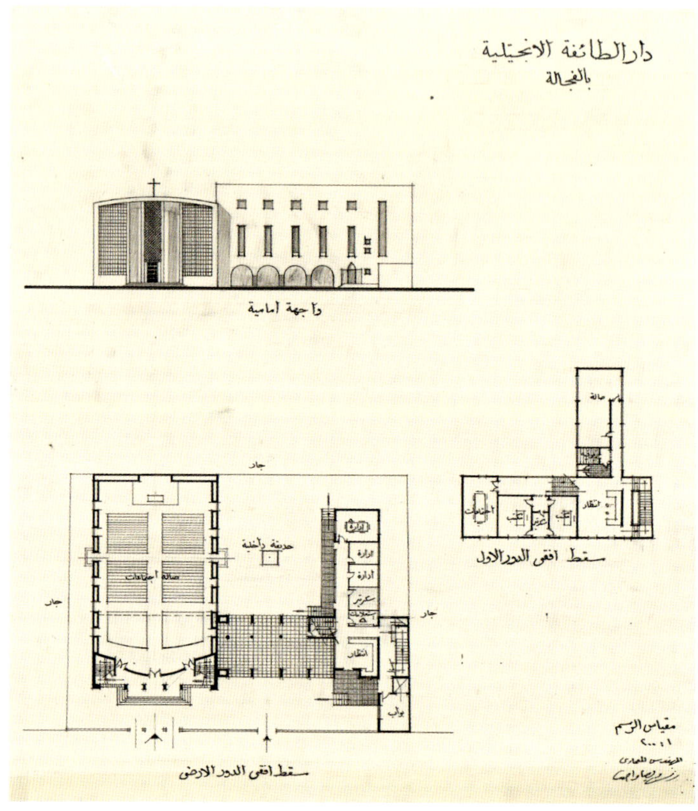

FROM TOP LEFT, CLOCKWISE:
Proposal 1 for the community center and offices showing main elevation (top) and plan (bottom).
Proposal 2 for the community center and offices showing main elevation (top left), first-floor plan (right), and ground-floor plan (bottom left).
Proposal 3 for the community center and offices, most likely not by Wissa Wassef.

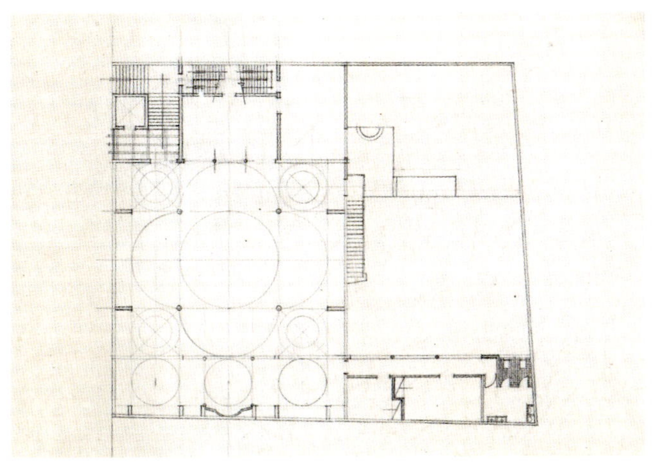

Plan of proposal 1 for a church.

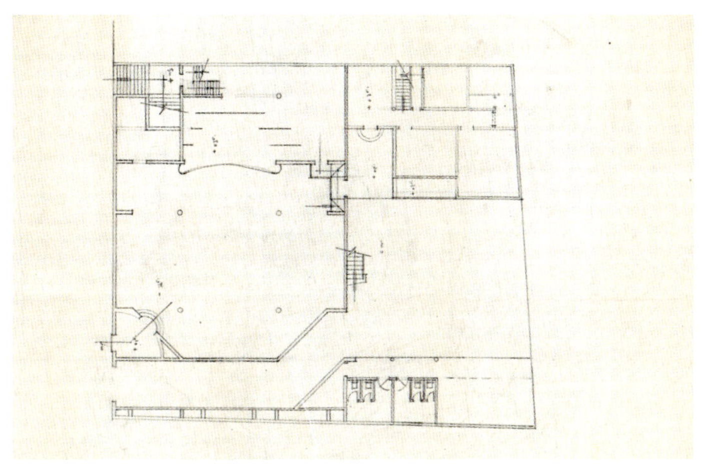

Plan of proposal 2 for a church.

Side elevation for proposal 1 of a church, showing one façade treatment alternative.

Side elevation for proposal 1 of a church, showing other façade treatment alternative.

COPTIC CATHOLIC PATRIARCHATE CHURCH

Date: 1962

Location: Harat al-Khukha, Old Cairo, Cairo

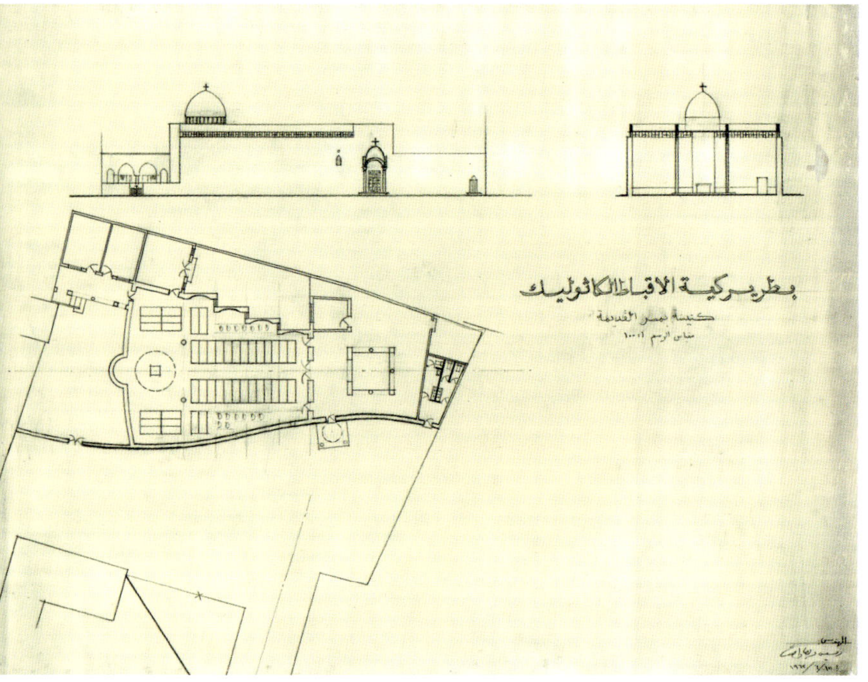

Proposal 1 plan (bottom), main elevation (top left), and section (top right).

The cadastral map included among Wissa Wassef's drawings for the design of this church reveals that part of the site was originally occupied by the Coptic Catholic Church of the Virgin Mary. Wissa Wassef designed two proposals for the replacement of the older church with a newer building.

The first proposal introduces an undulating wall, which acts as the wall into the church complex but also as the eastern wall of the church. The western wall is staggered to reflect the curve of the other wall, while also providing indirect lighting. It is an interesting hybrid of traditional elements of Coptic churches and contemporary design. The east wall is plain but for the doorways and a minimalist continuous strip of clerestory windows that surrounds the elevations to light the church interior. The second proposal is similar to the first, except that the church is rotated to face northeast–southwest instead of north–south, and its plan resembles that of an auditorium, with staggered walls on either side.

The older church was demolished, but a new church was never built. Instead, over the years the space the church once occupied developed into a street known as Harat al-Kanisa (Church Lane), lined with small residential buildings. The school that was originally next to the church was later converted into a workshop, which was demolished around 2016–18. It is unknown, even to the current Coptic Catholic Patriarchate, why Wissa Wassef's proposal was not implemented, or why the old church was demolished if the new proposal was never realized. A plausible explanation is that the demolition took place prior to finalizing the permits for the new building, which were not granted—or that the Patriarchate decided to drop the project, preferring a different location for its new church.

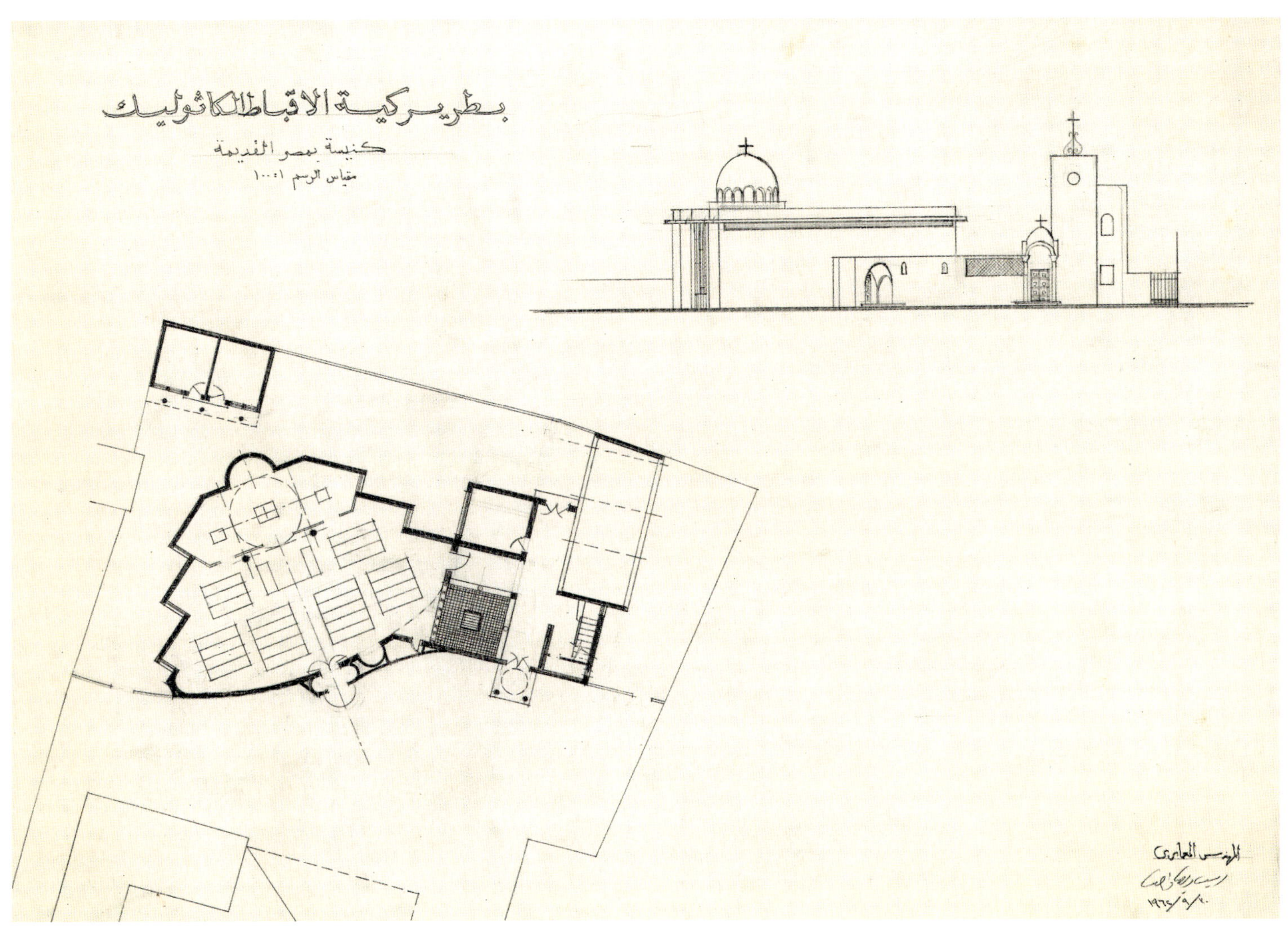

Proposal 2 plan (bottom) and main elevation (top right).

CATHEDRAL OF ST. MARK AND ANBA RUWAYS COMPOUND

Date: 1964

Location: Ramses Street, Abbasiya, Cairo

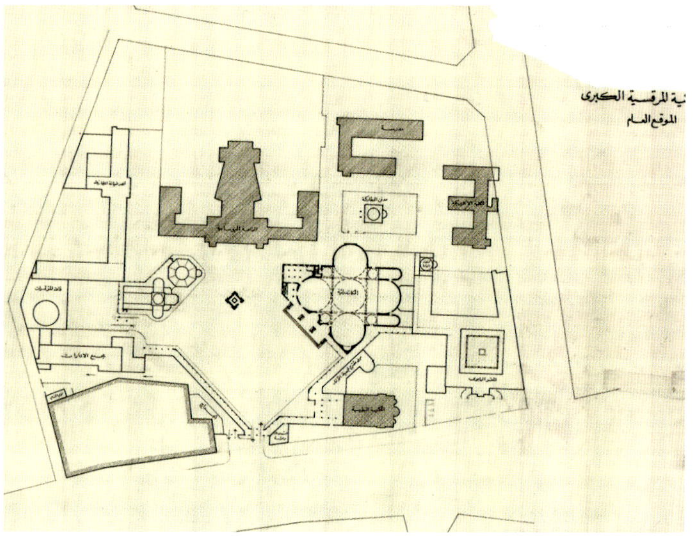

Site plan.

This project consists of Wissa Wassef's entry to the competition[7] for the development of the Anba Ruways compound and the construction of St. Mark's Cathedral. This is an area of historical religious importance dating back to the tenth century, which has undergone many changes in the centuries since.[8]

The proposal suggested preserving some buildings that existed in the compound; these included the al-Butrusiya Church (officially the Church of St. Peter and St. Paul), the clerical college, the school, and the Eusabian Hall (now known as al-Murqusiya Hall).[9] To the east of this hall, Wissa Wassef proposed a mausoleum for the burial of the patriarchs.

The general plan proposes the introduction of the Cathedral of St. Mark at the center of the compound with a stand-alone bell tower; leading from it to the west is the papal residence, and southward it connects to al-Butrusiya via a domed cloister and a building for hosting historic Coptic artifacts.

This cloister opens to highlight al-Butrusiya and runs south to the main gate and then continues on a perpendicular to connect with the majority of the proposed buildings: administrative block, conference hall, and the bishops' guesthouse. In front of the conference hall and a large plaza are two small churches. Together these two churches, the cathedral, and the cloister create a rectangular court or atrium.

The two unnamed churches on the western side of the court are captioned "reconstructed churches." It is possible that these are the proposals for the Church of the Holy Virgin Mary and St. Pshoi, and the Church of the Holy Virgin Mary and Anba Ruways—the two replacement churches that Pope Kirullus VI decided to build after discovering that the Church of the Virgin Mary would have to be demolished for construction of the cathedral.[10]

Awad Kamel Fahmy won the competition and, in his design, implemented and inaugurated in 1968, these churches were rebuilt under the new cathedral, which is elevated off the ground and has monumental steps leading up to it.[11]

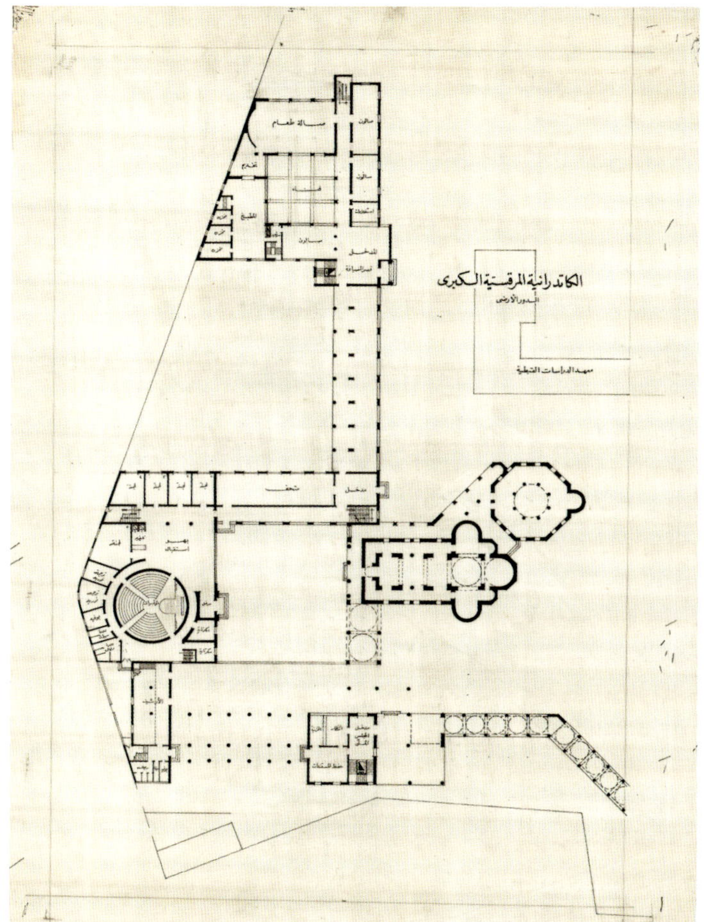

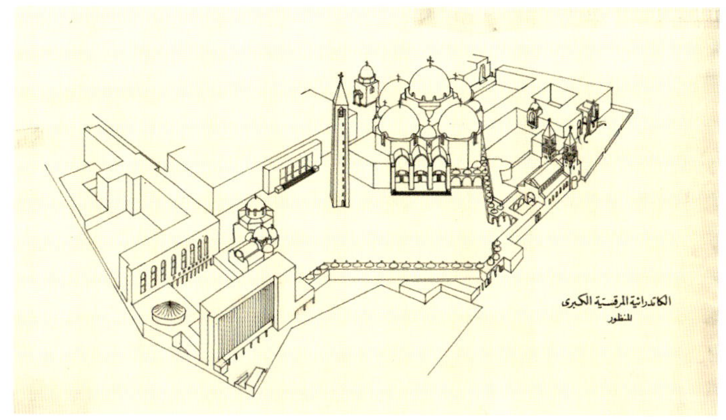

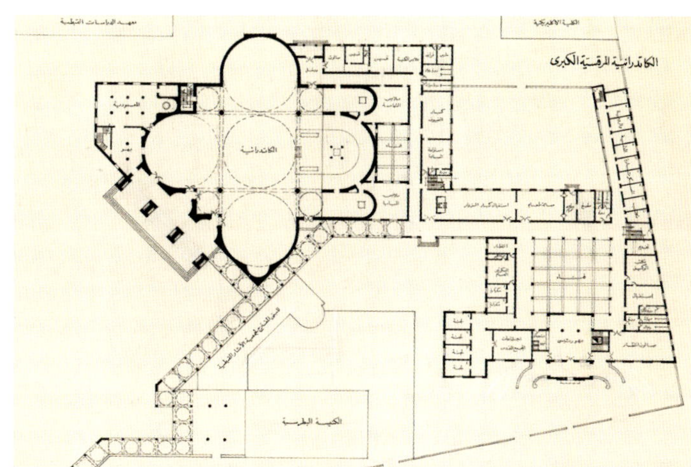

FROM LEFT, CLOCKWISE:
Plan of the reconstructed churches, administrative block, conference hall, and bishops' guesthouse.
Axonometry of the proposed buildings within the complex.
Plan of the cathedral and papal residence.

East elevation of cathedral and section through papal residence (left), and longitudinal section through cathedral (right).

Main elevation of cathedral (left) and transversal section (right).

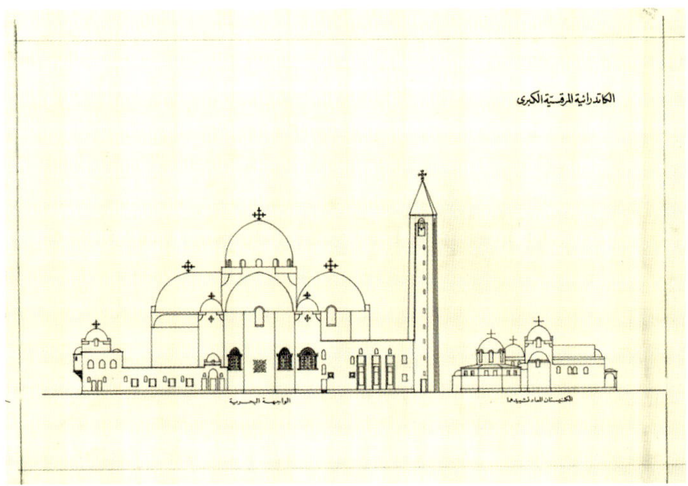

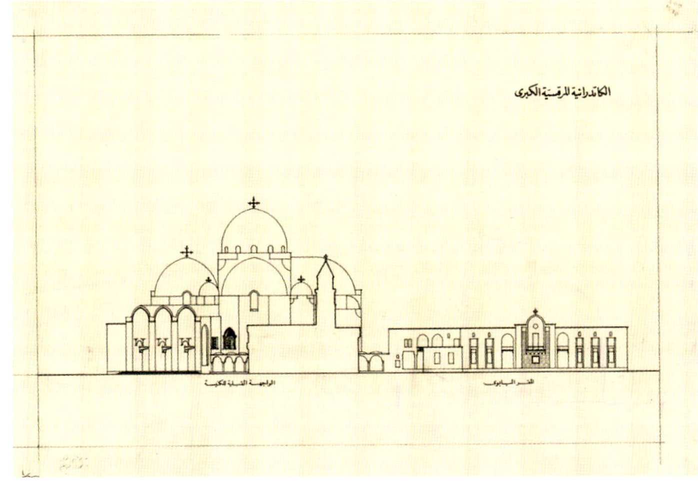

North elevations of cathedral (left) and reconstructed churches (right).

South elevations of the cathedral (left) and the papal residence (right).

HELIOPOLIS CHURCH THEATER AND CLUB EXTENSION

Date: Unknown
Location: Heliopolis, Cairo

This project is for the theater and community club building as part of an extension to a church in Heliopolis. The church for which this project was designed remains unidentified, and as such its status is unknown.

The design of the theater and community services building takes on elements from traditional Coptic church architecture in its elevations and sections, while introducing a contemporary plan. It is a unique hybrid of traditional and modern architecture. In one proposal, the main entrance leads to a domed space with an administration office on the right and a foyer on the left, reminiscent of a narthex. It opens to a central nave topped by three domes that faces the stage. The right aisle wall follows a folded plane with a gallery overhead, topped with half domes, reached via a spiral staircase in the main space. In contrast, the left aisle has a staggered façade to allow for natural lighting, a flat roof, and no gallery. Near the stage there is a door that connects to the three-story community services building, giving the extension an overall L shape. A small corridor separates this building extension from the church. In the top left corner of the plot there is a playground/sports area.

The second proposal is quite different in its treatment of the main theater hall, while keeping the service building, entrance, and main elevation the same. The plan consists of the stage area, in front of which is a domed double-height audience area that sits two steps lower than its surrounding ambulatory. The front arch supporting the dome is conveniently used to frame the stage and support the stage curtain. The back of the ambulatory can also act as an audience space. The whole ambulatory takes the form of a gallery on the first floor. In this case, the rear of the ambulatory is topped by a dome, its left side by a half dome, and the right by a flat roof.

Proposal 2 main elevation. The only difference between it and the one for proposal 1 is the positioning of the domes to reflect the plans.

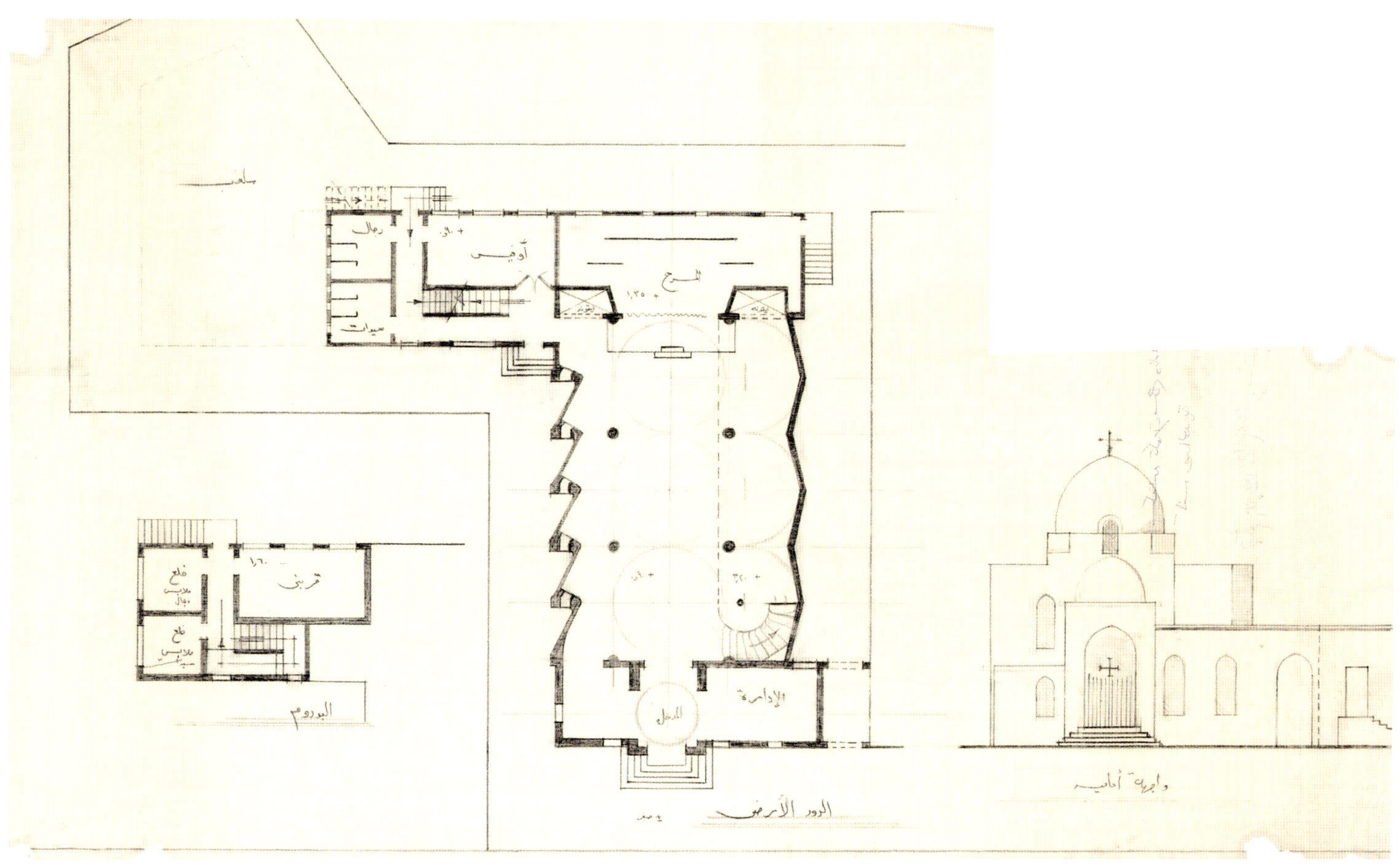

Proposal 1 basement plan (bottom left), ground-floor plan (center), and main elevation (bottom right).

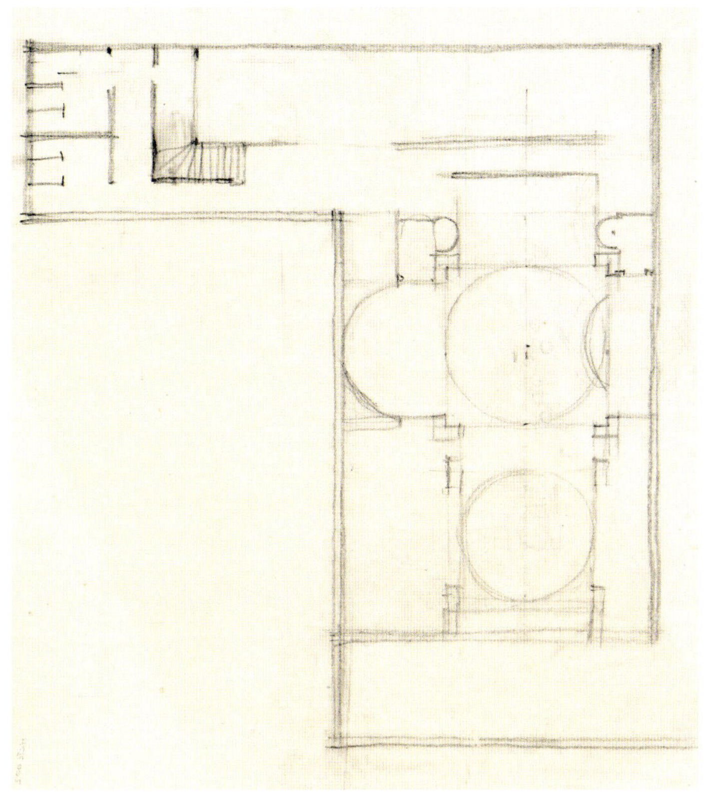

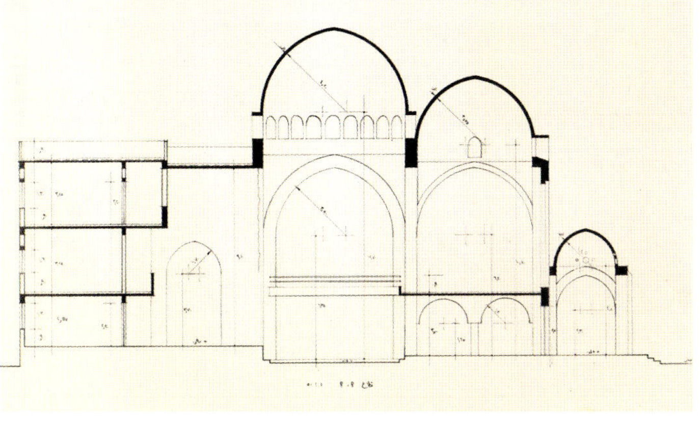

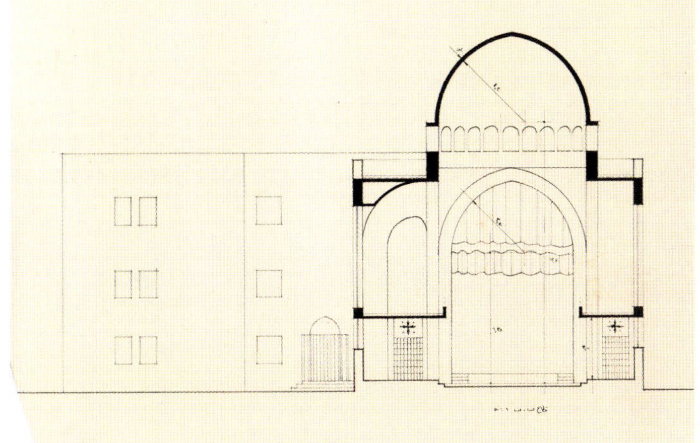

FROM LEFT, CLOCKWISE:
Proposal 2 ground-floor plan.
Proposal 2 longitudinal section.
Proposal 2 transversal section.

ICONOSTASIS AT THE COPTIC CATHOLIC CHURCH OF FAGGALA

Date: Unknown
Location: Yusuf Pasha Sulayman Street, al-Daher, Cairo
Alternative names: Église Copte Catholique de Faggala, St. Antonious Coptic Catholic Cathedral, St. Antoine Coptic Catholic Church

This church was designed by Gabriel Aclimandos, including a proposal for a *fer forgé* (wrought-iron) iconostasis.[12] On the other hand, Wissa Wassef also designed an iconostasis for this church, fitting perfectly within Aclimandos's architectural design. One of the unique features of Wissa Wassef's design is its replacing of the square panels of a traditional screen of wooden joinery (composed of squares and crosses) with *mashrabiya*-type lattice squares. It is unknown if Wissa Wassef's design was installed and replaced later or never implemented.

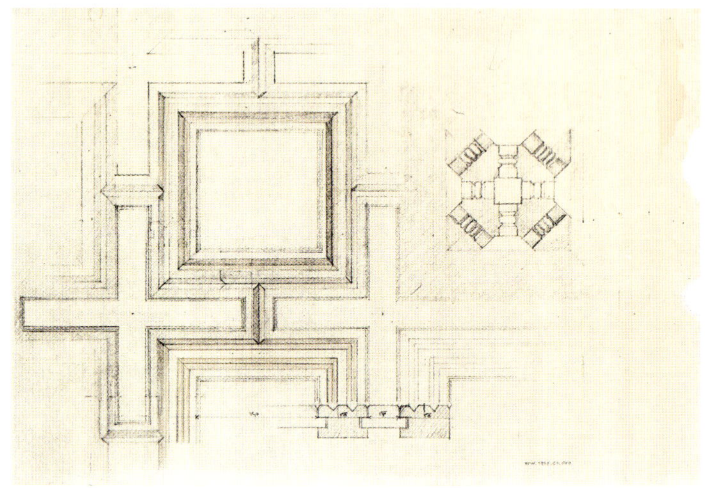

Detail of iconostasis wood paneling and lattice.

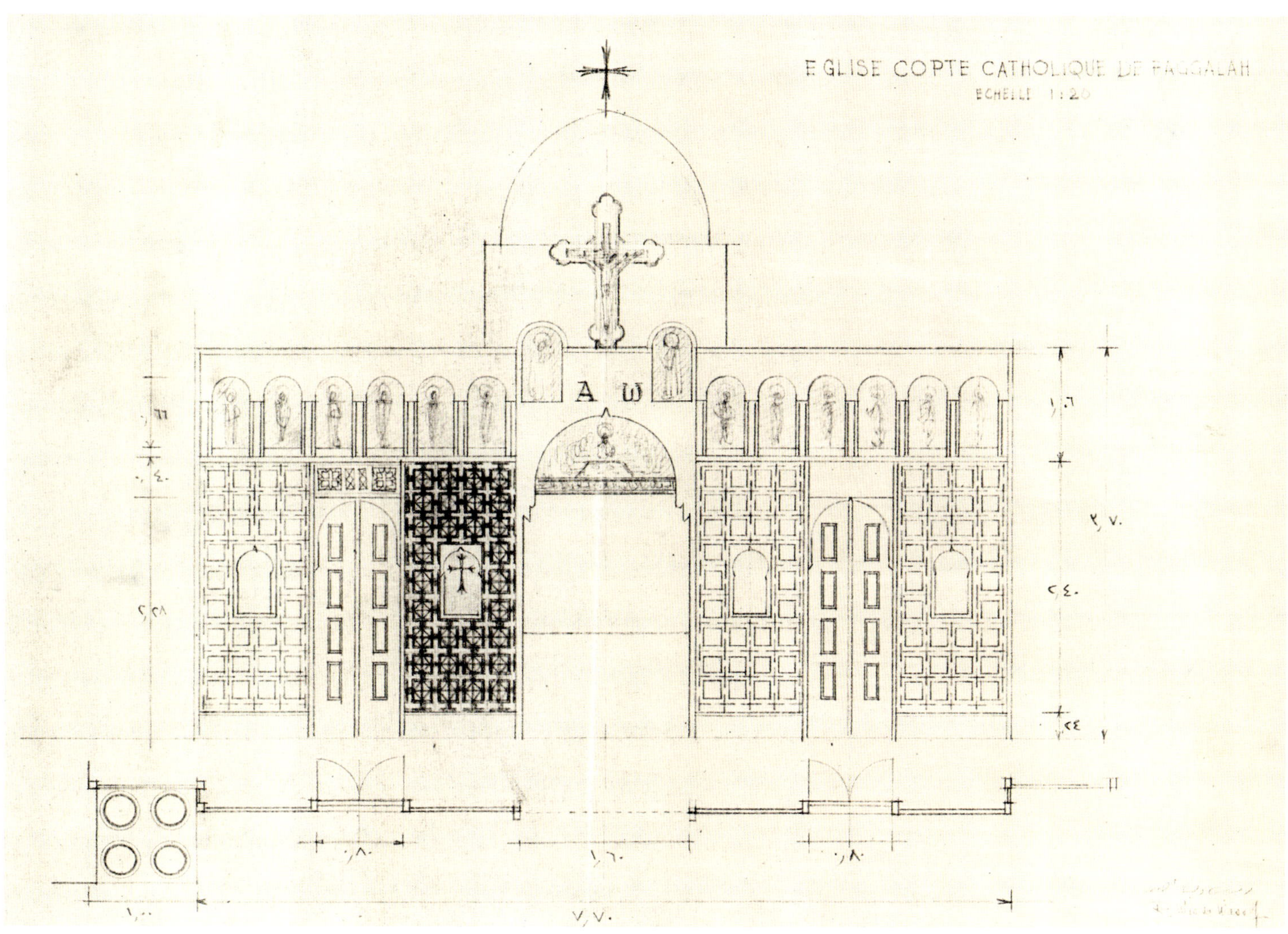

Elevation of iconostasis.

UNIDENTIFIED CHURCH COMMUNITY SERVICES BUILDING

Date: Unknown
Location: Unknown

This project consists of a church community services building, designed as a learning space with classrooms on the ground and first floors while including changing rooms in the basement. The ground floor contains a small chapel, and this whole level is connected via a small corridor to what is presumed to be the main church building.

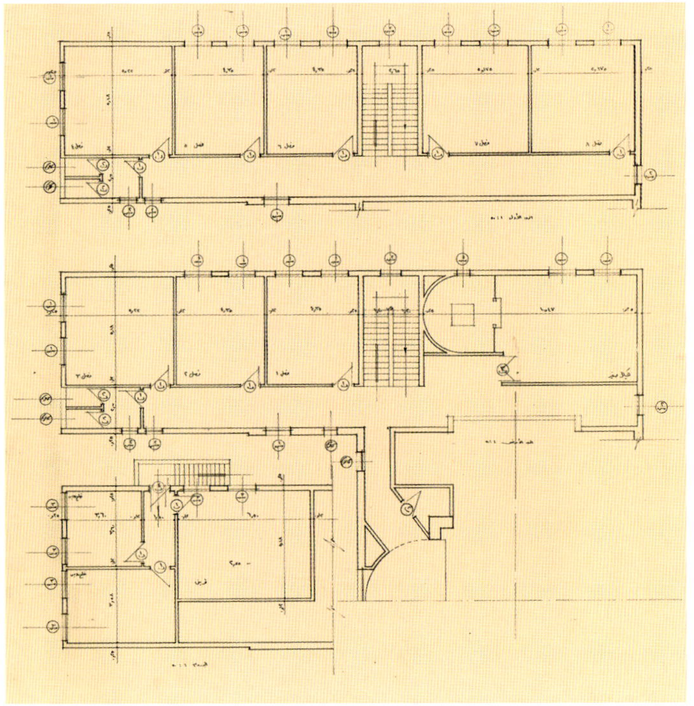

First (top), ground (center), and basement (bottom) floor plans.

UNIDENTIFIED CHURCH 1

Date: Unknown
Location: Unknown

In this unidentified church, Wissa Wassef put most of the effort into the design of the sanctuary. What makes this design different from his other ecclesiastical work is that the sanctuary is not bounded by walls, making its circumambulation possible. Originally a security feature that was frequently implemented in churches in Upper Egypt during times of turmoil to grant the clergy a direct exit, this evolved as a design feature.[13] Hence, it is likely that this church's intended location was in Upper Egypt.

The altar has a Coptic cross on the front that is embedded within a geometric pattern. On top of it is a cross supported by a base and flanked by candlesticks. Over the altar is a ciborium, and these features are surrounded on all four sides by the iconostasis. The front of this screen, facing the nave, is made up of a *mashrabiya* lattice with an opening through which to enter the sanctuary, which is elevated by two steps. The back is made of traditional wooden paneling and has a large icon of the Virgin Mary. The paneling and iconostasis extend at a lower height toward the walls of the church to separate the east entrance behind the altar from the nave. The other sides follow the *mashrabiya* lattice.

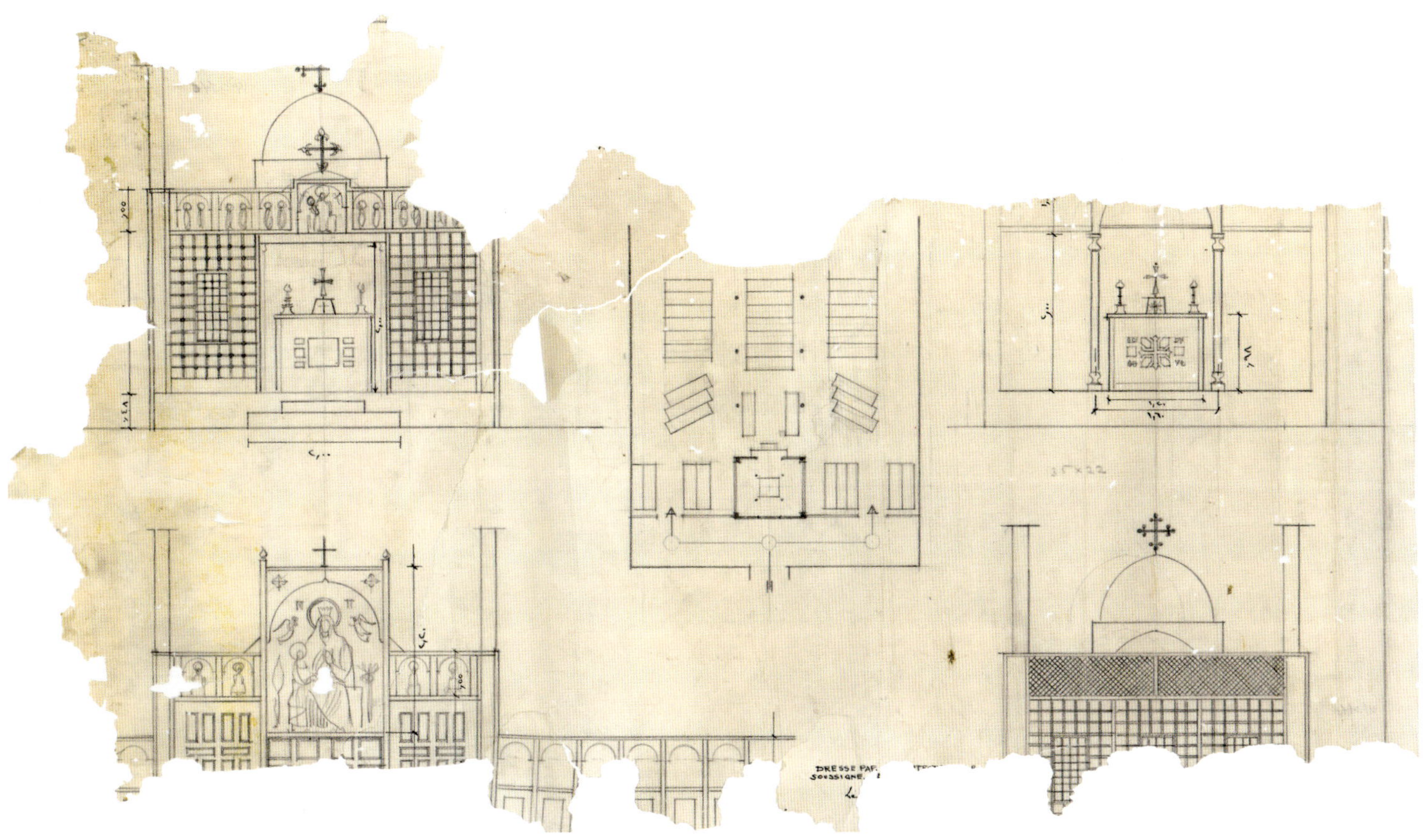

Partial plan of church (center), front elevation of sanctuary and iconostasis (top left), back elevation of sanctuary and iconostasis (bottom left), side elevation of sanctuary and iconostasis (bottom right), front elevation of altar (top right).

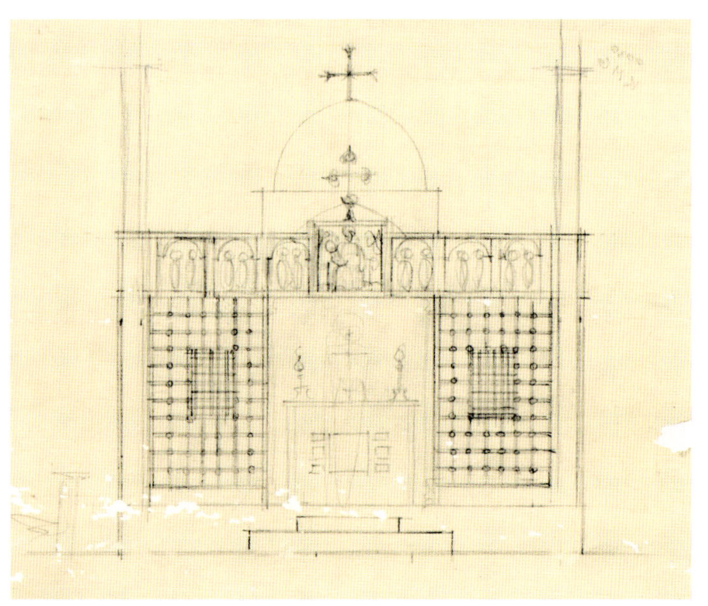

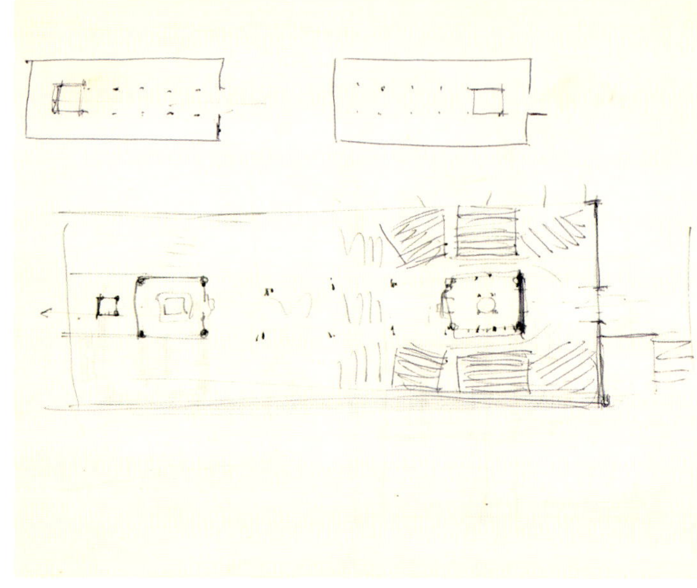

FROM TOP LEFT, CLOCKWISE:
Front elevation of sanctuary and iconostasis.
Sketch of plan.
Sketch of back elevation of sanctuary and iconostasis.

UNIDENTIFIED CHURCH 2

Date: Unknown
Location: Unknown

There are two proposals for the design of a church on a long rectangular plot. In the first one, the building's entrance overlooks a large atrium with central steps climbing up to the narthex. The church has a telescopic plan and section, and its sanctuary consists of an elevated platform behind which is an apse. Behind the sanctuary is a courtyard leading to a community services building; in two of the sketches, this courtyard includes a domed cloister.

The second proposal has a similar layout, but the form of the church is different. This church follows a triconch plan; its sanctuary is backed by a flat wall with a niche, above which is a cross and then an oculus. The church seating in the transept is suggested as being laid out radially from the altar. The church follows a Byzantine style, particularly in its treatment of the domes and half domes. Its entrance is similar to that of the first proposal in plan, except that the entrance courtyard and narthex are significantly smaller in order to accommodate a larger church capacity and community services building.

However, an elevation drawing exists only for the second proposal, showing a domed arcade, comprsing a set of three arches, embedded in the recess of a triumphal arch containing a cross, as a sort of hybrid between *doksar* and narthex.

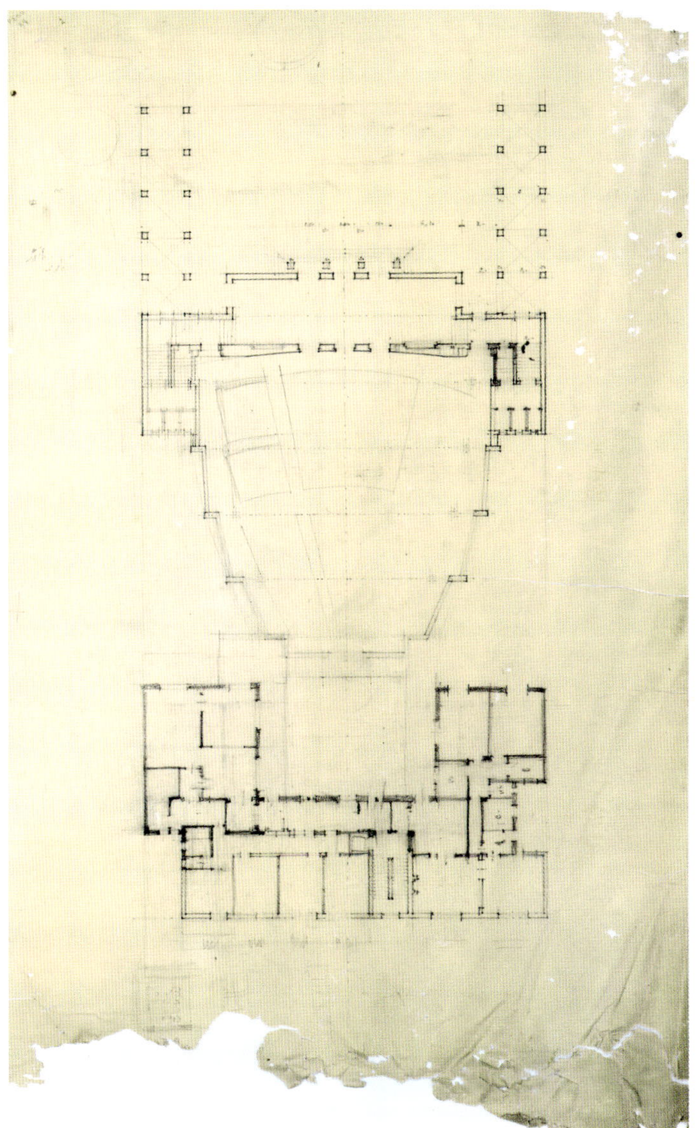

Proposal 1 plan.

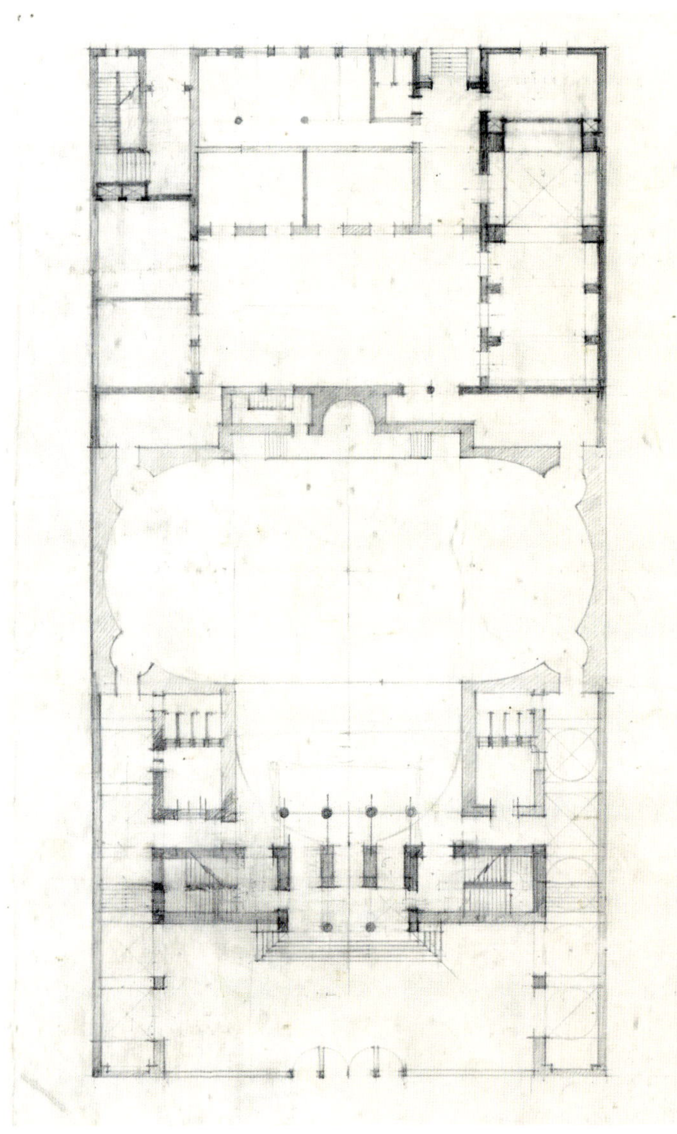

Proposal 2 plan development.

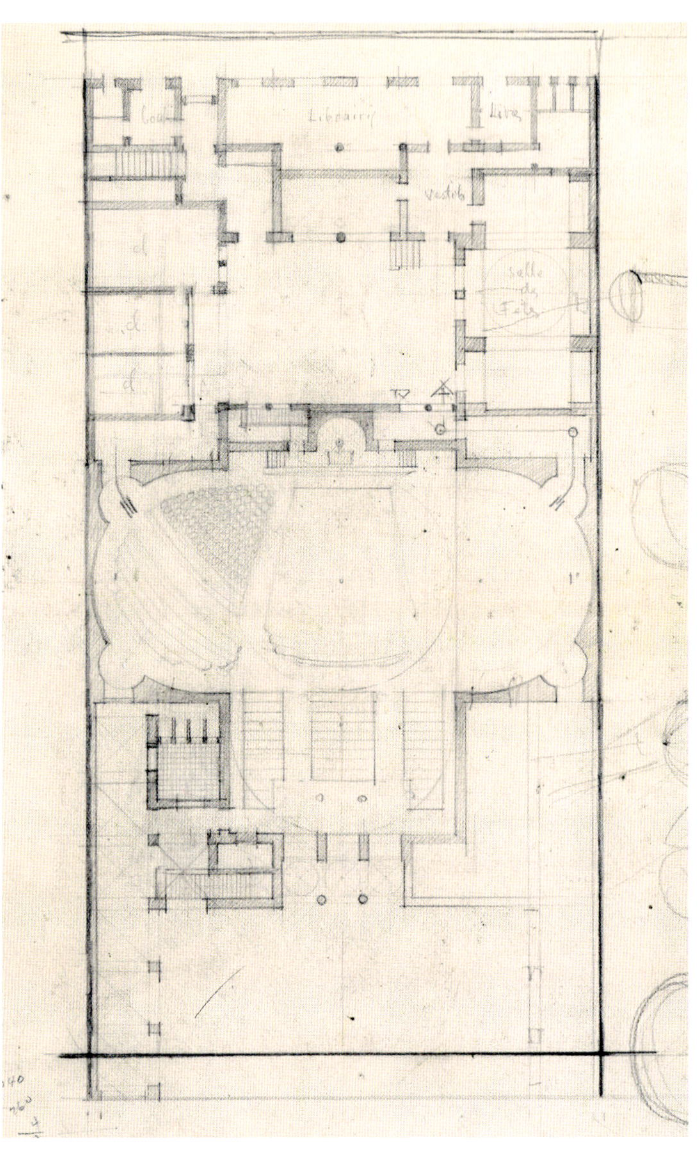

Proposal 2 plan development with different service buildings.

Proposal 2 main elevation.

Proposal 2 section showing altar.

VILLA FIKRY BOUTROS

Date: 1947
Location: Manshiyat al-Bakri, Cairo

Wissa Wassef designed this villa for his mother's cousin Fikry Boutros. There are two proposals for the residence—the earlier one contemplated a more compact layout for the villa while the later proposal, dated seven months after the first, is more linear in layout, providing a greater feel of spaciousness.

The elevations are simple, but are given character through the variety of their fenestration. This proposes integrating plain rectangular windows with wrought-iron rails, plain grilled windows, a *mashrabiya*, a double-arched window with shared railing, stained-glass stucco panels, a claustra opening, and a stone portal framing the entrance door.

The design was completed, but the owner ultimately changed his mind and decided to build a villa in Upper Egypt instead.[14]

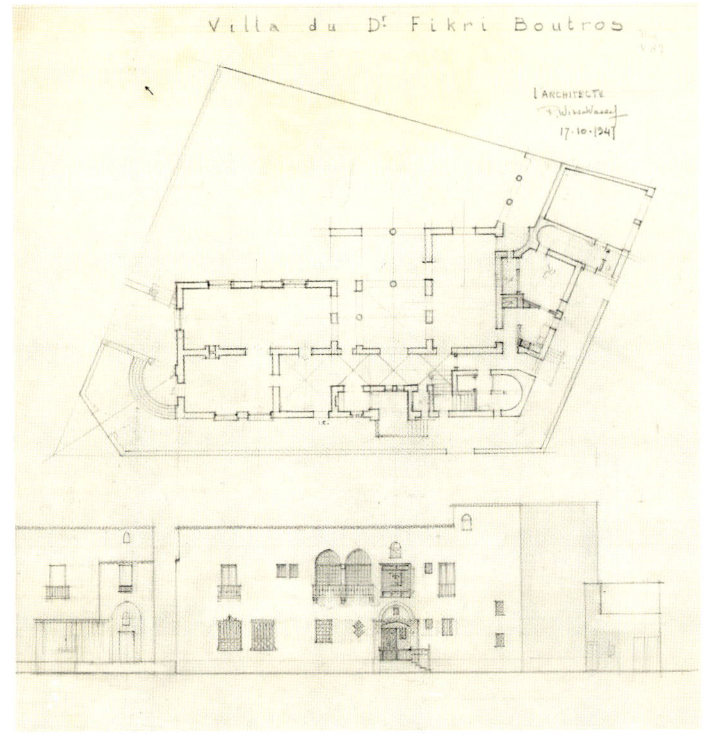

Proposal 2 ground-floor plan (top), southwest elevation (bottom right), northwest elevation (bottom left).

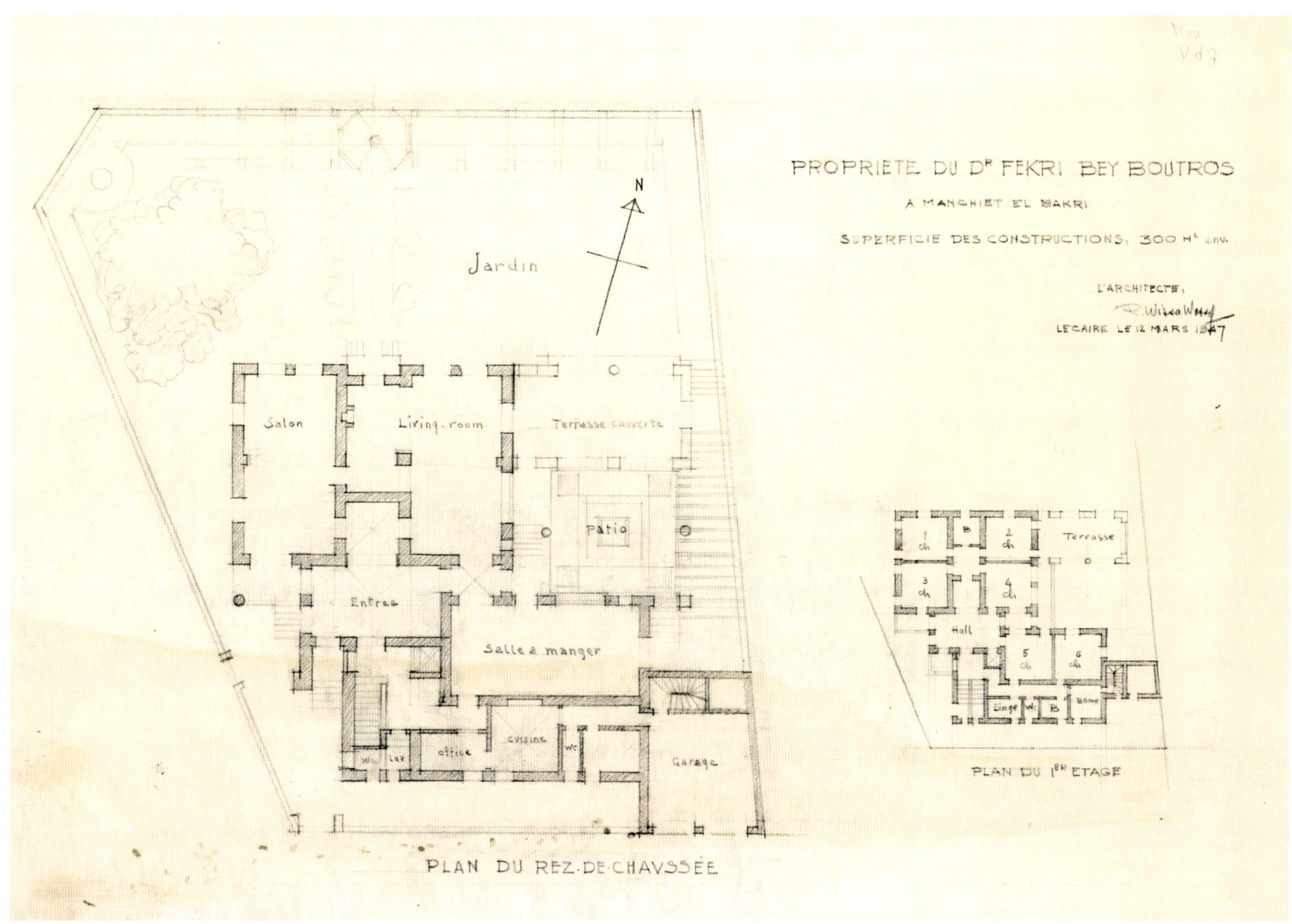

Proposal 1 ground- and first-floor plans.

VILLA AL-AMIRA NAIMA IBRAHIM

Date: 1948
Location: al-Manyal, Cairo

This villa was designed for Princess Naima Ibrahim Hilmi (1886–1950), also known as Princess Naima Surraya—the daughter of Ibrahim Hilmi Ismail and Princess Nazima, and spouse of Mustafa Sürreyâ Bey Bozcaadali.[15] It is likely that she commissioned Wissa Wassef to design the residence in 1948 but that construction never started before she died two years later.

The proposed villa was quite large, containing on the ground floor a large entrance vestibule, office, hall, living room, patio, loggia, and dining room with an adjacent food-service room including a dumbwaiter, and on the first floor a gallery, loggia, large master *en suite* bedroom including an adjacent hall, two other bedrooms, and a bathroom. Designed to be serviced by staff, the villa had the kitchen, laundry room, storage, and staff bedrooms in the basement, while the roof had an additional maid's bedroom and linen room.

The design of the elevations takes its inspiration from Islamic and vernacular architecture, including doorways, *mashrabiya*s, stone claustra, and window openings, and how these are used collectively in a variety of configurations.

OPPOSITE FROM TOP LEFT, CLOCKWISE:
Basement plan.
Windows and carpentry details.
Sections of the house.

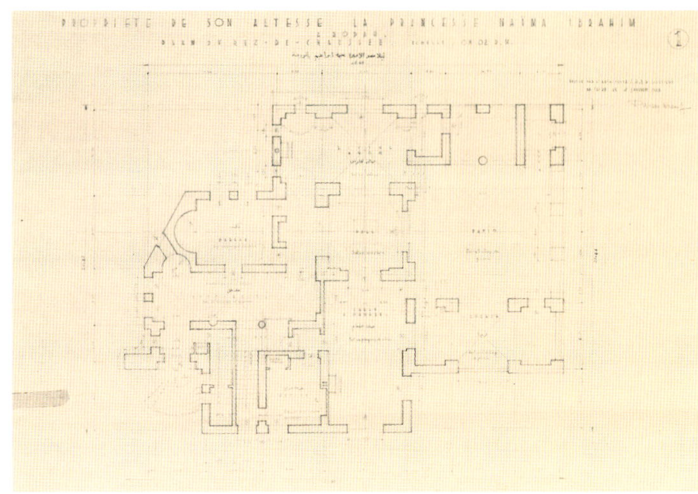

Ground-floor plan.

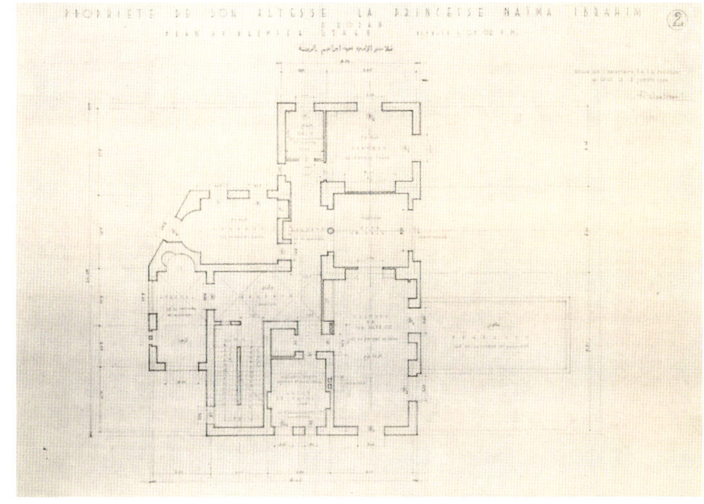

First-floor plan.

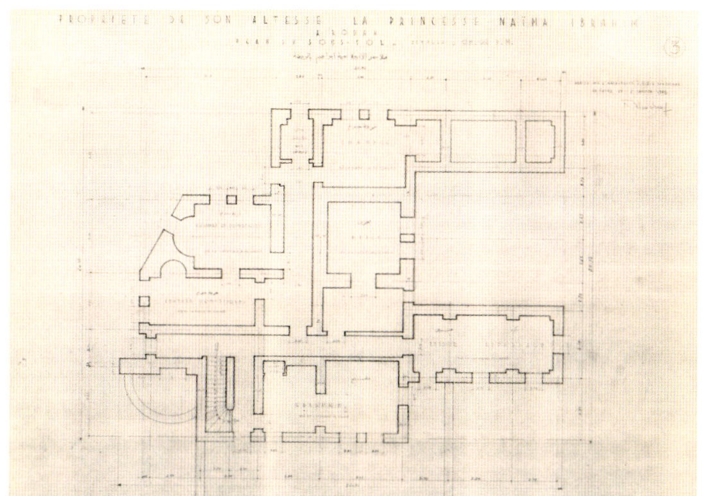
3

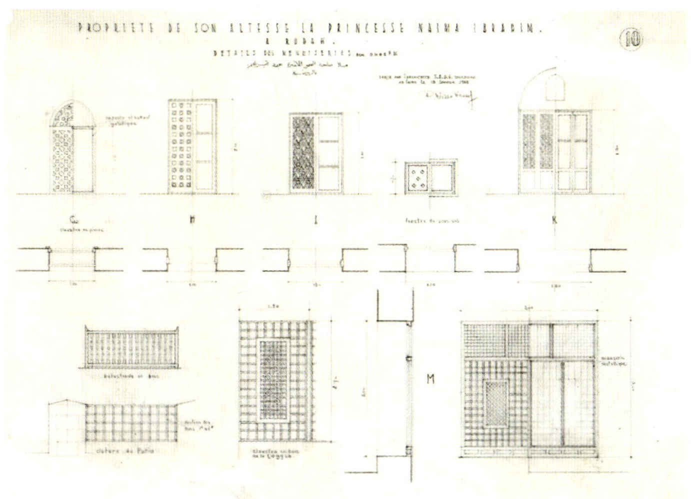
10

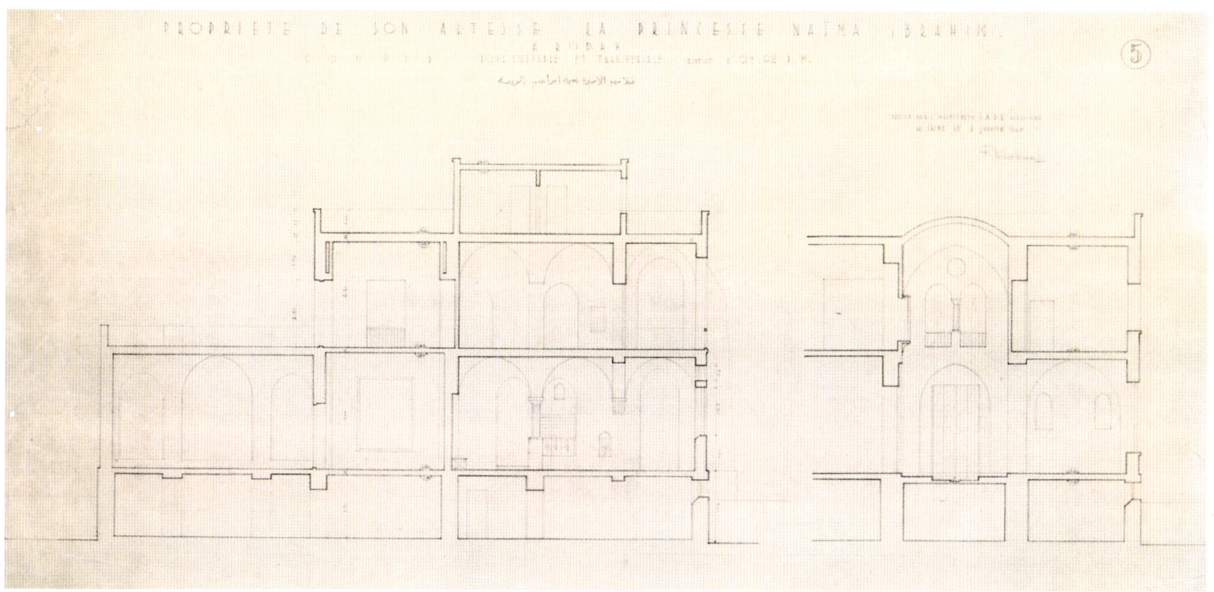
5

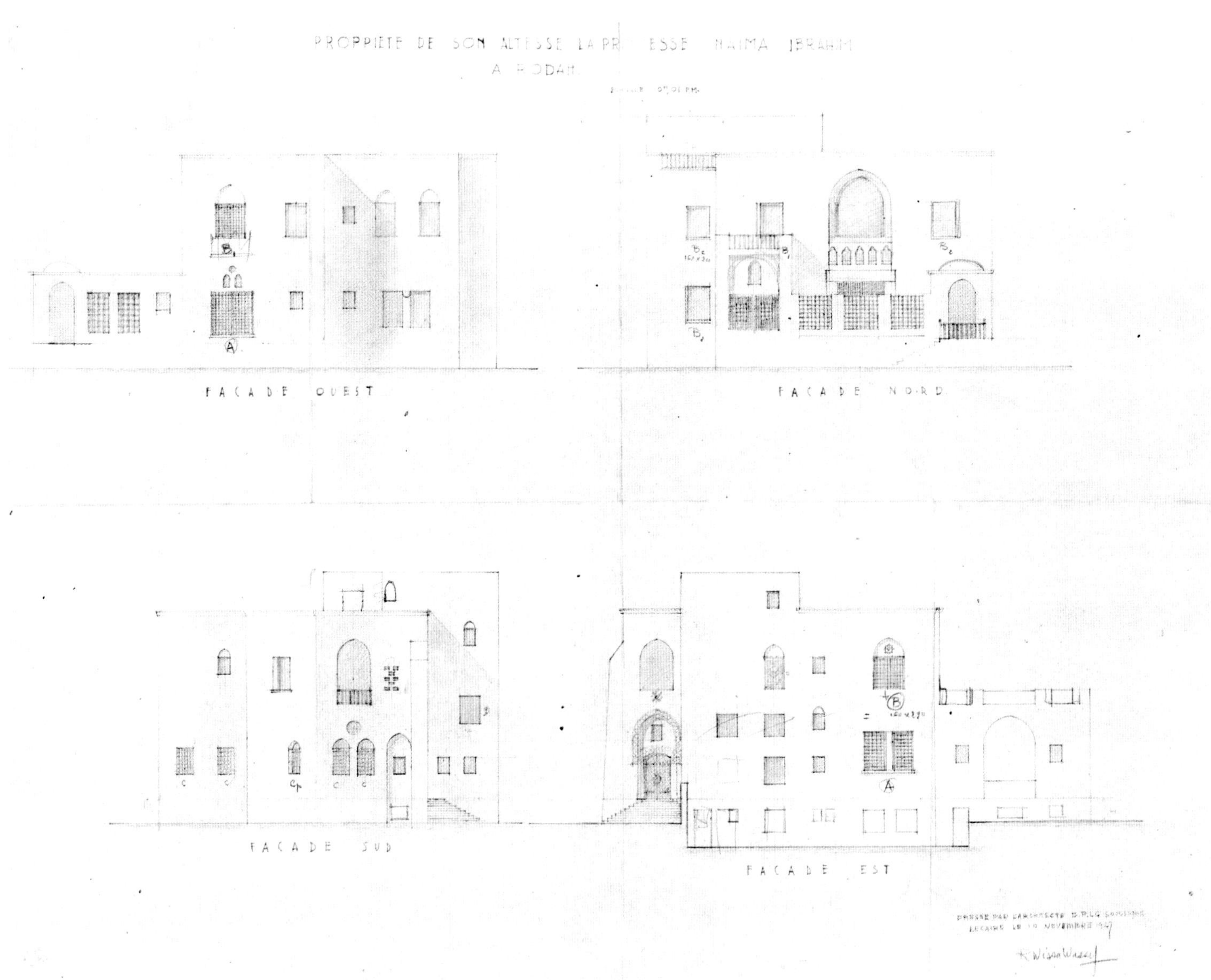

West elevation (top left), north elevation (top right), east elevation (bottom right), and south elevation (bottom left).

AUGONIE ABDEL SAYED AND HABIB GEORGI BEACH HOUSE

Date: c.1952
Location: Abu Qir

Augonie Abdel Sayed, Wissa Wassef's mother-in-law, suffered from asthma. It affected her greatly in summer when the humidity was high in Cairo, so she and her family would spend summers in Abu Qir, which was less humid than Alexandria. Around 1952, Wissa Wassef designed a summer house for his in-laws on the beachfront there. The house was built by the contractors Sharubim and Farag Akladious.[16] A couple of years later, in 1956, Wissa Wassef also built a beach house for his mother and family at Abu Qir. Between 2001 and 2003—long after the deaths of Abdel Sayed, Georgi, and Wissa Wassef—the houses were sold. The new owner demolished them to make way for a high-rise building, following the urbanization trend that was taking the small coastal town by storm.

FOLLOWING PAGE, FROM TOP LEFT, CLOCKWISE:
Main elevation facing north.
Section through patio.
Section through domed living room or *qa'a*.

The design of the beach house takes its inspiration from vernacular and Islamic architecture, consisting of a single-story villa with a varied roofline. With its three bedrooms, large living space, loggia, terrace, two bathrooms, and kitchen, Wissa Wassef plays around with three compositions. The living space is highlighted with a high dome, while the loggia is roofed with smaller domes. No doubt the flat layout of this house, combined with the passive cooling systems proposed, would have made it an ideal summer house with a cool Mediterranean breeze.

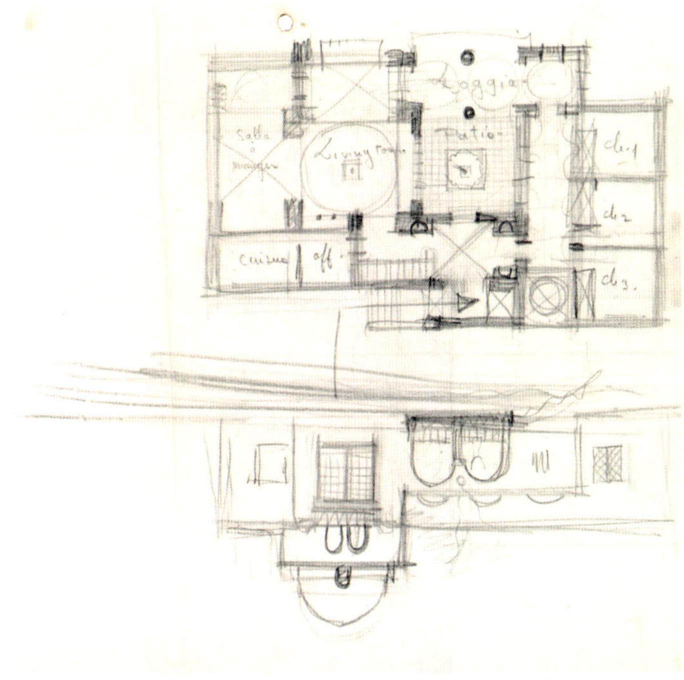

Plan of the beach house with its elevation.

BERLANTY YOUSSEF BEACH HOUSE

Date: 1955
Location: Abu Qir

Wissa Wassef designed two beach houses in Abu Qir, the first for his in-laws Augonie Abdel Sayed and Habib Georgi, and four years later one for his mother Berlanty Youssef. The families would often take their vacations there in the summer due to Abdel Sayed's asthma. Despite having spent many summers there, they took no photographs of the latter house. The family sold the property between 2001 and 2003 after the deaths of Youssef and Wissa Wassef. It was eventually torn down and replaced with a high-rise building.

This modest two-story beach house follows the style of 1950s residential architecture. It is designed to accommodate a large family, containing six bedrooms, a large living room, three kitchens, and four bathrooms. One of the curious features of the drawings is that the ground-floor plan is split between the sheets of paper, with the main functions on one sheet and the garage, service room and bathroom, and secondary staircase on the other. This could be interpreted as Wissa Wassef designing the residence for phased construction or proposing a small and a large version of the house.

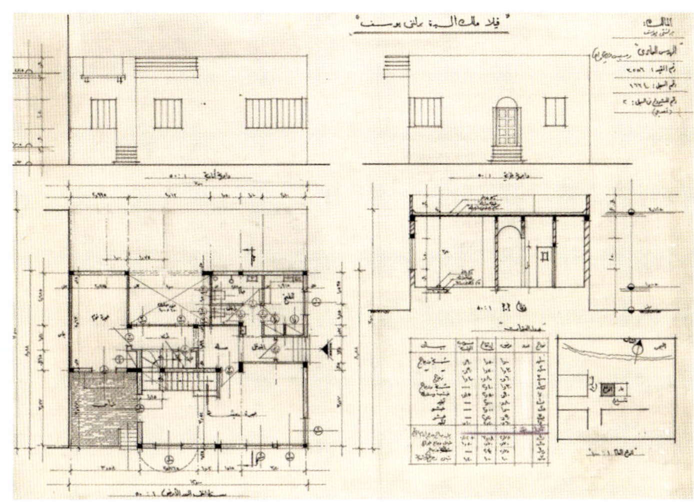

Main northern elevation of ground floor (top left), side elevation of ground floor facing west (top right), section and location sketch (bottom right), ground-floor plan (bottom left); in all cases excluding garage and services area.

FOLLOWING PAGE:
Main elevation facing north (top left); side elevation facing west (top right); first-floor plan (bottom right); back elevation facing south (bottom left); and ground-floor plan of garage, service room, and service staircase (middle left).

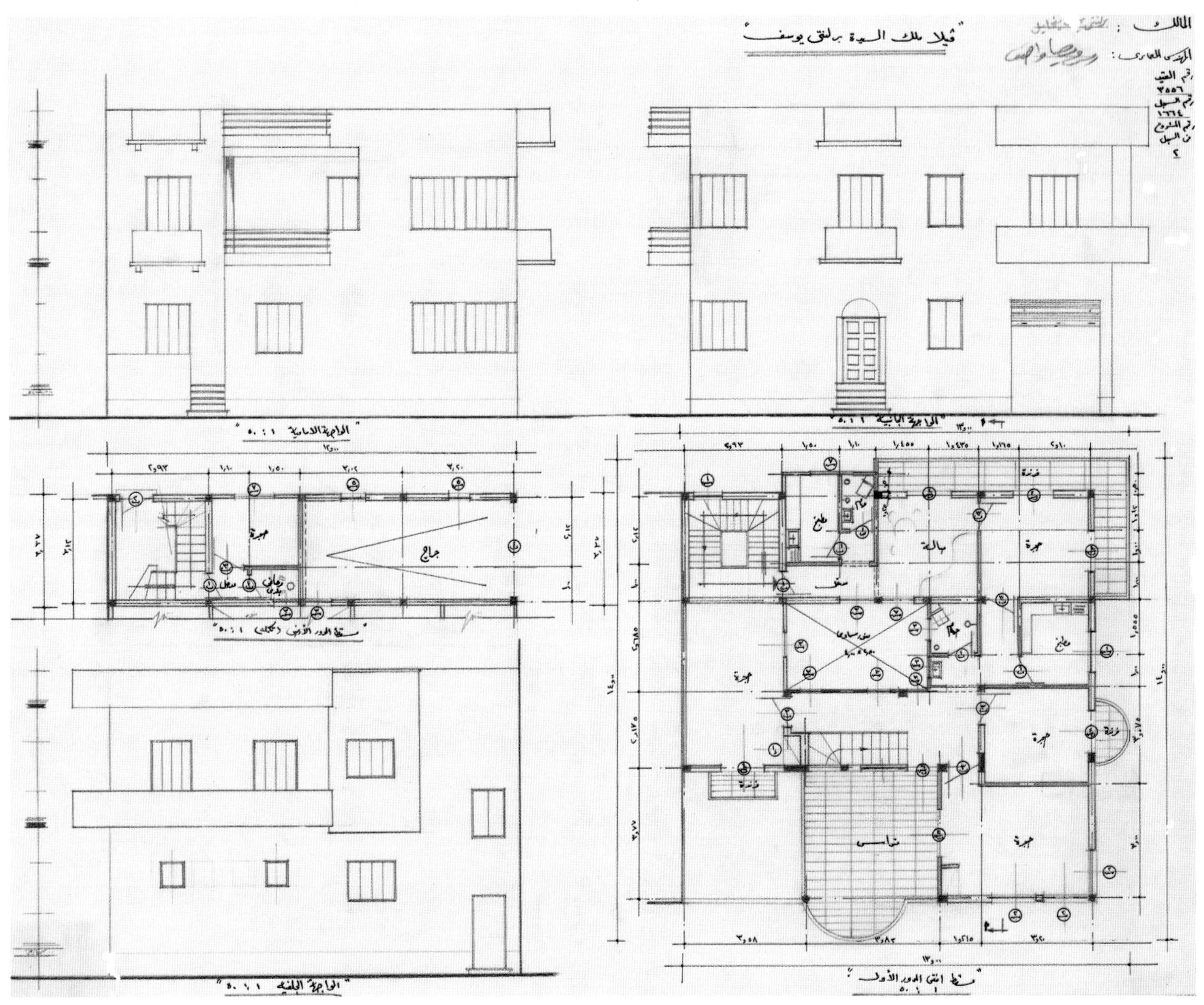
الواجهة الامامية
جراج
حجرة
الواجهة الجانبية
صالة
مطبخ
تراس
الواجهة الخلفية

APARTMENT BUILDING ON SHEIKH RIHAN STREET

Date: 1960
Location: Sheikh Rihan Street, Abdin, Cairo

This apartment building would have been located on Sheikh Rihan Street. It is challenging to identify the exact location and whether it was ever built. The design of this seven-story building follows the style of buildings from that period: a minimalist elevation accentuated with a few vertical lines. The entrance to the building also reflects this late-1950s/early-1960s style with what appears to be a glass-block wall framing the door, which has semicircular handles that close together forming a circle.

There are two interesting features in this building. The first is that it does not maintain a uniform height, being almost split in two with the half facing the 17-meter-wide main street reaching a height of seven floors while the rear overlooking the 6-meter-wide side street reaches only a height of five floors. The second interesting feature is that the top two floors of the five-story portion collectively form a duplex apartment, acting as a penthouse despite it being lower than the other half of the building.

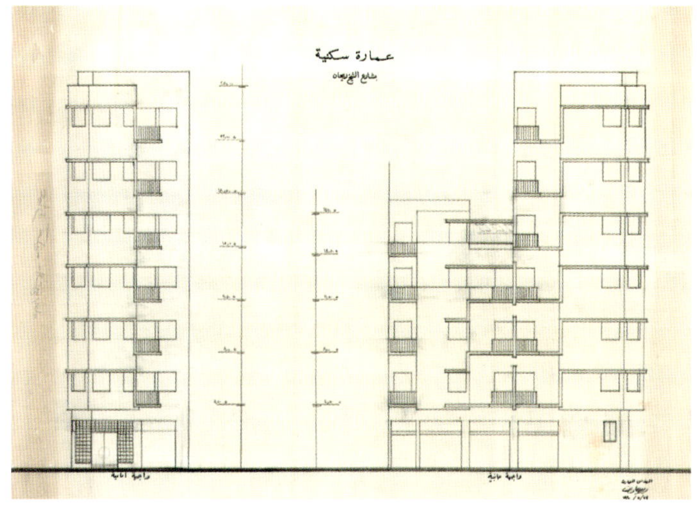

Main elevation (left), side elevation (right).

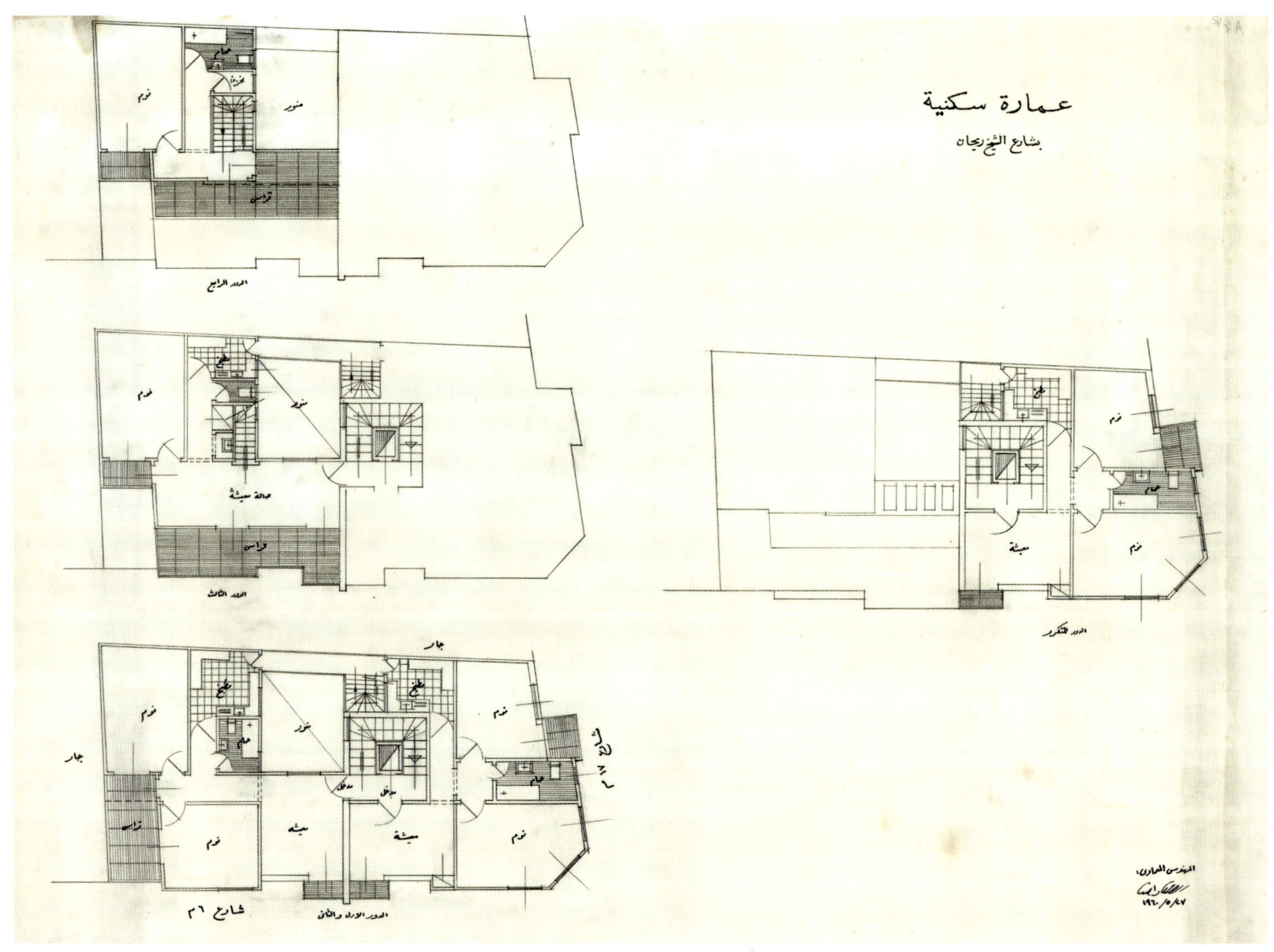

Fourth-floor plan (top left), third-floor plan (middle left), first- and second-floor plan (bottom left), typical floor plan (right).

APARTMENT BUILDING ON CLOT BEY STREET

Date: 1960
Location: 17 Clot Bey Street, Downtown, Cairo

Labeled as building no. 17 on Clot Bey Street, not much else is known about this structure or whether it ever existed. Due to the changing nature of Clot Bey Street from the 1950s onward into a largely commercial thoroughfare, the ground floor is designed to accommodate four stores overlooking the main street and corner. A linear staircase leads up to the doorman's quarters and the apartments. Each floor comprises a small apartment that cleverly adjusts to the angles of this odd-shaped plot, surrounded by three streets.

Like some of Wissa Wassef's other residential work from this period, the building elevations follow the minimalist style of the late 1950s and early 1960s, emphasized with sharp lines and smooth curves. The drawings are cosigned with Badie Habib Georgi, Ramses's brother-in-law, who was an architectural student in the late 1950s and sometimes inked some plans for Wissa Wassef.[17]

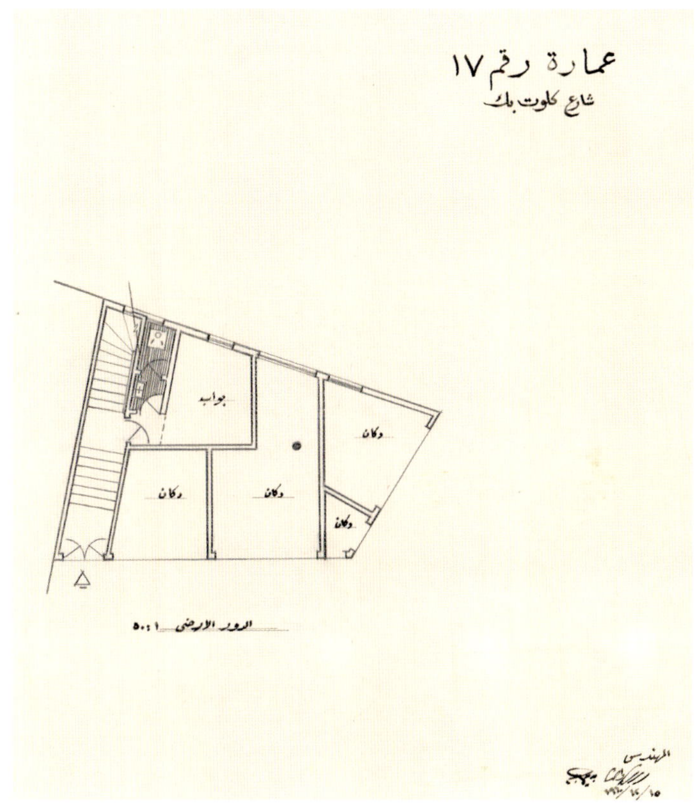

Ground-floor plan.

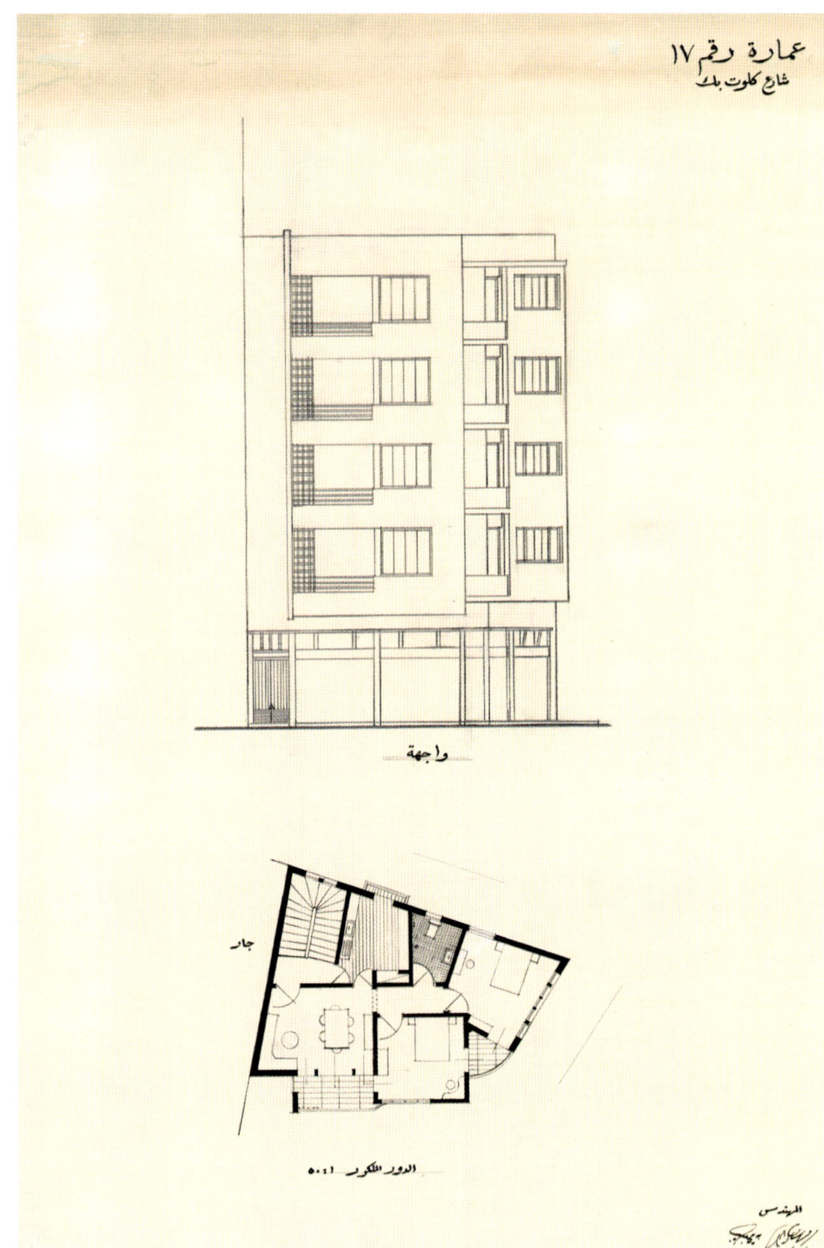

Main elevation and typical floor plan.

BUILDING NUMBER 34 AND 36

Date: 1960
Location: Unknown

Following the late-1950s/early-1960s style, this residential building is characterized by the linearity of its façade design.

Located between two parallel streets, not much else can be discerned about the location or owner of this building, labeled only with its number on the two unnamed streets. The typical floor plan of this L-shaped building is divided into two apartments with the stairs and ventilation court at the center of the L. By contrast, the ground floor is divided into an apartment, the doorman's quarters, and two stores, with the option of turning one of the rooms of the apartment into a third store. Badie Habib Georgi's signature appears next to Wissa Wassef's; at the time, he was ending his studies and sometimes aided Wissa Wassef in drafting plans.

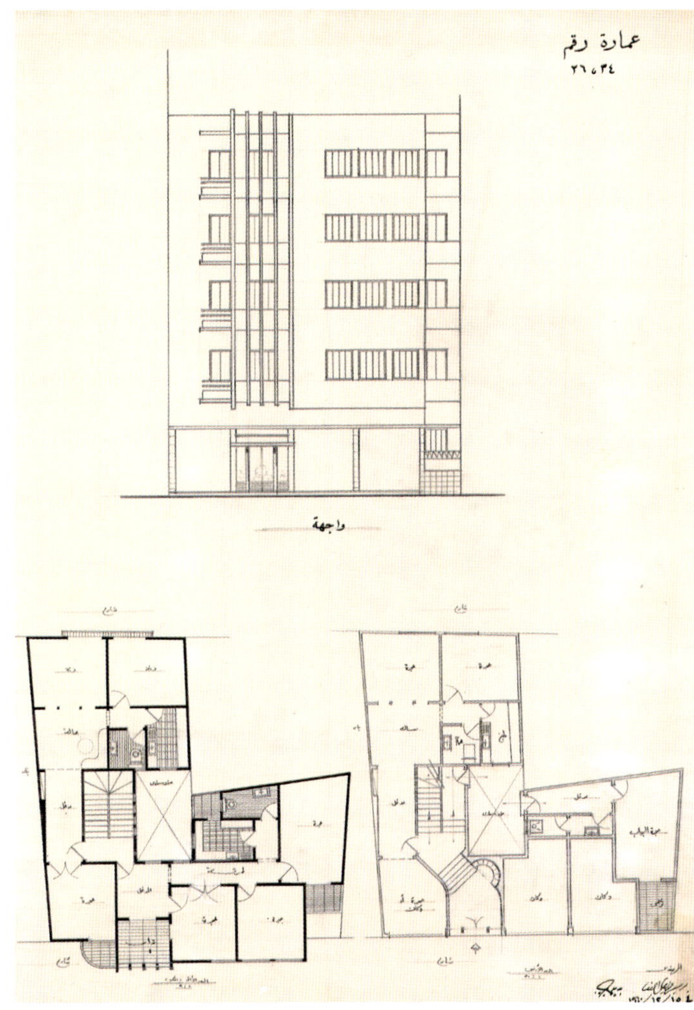

Main elevation (top), ground-floor plan (bottom right), and typical floor plan (bottom left).

ZEINAB BADAWI HOUSE

Date: 1965–66
Location: Harraniya, Giza

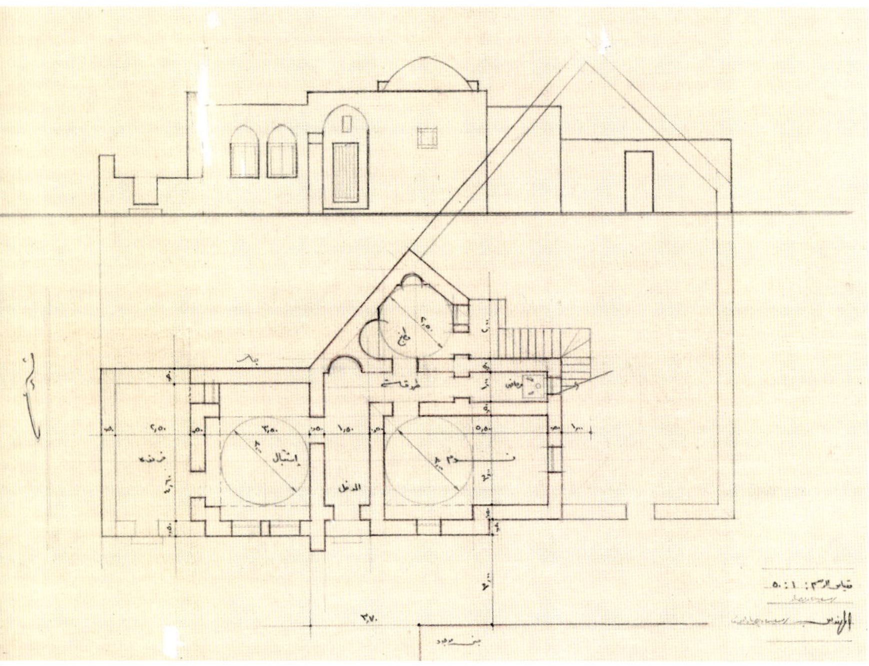

Ground-floor plan and elevation.

This house was designed for Zeinab Badawi, one of the weavers at the Ramses Wissa Wassef Art Center. Wissa Wassef designed it following her specific needs and those of her family's lifestyle in a rural village. Eventually she sold the house and its garden. The new owners demolished it around 1999–2001.

The modest single-story dwelling was composed of an entrance hall, a reception area that opened onto a veranda, a bedroom, toilet, and kitchen. The kitchen led to an enclosed garden and a staircase providing access to the roof. The most peculiar aspect of this house was the shape of its kitchen: with its almost trapezoidal form having two corners converted into round niches, it is hard to envision how this space would have been furnished or used. Most likely, Wissa Wassef was simply following Badawi's specifications.

ADAM HENEIN HOUSE AND ATELIER

Date: 1968
Location: Harraniya, Giza

View of the garden containing *Adam's Ship*, still present today.

Like many creatives who followed Wissa Wassef to Harraniya, Adam and Nessim Henein also moved there. The two brothers built houses next to each other. Adam Henein, a prominent sculptor, chose Wissa Wassef to design his residence. A stand-alone studio was built some years later.[18] This house is a true testament to Wissa Wassef's generosity. Henein had requested construction stop, as he could not continue funding it. Hearing this, Wissa Wassef purchased *Donkey*, a sculpture that Henein was working on, so that the latter could put that money toward finishing the house.[19] This sculpture would later become one of the highlights of Henein's portfolio from the 1960s; it is currently part of the Ramses Wissa Wassef Art Center landscape.

The house was quite modest, serving Henein's basic needs, with limestone foundations and mud-brick walls and roofing.[20] The ground floor contains a small entrance lobby that leads to the kitchen, which includes the dining area, stairs, and—through a bent corridor—the living spaces. Attached to the latter is a small study. The first floor has two bedrooms, a bathroom, and a terrace. All rooms are domed, with the exception of two *iwan*s that open to the living space, which is roofed by the main dome. The workshop was a separate component from the house.

Part of the garden still serves as Henein's quarry-stone store and workshop for larger pieces, while the remainder is a sculpture garden that was brought together with Henein's *Adam's Ship* (2000–2004) as its centerpiece—a literal and figurative vessel for his life's work, creating harmony in the curation of the garden.

In 1995 Henein commissioned Ikram Nosshi, Wissa Wassef's son-in-law, to modify the bedroom, converting it into a master bedroom with *en suite* bathroom to improve accessibility for his wife 'Afaf, who was growing frail. Eventually, Henein demolished the house and studio to build his museum. Designed by Wissa Wassef's student Suheir Salih[21] and inaugurated in 2014, the museum houses the carefully curated lifeworks of Adam Henein—or, as it is also known, his "life of creativity."[22]

View of the transition zone of the central dome, 1983/1984.

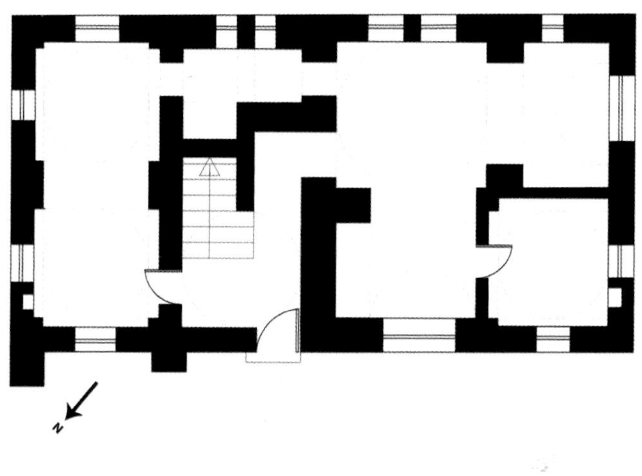

Ground-floor plan.

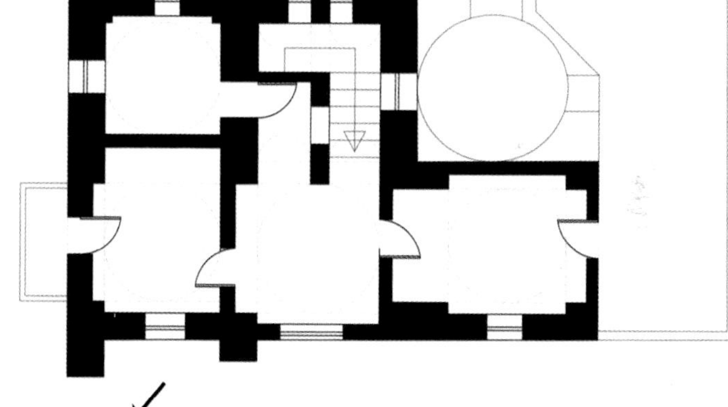

First-floor plan.

OPPOSITE, FROM TOP LEFT, CLOCKWISE:
Exterior shot of the east corner, 1983/1984.
View of one of the *iwans* forming part of the living space, 1983/1984.
View of the other *iwan* being used by Adam Henein as a small studio, 1983/1984.
Upstairs hall leading to the two bedrooms and bathroom, 1983/1984.

ABUL-'ENEIN WEEKEND HOUSE

Date: c.1968
Location: Harraniya, Giza

This small house and studio was built for the artist and playwright 'Abd al-Ghani Abul-'Enein. Built of stone, clay, and mud, it acted as a weekend retreat, made up of two rooms and a bathroom. In 1979 Ikram Nosshi, Wissa Wassef's son-in-law, added a two-story studio that was used as a museum for Reaya al-Nimr's private collection. Al-Nimr, Abul-'Enein's wife, had spent a lifetime collecting items related to the tangible and intangible heritage of Egypt and the wider region, including traditional clothing and jewelry.[23] At one point she had been the partner of Shahira Mehrez, renowned researcher of Egyptian costumes and jewelry and designer of heritage-inspired apparel.

Abul-'Enein passed away in 1998, and al-Nimr in 2006, without children. Other family members inherited the property, which was sold soon afterward and demolished by the new owners. Items from al-Nimr's and Abul-'Enein's collections now form part of the permanent exhibition on Arab Folk Art at the Bibliotheca Alexandrina.

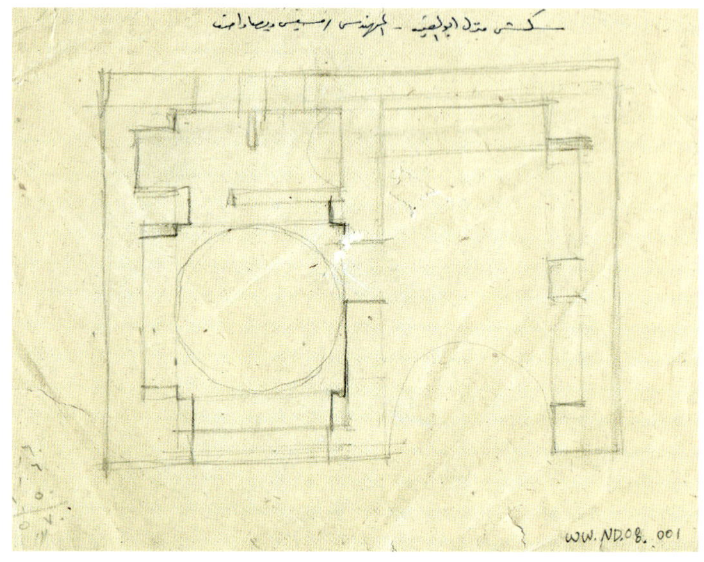

Sketch of ground-floor plan.

STUDENT PROJECT: VILLA

Date: Unknown
Location: Unknown

One of the plans for this residence is annotated with the word *superflu* (superfluous), and another one with *bacalauréat*, suggesting that it was one of Wissa Wassef's university projects. The house has a series of communal spaces surrounding a tiled courtyard with a fountain that looks out to the garden. These spaces are connected from behind with a corridor that leads to the other rooms. The villa has a large garden containing a pool and what appears to be a large rectangular garden bed divided into a uniform grid.

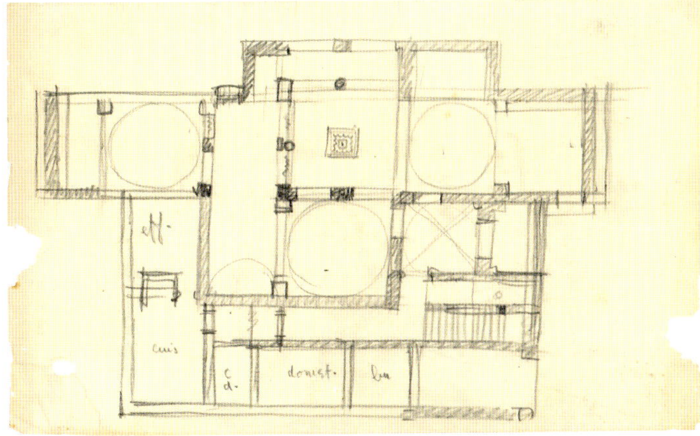

Ground-floor plan.

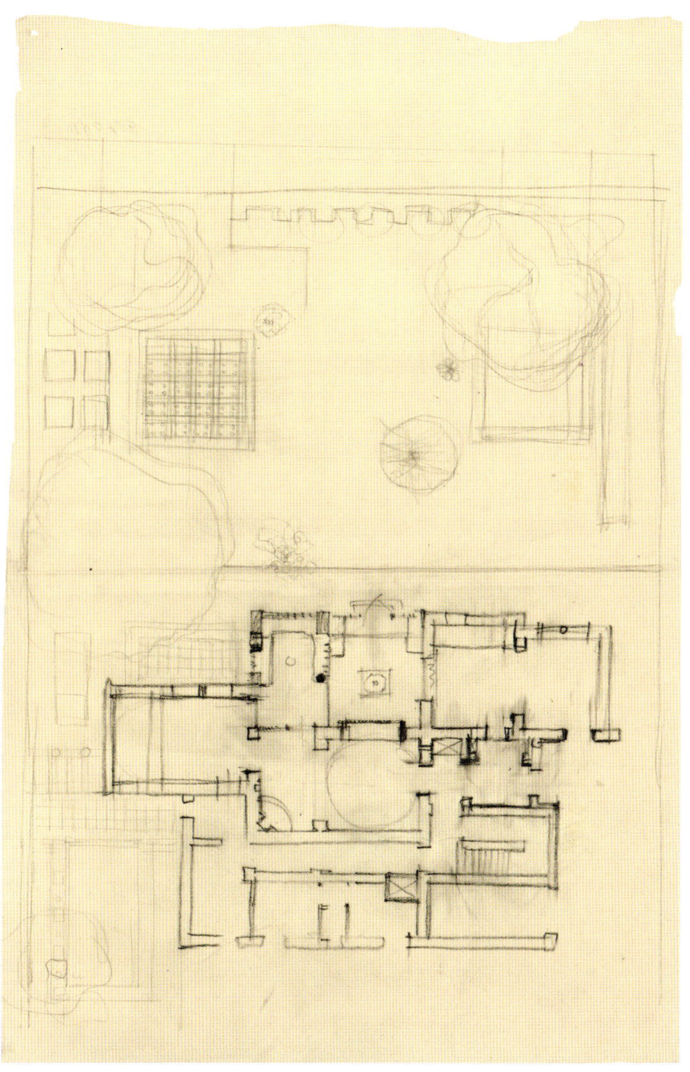

Site plan including landscaping and draft ground-floor plan.

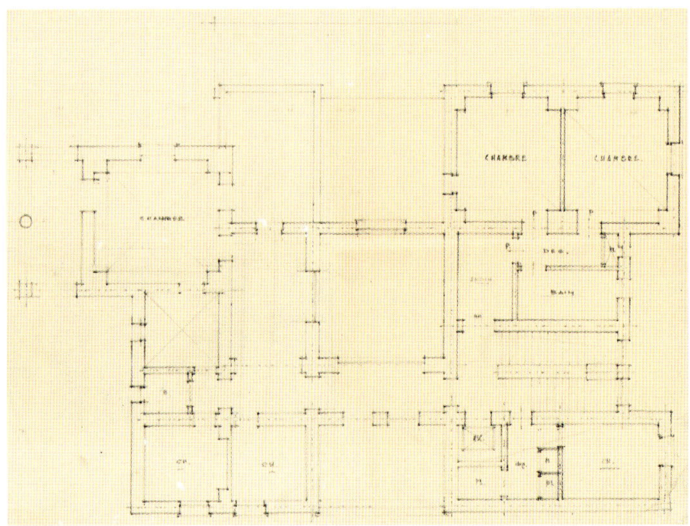

First-floor plan.

Draft plan and elevation.

UNIDENTIFIED APARTMENT BUILDING 1

Date: Unknown
Location: Unknown

This unidentified multiple-family house has an unusual layout. One enters the building to be faced with the stairwell; from it, one can access one apartment on the ground floor or two apartments on each subsequent level. The ground floor also contains a garage on the southern side. The building's north-facing apartment shifts at an angle of 15 degrees. Its main living space has a wall facing the street that is curved on the interior and angular on the exterior, creating an interesting play on geometry.

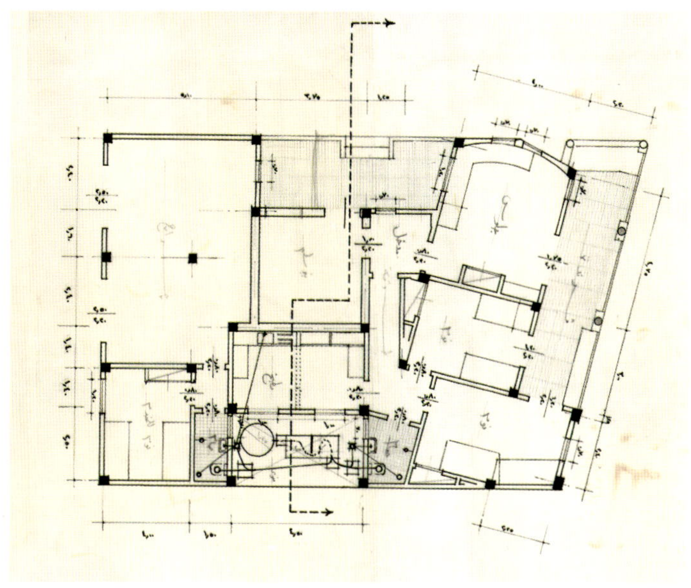

Ground-floor plan.

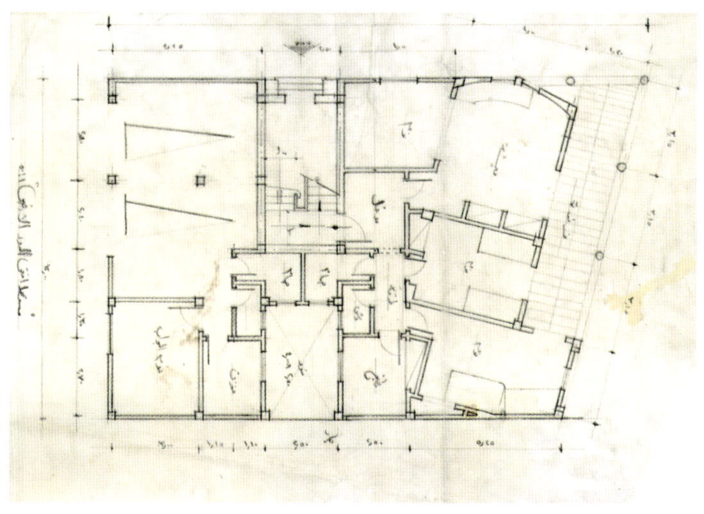

Alternative ground-floor plan with different treatment of the building entrance.

UNIDENTIFIED APARTMENT BUILDING 2

Date: Unknown
Location: Unknown

Not much can be said about this project from an architectural point of view. It appears to be a proposal for an apartment building on a plot that used to have a villa. The sketches vary from proposals for dividing the garden to the zoning of the building in plan.

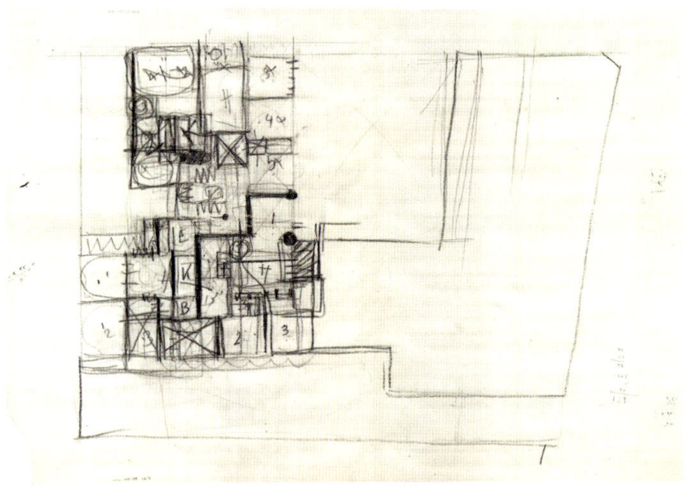

General zoning of apartment building.

General zoning of one of the apartments in the building.

UNIDENTIFIED VILLA 1

Date: Unknown
Location: Unknown

The unique feature of this design is that it is one of the only residential projects for which Wissa Wassef drafted the whole landscaping of the garden. The landscaping is inspired by traditional four-quadrant Islamic gardens, in which each of the quadrants is planted with trees. The periphery of the garden is articulated with either a wooden pergola or a unique paving system. To the side, what appears to be a stepped platform with a central fountain has been added, contributing to the Islamic garden elements found in this design. The house has a courtyard framed on two sides by a vaulted cloister, which opens onto the garden. As in his other residential projects, Wissa Wassef has incorporated a *qa'a* within the house.

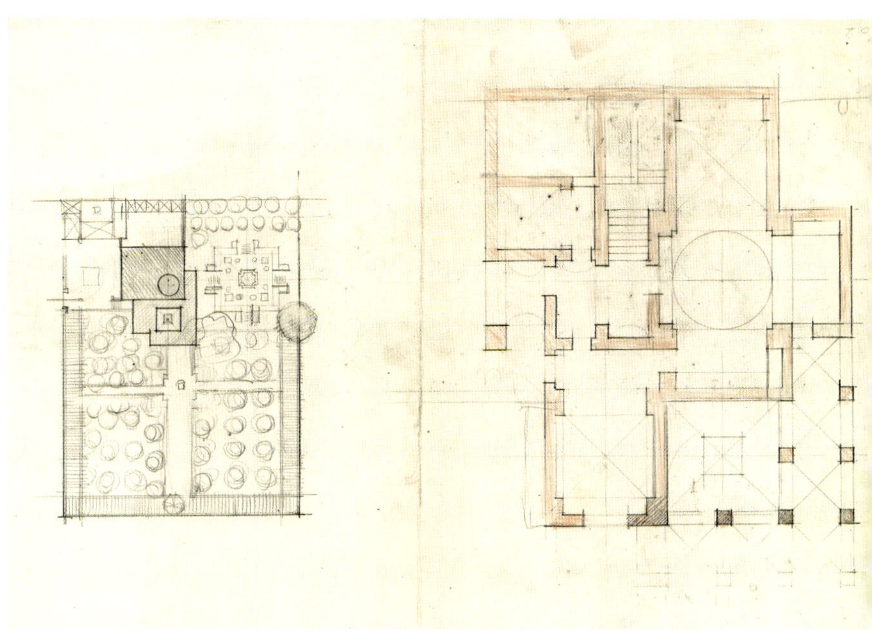

Site plan and ground-floor plan.

Main elevation with further articulation and modifications.

UNIDENTIFIED VILLA 2

Date: Unknown
Location: Unknown

In this villa Wissa Wassef starts to experiment with reinterpreting traditional domestic features, introducing a domed double-height *qa'a* and, situated diagonally from it, a second space that also appears like a *qa'a* but instead is single-height and lacking a dome, while maintaining the *durqa'a*. A courtyard is aligned between the two *qa'a*s; one of its sides integrates elements of a *takhtabush*, providing a shaded entrance from the garden split in two, which also allows for the cooling of the house.

The other side of the courtyard is framed with a window looking out but covered with a pergola. The main entrance steps are protected by a protruding wall containing an opening.

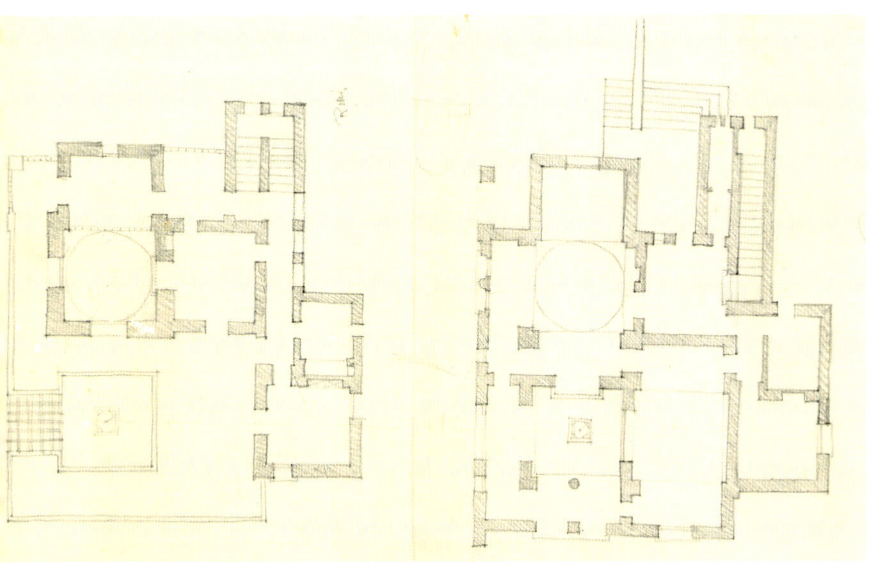

Ground-floor (right) and first-floor (left) plans.

Main elevation.

UNIDENTIFIED VILLA 3

Date: Unknown
Location: Unknown

One of the curious features of this project is that no plans have been identified in the collection matching this series of elevations and axonometric drawings. In each sketch Wissa Wassef explores the articulation of fenestration patterns integrating minimalist openings with more detailed traditional formats, as well as the effect of protruding and recessing walls and how they all work together to give form to the house.

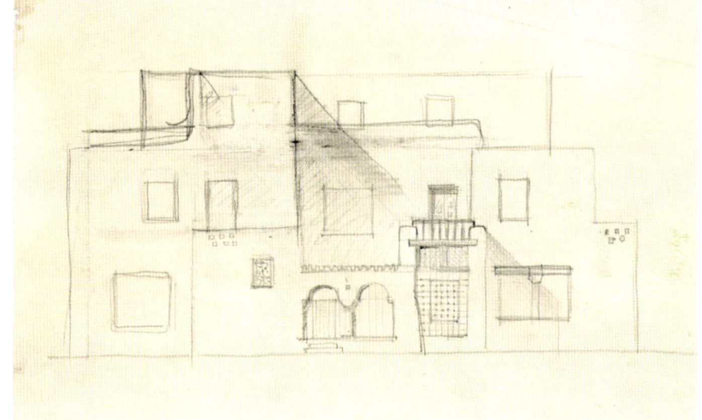

FROM TOP, CLOCKWISE:
House axonometry.
Elevation draft.
Elevation draft.

UNIDENTIFIED VILLA 4

Date: Unknown
Location: Unknown

This villa design takes inspiration from three different styles of architecture: its forms are based on vernacular structures, the influence of Islamic architecture can be seen with the integration of *mashrabiya* windows, while pharaonic monumentality can be sensed in the pylon-inspired protrusion. The beautifully drawn elevation and perspectives reveal the harmony in the design between the built and the void, the light and the dark, the human-made and the natural.

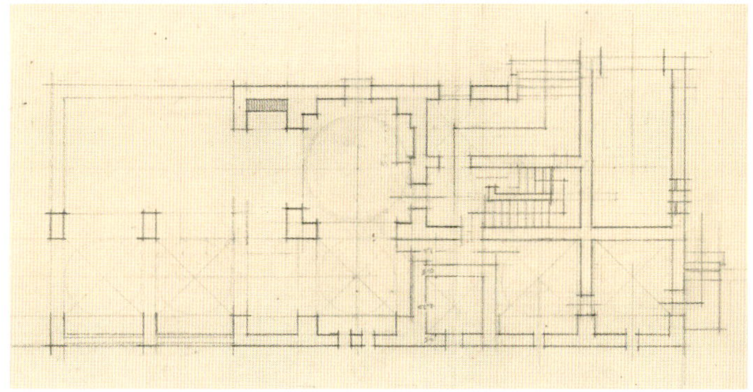

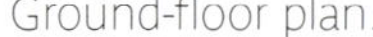

Ground-floor plan.

House perspectives.

Main elevation.

UNIDENTIFIED VILLA 5

Date: Unknown
Location: Unknown

This villa is carefully designed to provide living spaces with varying degrees of privacy. Upon entering the house, there is a vestibule that opens into a long corridor leading down the house and a domed living area. The latter leads to the second living area, through a variation of a *magaz* (axially broken entrance), creating privacy between the two spaces. It can also be accessed from the entrance through the long corridor. This second living space then opens onto a private *hawsh* that connects with the garden. Upstairs there are two bedrooms with a bathroom each.

The elevations of the villa are quite minimal, relying entirely on the form and how light hits it to convey its expression.

North elevation.

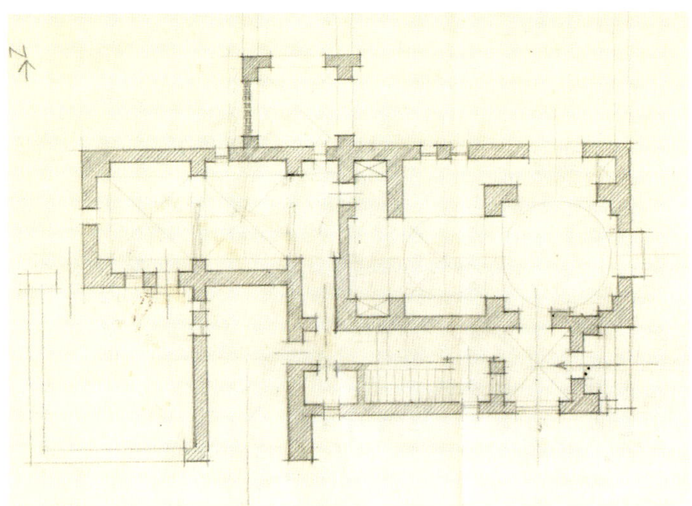

Ground-floor plan.

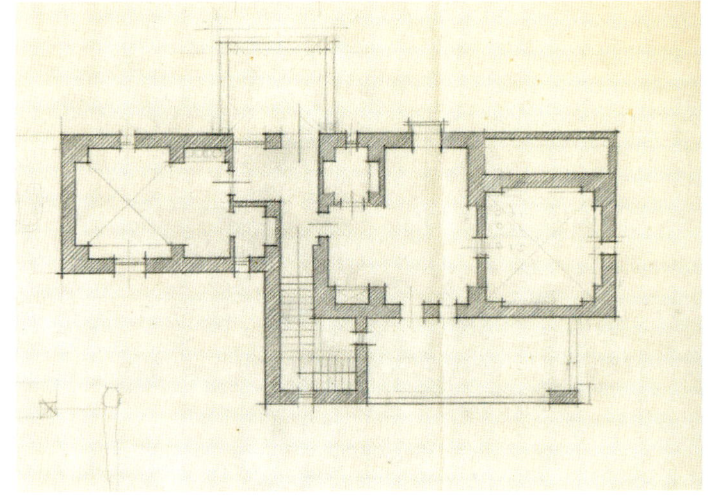

First-floor plan.

South elevation.

EDUCATIONAL AND CULTURAL

GRADUATION PROJECT: OLD CAIRO POTTERS' HOUSE

Date: 1935
Location: Old Cairo

Wissa Wassef's graduation project reveals a lot about who he was to become as an architect and educator. He chose to design a facility for craftspeople, a vocation that would become the focus of his architectural and educational work.

Already one can see how traditional architecture influences his work, even while adopting the contemporary style, taking cues from different eras of Egypt's history in the architectural features and detail of the section drawing.

In this project situated on the bank of the Nile in Old Cairo, he demonstrated spectacular attention to detail, providing in his drawings the context of the city around him. Looking at his elevation, it contains a Cairene skyline on the east and felucca masts on the west. At the time feluccas were still an important form of transportation and would have been plentiful along the Nile.

The ground-floor plan contains rooms for activities that can be considered more public than domestic. These include five pottery cubicles arranged linearly in the northern wing, and three rooms whose function can act as living, study, or reception rooms in the southern and western wings. The northwestern corner contains the kiln used to fire the pottery. Although the drawings for the upper-floor plan are missing, it is safe to assume that it would have contained the dormitories for the craftspeople.

Axonometries.

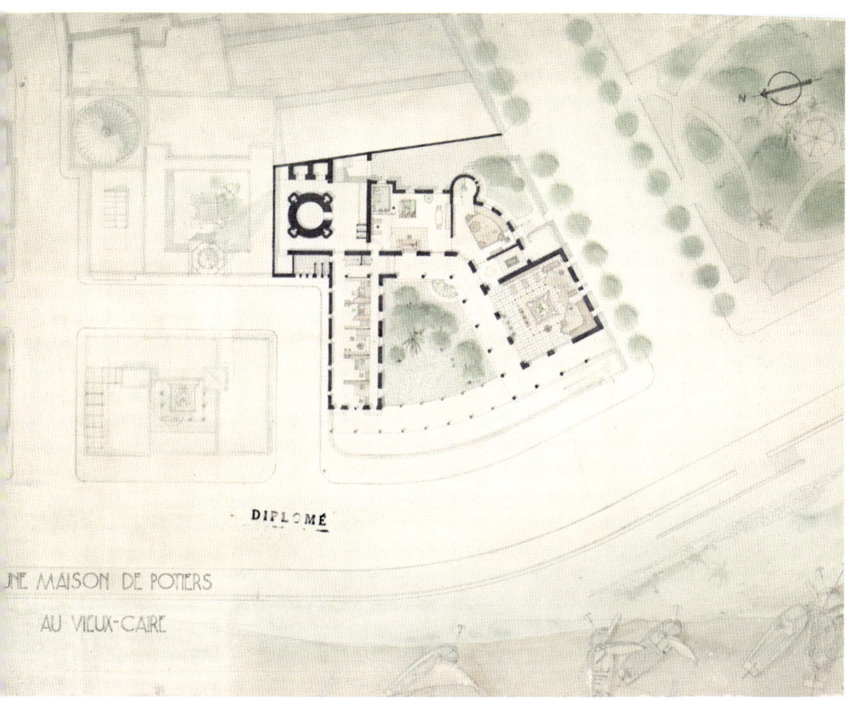

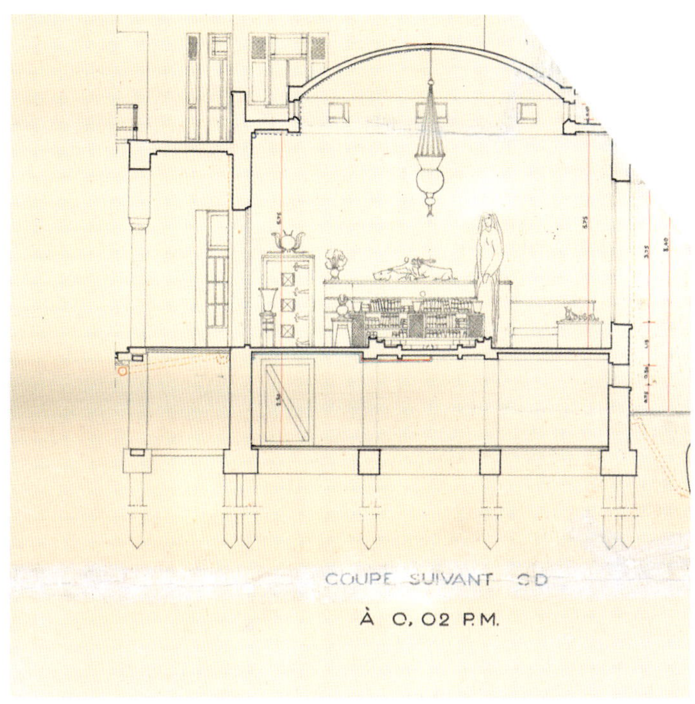

FROM TOP LEFT, CLOCKWISE:
Site plan of the Potters' House in Old Cairo, with surrounding traditional houses.
Section showing the furnishings of one of the living spaces.
Elevation of Potters' House in Old Cairo.

SMALL RENOVATION AT COLLÈGE FRANÇAIS DU DAHER

Date: 1939
Location: 45 al-Daher Street, al-Daher, Cairo
Alternative names: Mission Laïque Française du Daher, Collège Français de Garçons, Collège des Garçons du Daher au Caire

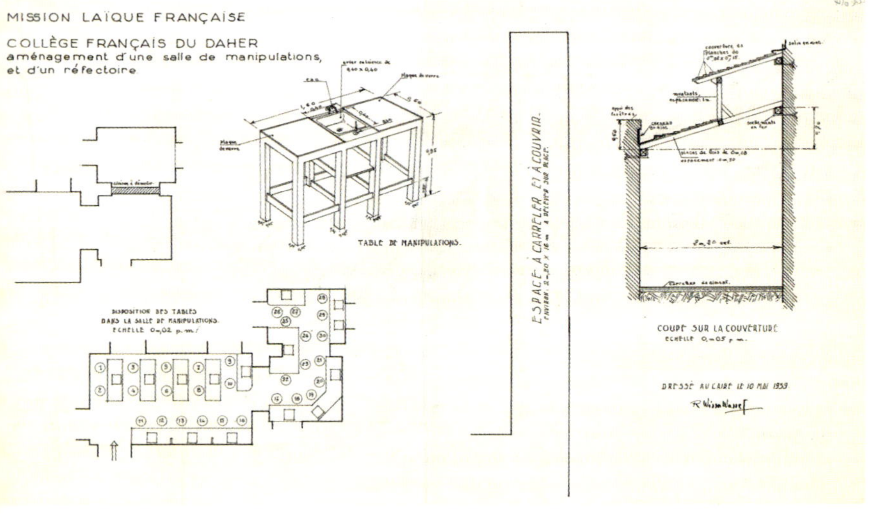

Proposed intervention at the school, including specialized furnishing and carpentry.

The drawings for this project are titled Mission Laïque Française—Collège Français du Daher. The school was most commonly known as Collège des Garçons du Daher au Caire or Collège Français de Garçons.[24] It was established in 1914, replacing Collège Esnault, one of the first schools supported by the Mission Laïque in Egypt.[25] In 1934 it was decided that the school would relocate to a larger campus at 45 al-Daher Street,[26] though it is unclear when exactly the school opened at the new location.

It is not clear either whether Wissa Wassef's project was a small renovation conducted when the school moved to the al-Daher Street campus, to prepare the building for its new function, or after it had been operating for some time at the new location. The drawings show an intervention comprising the installation of a food and materials-manipulation classroom, and a roof system for a previously open corridor.

Wissa Wassef also designed the furnishings of the classroom to accommodate its specific learning objectives. It is unknown whether he contributed any other intervention at the school.

At some point the institution was converted into a commerce school, and ultimately changed to the al-Daher New Secondary School for Girls at the beginning of the twenty-first century. There is no information pinpointing when the original building was demolished.

FARUQ I UNIVERSITY DORMITORY

Date: 1945
Location: Ahmed Zewail Street (formerly Tharwat Street), Dokki, Giza
Alternative names: Cité Universitaire Farouk 1er, Cairo University Dormitory

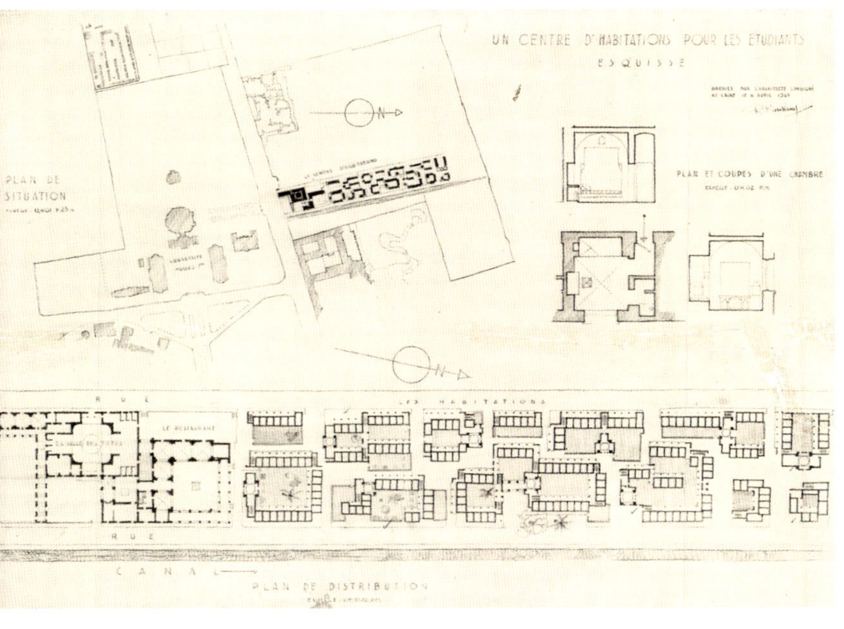

Proposal by Ramses Wissa Wassef and Hassan Fathy for the university dorms.

There are three proposals for the design of the dormitory complex for Faruq I University, now Cairo University, that involved Wissa Wassef. The first proposal is signed exclusively by him. It consists of a narrow plot of land with the public buildings at the front, followed by the residential units. The public buildings consist of a restaurant and an events hall, which shares many similarities with the unbuilt events hall that Wissa Wassef designed for the Lycée Franco-Égyptien d'Héliopolis. The proposal treats the dormitory complex like a village, with a main path that flows and turns with the buildings. Although all the residential units vary in size and layout, they each have a walled courtyard. A prototype for the rooms demonstrates inspiration from vernacular architecture: with a groin-vaulted ceiling, the room contains a *mastaba* bed and a desk with oriental inspiration—each embedded in a wall niche.

The second proposal is signed by Ramses Wissa Wassef and Hassan Fathy. It is a basic layout that takes its inspiration from the first proposal, but it is amplified, as the plot size has increased substantially.

The third proposal is signed by Wissa Wassef, Fathy, and Abu Bakr Khayrat. It builds on the second proposal but introduces a main central spine and plaza. Ultimately, none of the proposals was implemented.

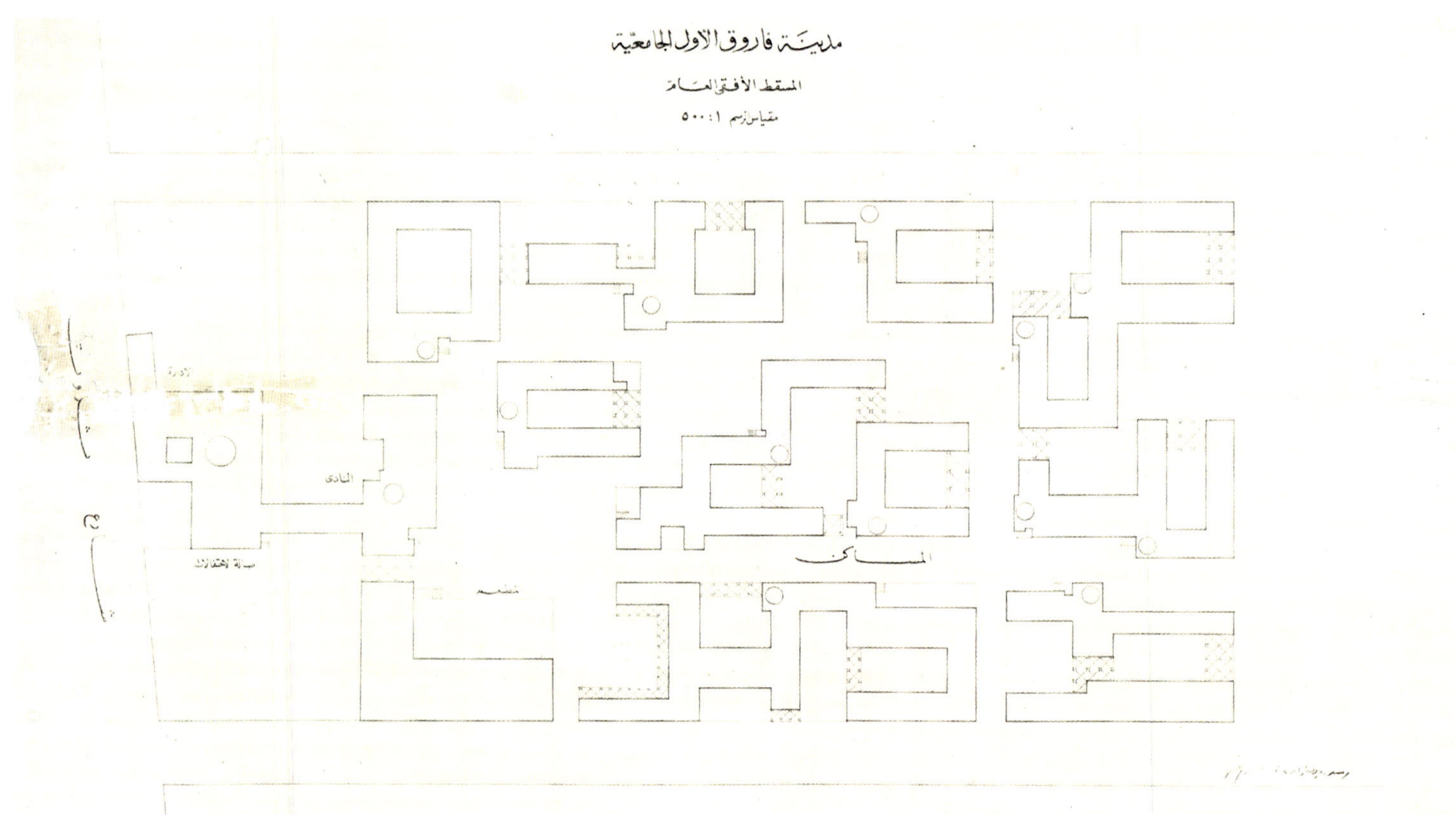

Proposal by Ramses Wissa Wassef for the university dorms.

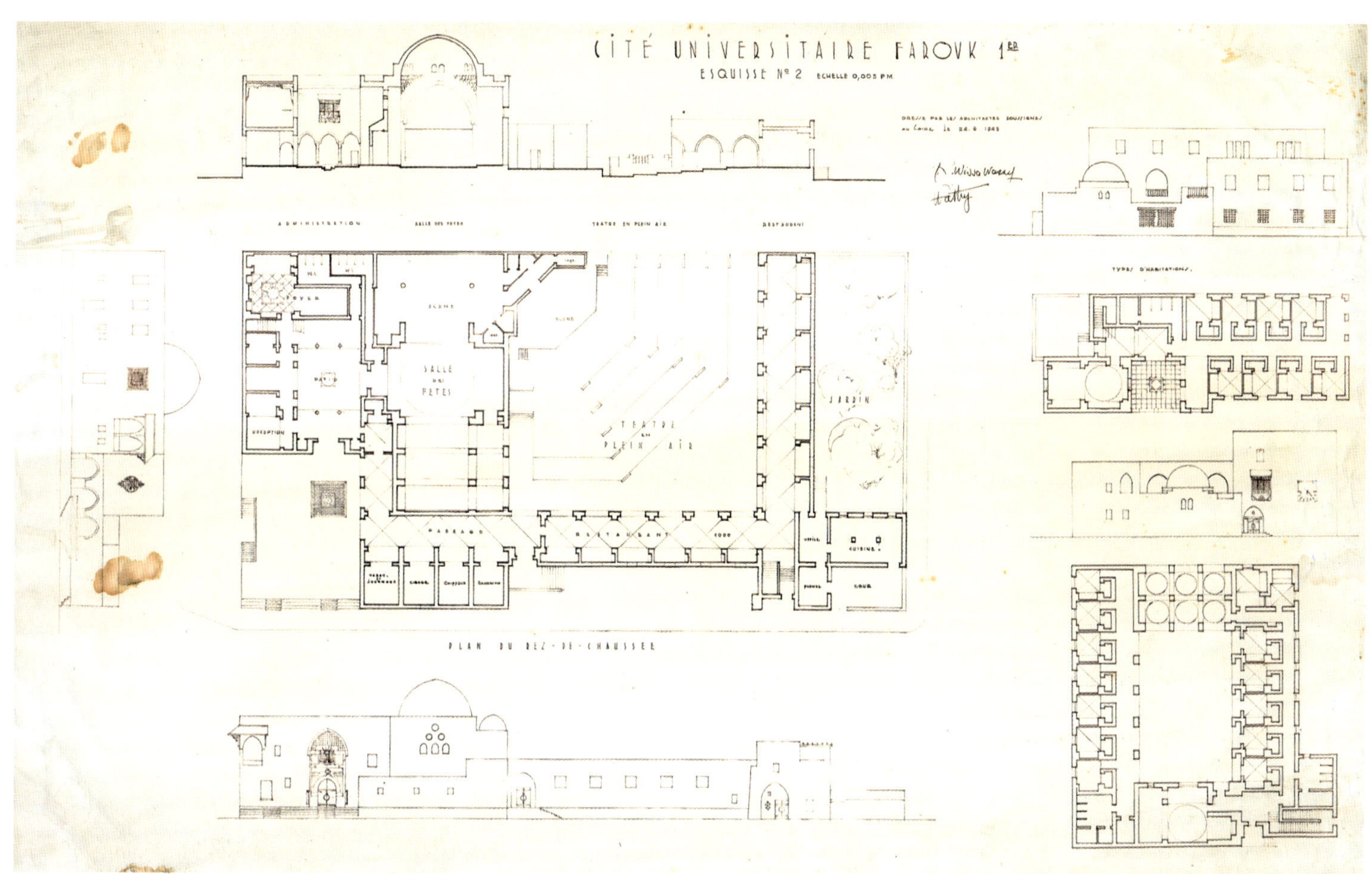

Plan of the theater and events hall in the proposal by Wissa Wassef and Fathy.

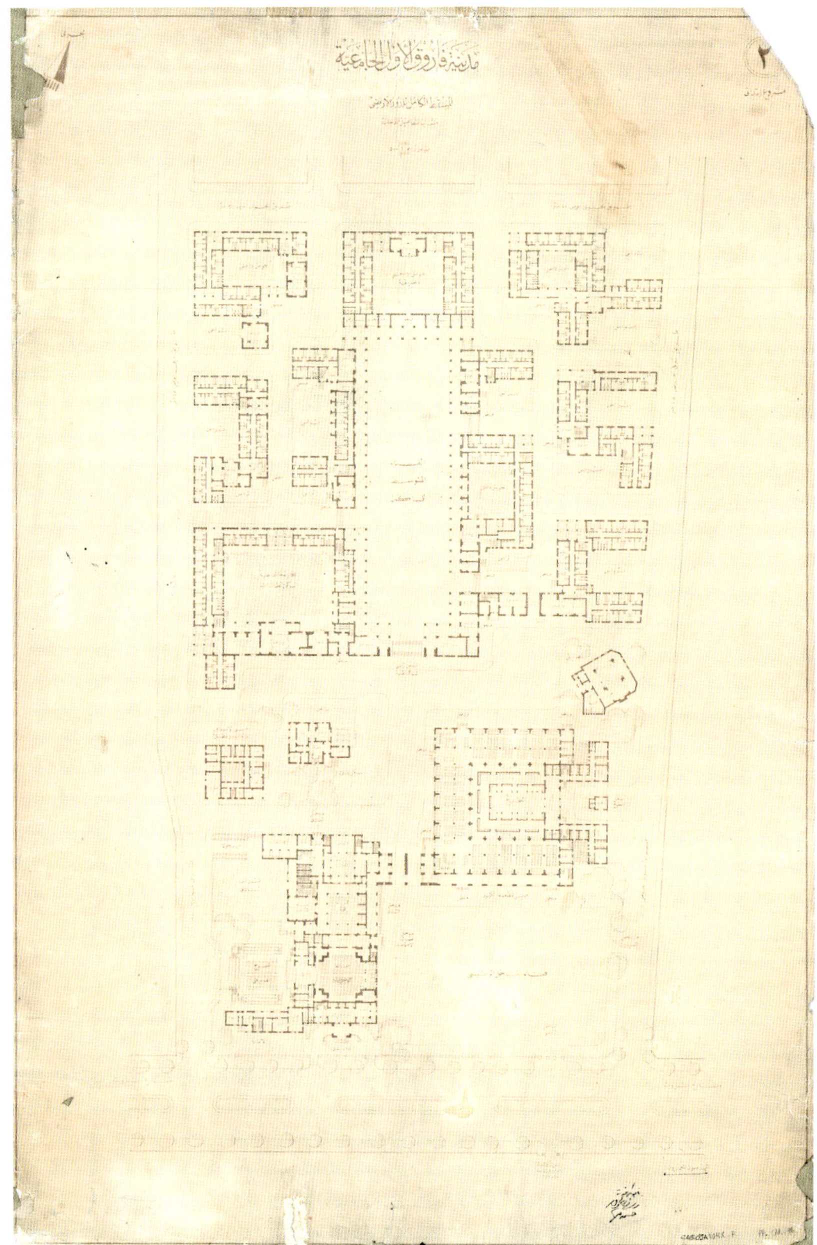

Proposal by Ramses Wissa Wassef, Hassan Fathy, and Abu Bakr Khayrat for the university dorms.

SCHOOL FOR ART AND HANDICRAFTS IN AL-QUBBA

Date: 1947
Location: Matariya Street, al-Qubba, Cairo
Alternative names: École Artisanale, Artisanal School

This artisanal boarding school preceded the Ramses Wissa Wassef Art Center, yet one can see the beginnings of the latter in this project, which also focuses on the connections between natural and creative environments. Although the area along Matariya Street is now urbanized, at the time much of the land in Matariya was used for agriculture and contained many *'izba*s. It is unclear if any part of the project was ever implemented.

There are two proposals for the scheme, yet both contain the same functions and layout principles. The school layout follows the essence of a typical Egyptian village, with winding paths of varying widths and a variety of courts. In plan, Proposal 1 has a more organic urban and architectural composition, lacking a formal grid throughout the project, while Proposal 2 is more modular.

The former seems to have been the leading proposal, as it was taken a step further with the drafting of detailed drawings containing dimensions. The school includes classrooms, workshops, administration offices, an exhibition gallery and museum, pottery kilns, dormitories, a large dining hall and kitchen, agricultural land, a small farm and farm house, and the director's quarters. A variety of fenestration was proposed throughout the project, creating an intimate and dynamic atmosphere.

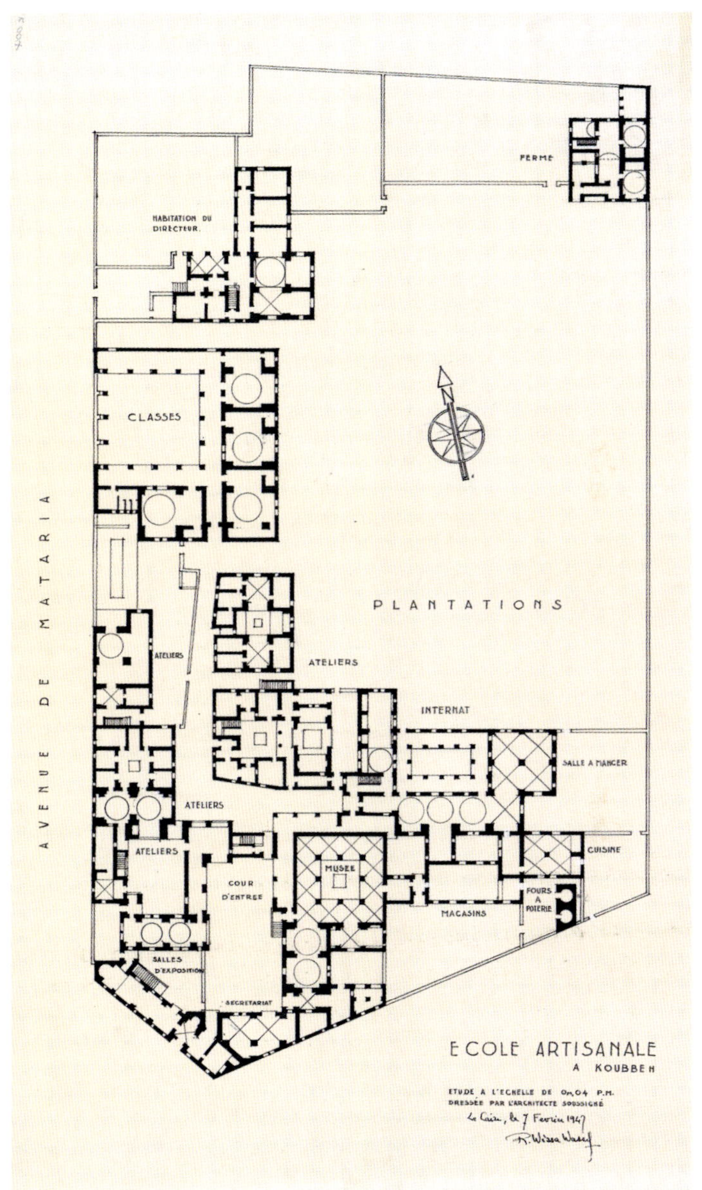

Ground-floor plan, proposal 1.

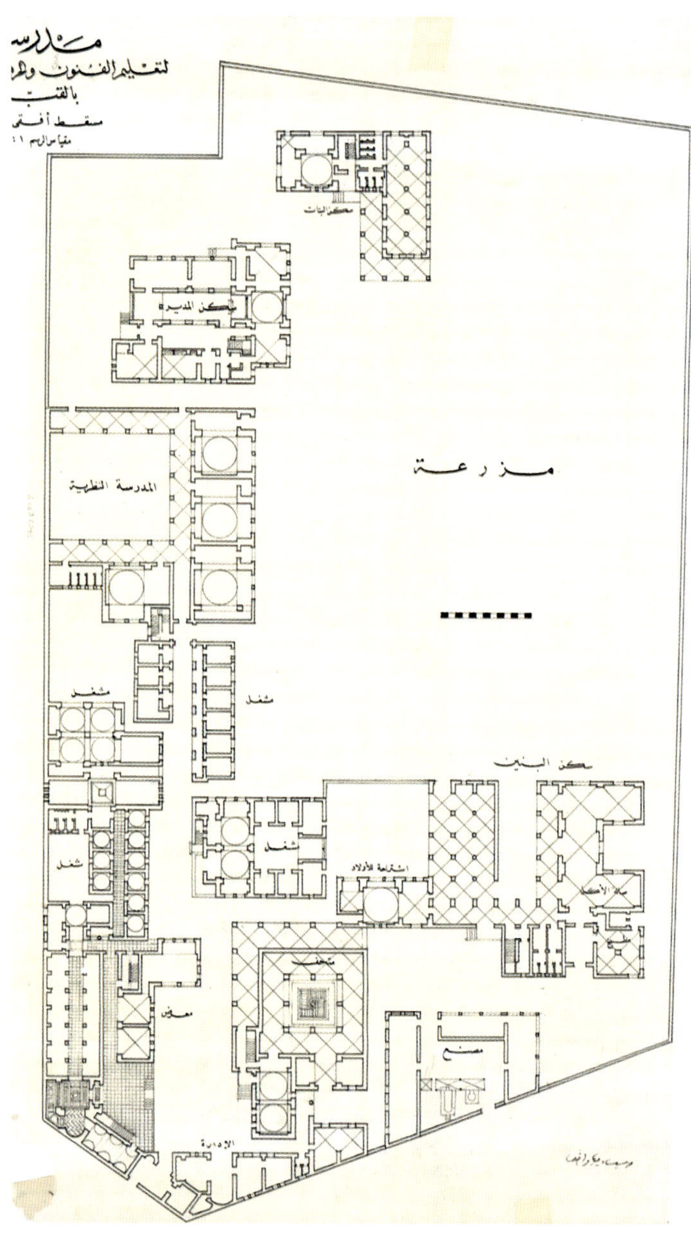

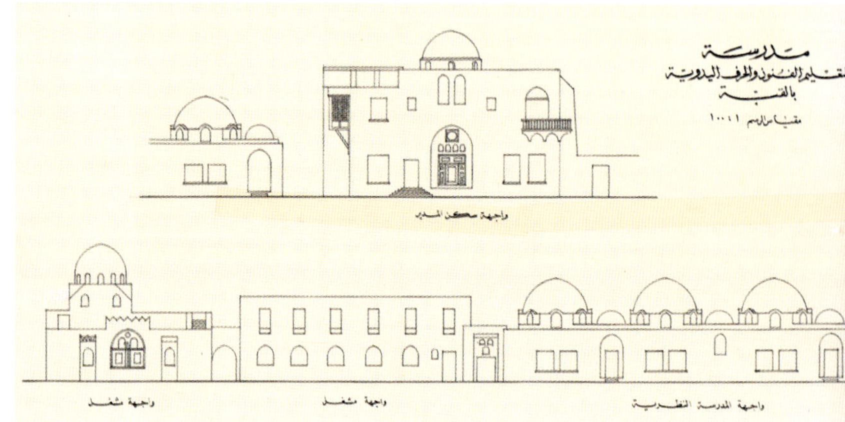

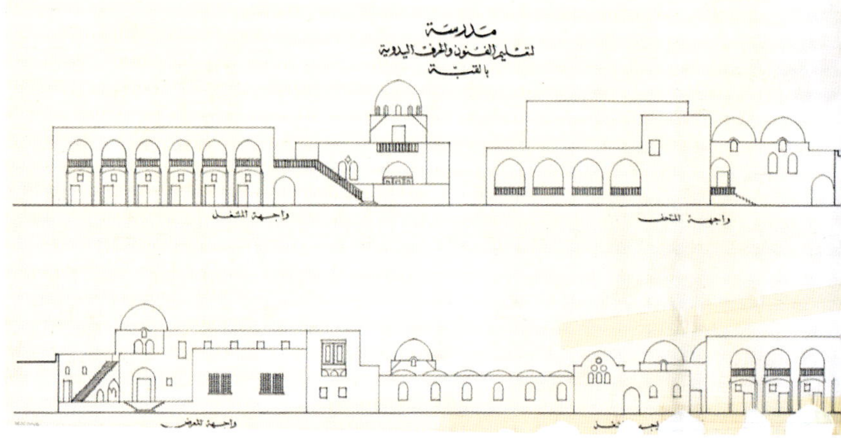

FROM LEFT, CLOCKWISE:
Ground-floor plan, proposal 2.
East elevations for the eastern workshops and the director's home, proposal 2.
West elevations for the eastern workshops and museum, and east elevations for the western workshops and exhibition, proposal 2.

ISMAILIYA SECONDARY SCHOOL

Date: 1949
Location: Intersection of Anwar al-Sadat and al-Madaris Streets, Ismailiya

Initially called the Ismailiya Secondary School, the institution is currently known as the Sadat Secondary Military School for Boys. According to the school administration, the building was built by Hussein Salem starting in 1948 and completed in 1950.[27] The drawings in Wissa Wassef's collection are dated 1949 and cosigned with Fuad Fikry, which raises the question of why his drawings have some parts that resemble the existing building while others do not. Was the school construction phased, and Wissa Wassef approached for the design of the main building after construction had started? Was Salem's role that of contractor or structural engineer—not involved in the architectural design? It is unclear if any part of the existing school was designed by Wissa Wassef.

The proposal shows a U-shaped building with an assortment of smaller units to the north, which contains a mosque and specialized classrooms such as the art studio, laboratories, and workshop. The ground floor of the west wing contains the school's more public elements such as the administration offices, theater, and reception courtyard; the north wing consists of classrooms; and the east wing contains the dining hall. The ground floor is quite accessible, as the circulation corridors are separated from the open spaces via arcades. The first floor is mostly used for classrooms. Overall, the scheme is quite classical in layout, with a central portal entrance to the classrooms and through to the specialized classrooms, another portal entrance to the administration suite, and a domed theater.

The design differs from the existing building, whose layout ended up following a rectangular shape with a chamfered corner so that the main entrance opens facing the street square. This diagonal wing was increased to a three-story height and has a curvaceous protrusion into the school yard. The articulation of the building is quite different from its classical plan, implementing a more modernist language. It has no ground-floor arcades, and all its windows are square or comprise long rectangular strips. The east wing as built had a pitched roof rather than Wissa Wassef's flat roof; it was demolished in 2014. The specialized classrooms, although in the same location, are significantly larger and follow a different morphology to that shown in the design.

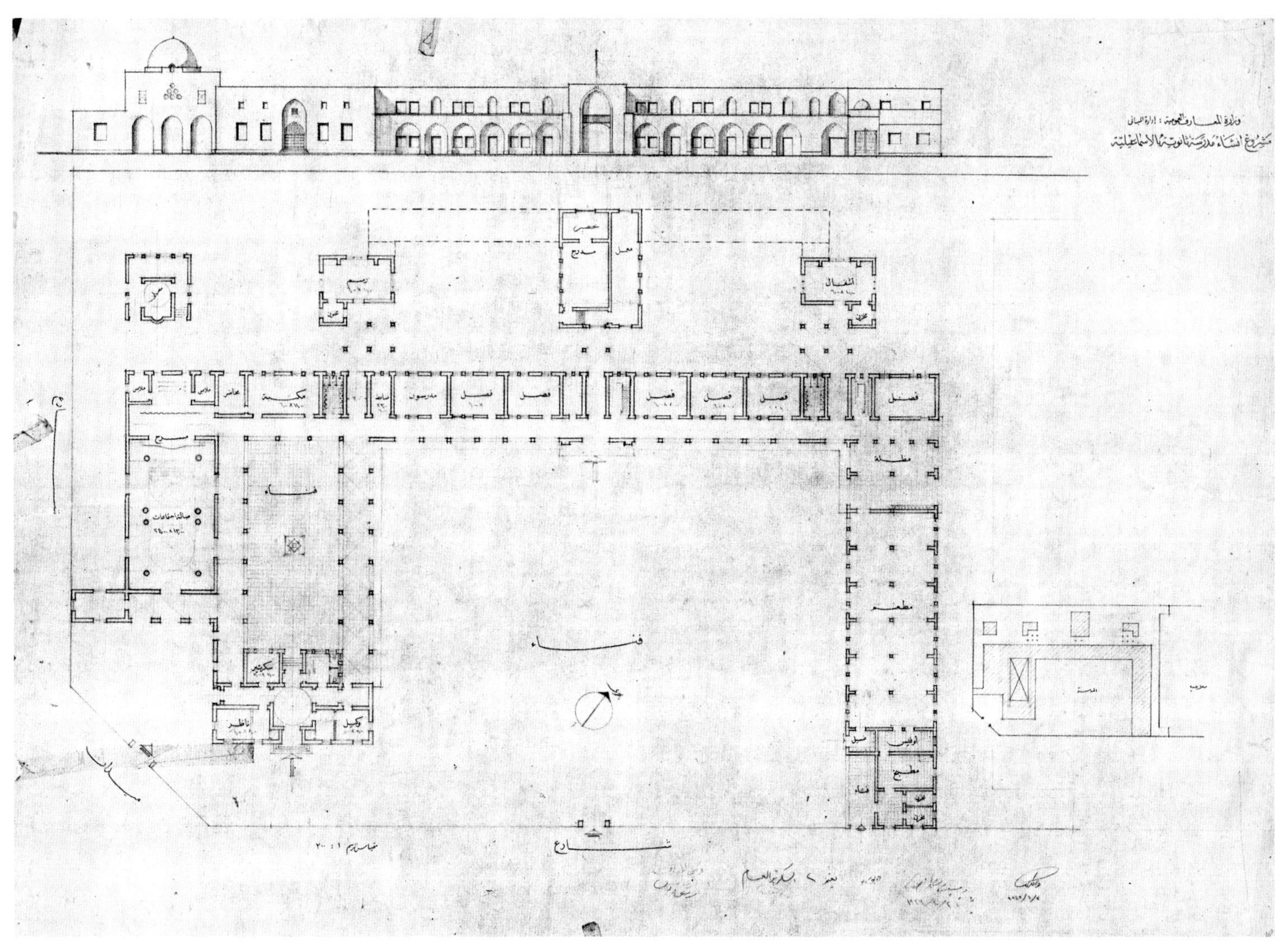

Ground floor plan of the school, including main elevation and site plan.

AMERICAN MISSION FOR GIRLS: EXPERIMENTAL PROJECT FOR FARMING

Date: 1955
Location: off Haram Street (Pyramids Road), Giza

The Experimental Project for Farming buildings are located at the entrance to the plot and consist of a rest house, stores, a red-brick farm complex containing animal pens, dairy facilities, stores, washroom, and toilet facilities, and, across a large *hawsh*, the farm residences. The dairy facilities include a milking parlor and working rooms allowing for the manufacture of butter and cheese. The whole complex is roofed with domes and vaults. The strip of farmers' residences is made up of five units, four of which have two bedrooms, a storage room, a corral, and a courtyard. The fifth has an extra two bedrooms instead of the corral; they all have stairs leading to an open rooftop. As part of the sanitary work, Wissa Wassef also designed a sewage treatment tank.

The project was proposed on a part of land owned since 1925 by the American University in Cairo (AUC) along the Pyramids Road. Here, AUC had plans to build a suburban campus but, pending realization, rented out subplots[28]—in this case to the American College for Girls (ACG), later renamed Ramses College for Girls.[29] In one of the drawings, the adjacent subplot is annotated "Esbeh ['Izbat] Cleland" (Cleland's farming estate), after Wendell Cleland, who was the head of the Extension Program (later the Division of Public Service) at AUC. This program was established in 1924 and aimed to provide educational, cultural, and medical services to Egyptians regardless of their background. These services took the form of public lectures, radio broadcasts, clinics, and more.[30] Around 1932 AUC sponsored the construction and operation of a small clinic on this land.

Following the Second World War, Cleland believed that programs related to postwar reconstruction would benefit both the university and the wider Middle East. Among the many projects that he proposed to AUC was the establishment of a "model dairy on Pyramids road farm . . . to . . . demonstrate the latest techniques of milk production and help train Egyptian farmers in modern methods."[31] Lacking funding, the projects were not implemented. In 1947 Cleland resigned from AUC and shortly after, late in 1949, the suburban pyramids campus idea was abandoned for good and plans for the sale of the land started. However, in June 1953, Cleland came back as interim university president until January 1955.[32] It is unclear if the individual pushing for the project implementation during this time was Cleland or Helen Martin, the principal at ACG. Wissa Wassef had mailed Martin the cost estimate for the proposals.[33] Despite this, it is unknown whether the model dairy project was ever implemented or was halted by the sale of the land.

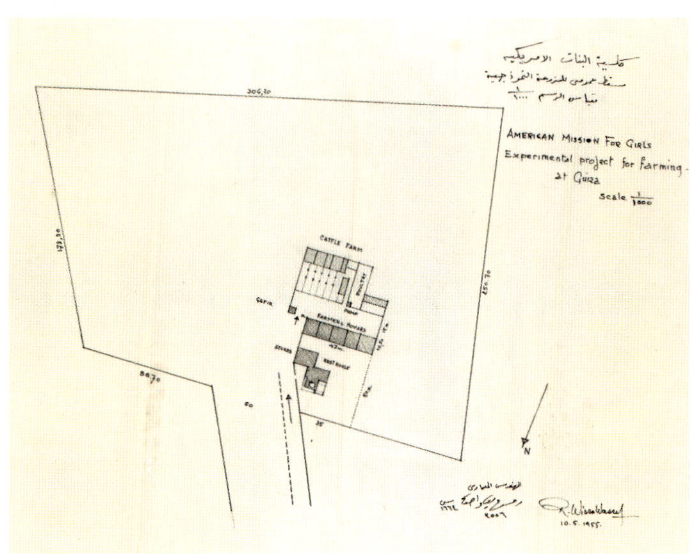

Site plan of farm and dairy farm facilities.

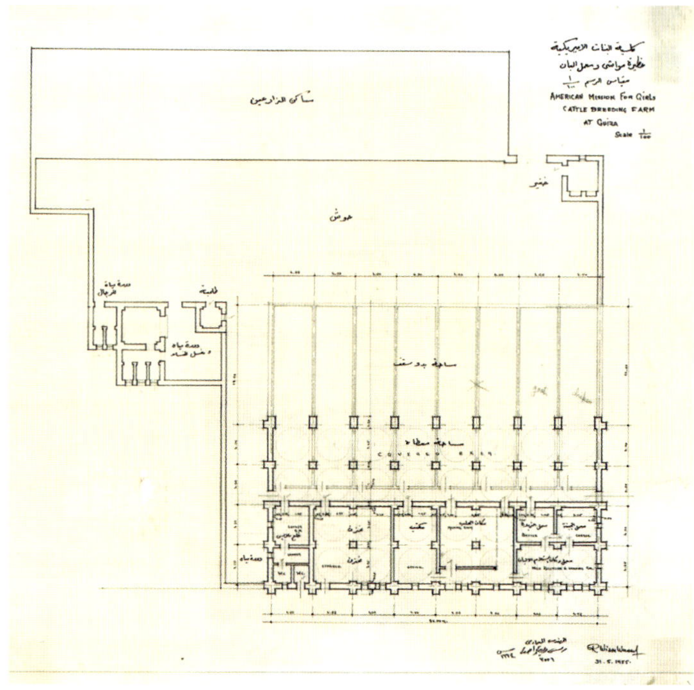

Plan of dairy farm facilities enclosure.

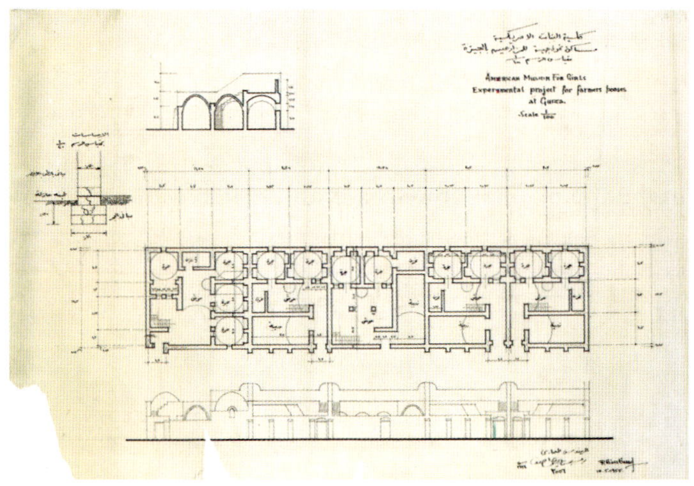

Plan of farmers' residences.

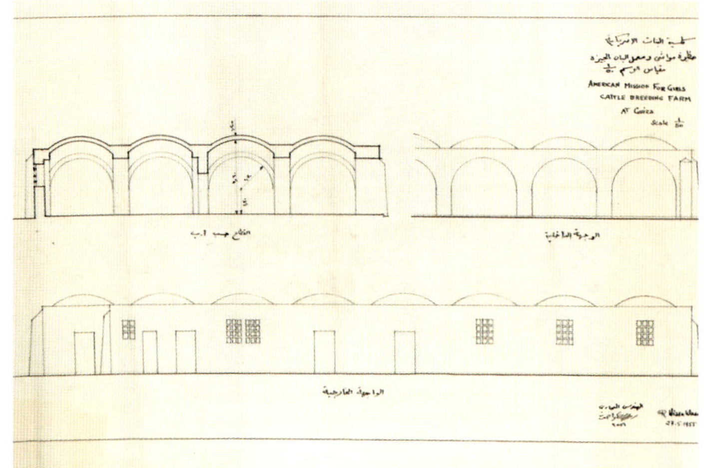

Elevation of farmers' residences.

OTHER

BANQUE MISR BUILDING AND HOTEL COMPETITION

Date: 1937
Location: Opera Square, Downtown, Cairo

Perspective.

This mixed-use development project was designed by Wissa Wassef for a Banque Misr competition requiring a hotel and residential building overlooking Opera Square and the Continental Hotel. It included residential apartments, terraces, a hairdressing salon, an antique shop, stores, an exhibition gallery, a gallery for Société Misr, a garage for twenty-five vehicles, and a hotel that included an events hall, restaurant, and cabaret, the latter a common feature in hotels of the time.

Wissa Wassef's Art Deco–inspired elevations and perspectives take their cue from pharaonic motifs, reminiscent of the architecture that was present in Downtown Cairo since the 1920s. The fez-wearing individuals portrayed in his colored drawings are a surprising touch that is a testament to Wissa Wassef's attention to detail and context in his work.

The winning entry of the competition was designed by the architect and musician Abu Bakr Khayrat, who had also studied architecture at the École des Beaux Arts de Paris, graduating in 1935.[34] The competition results were not implemented, however; instead, the Opera Cinema and Casino Badia, also known as Casino Opera, were inaugurated in 1940, becoming a landmark of the performing arts in Egypt until the 26 January 1952 Cairo fire that occurred in the aftermath of protests against the killing of police officers in Ismailiya by the British army.[35]

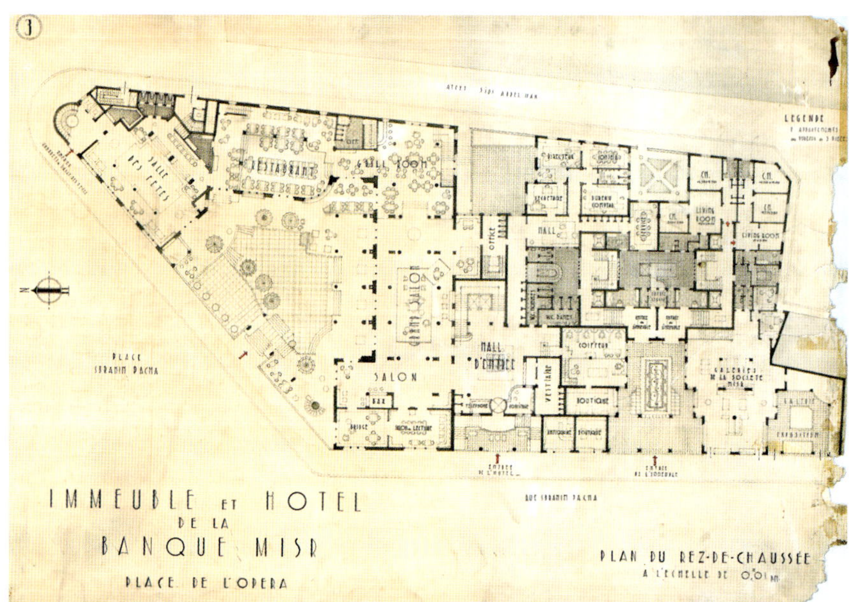

Ground-floor plan.

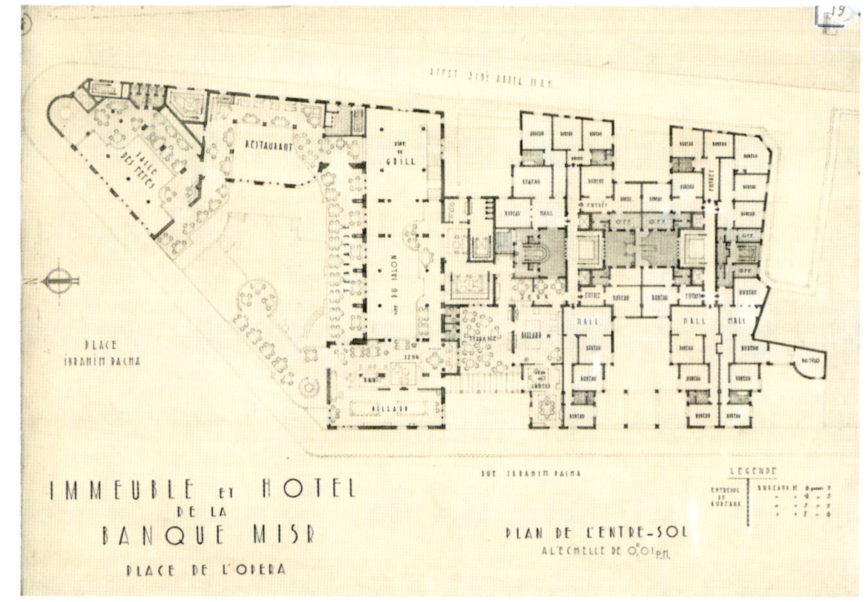

Mezzanine floor.

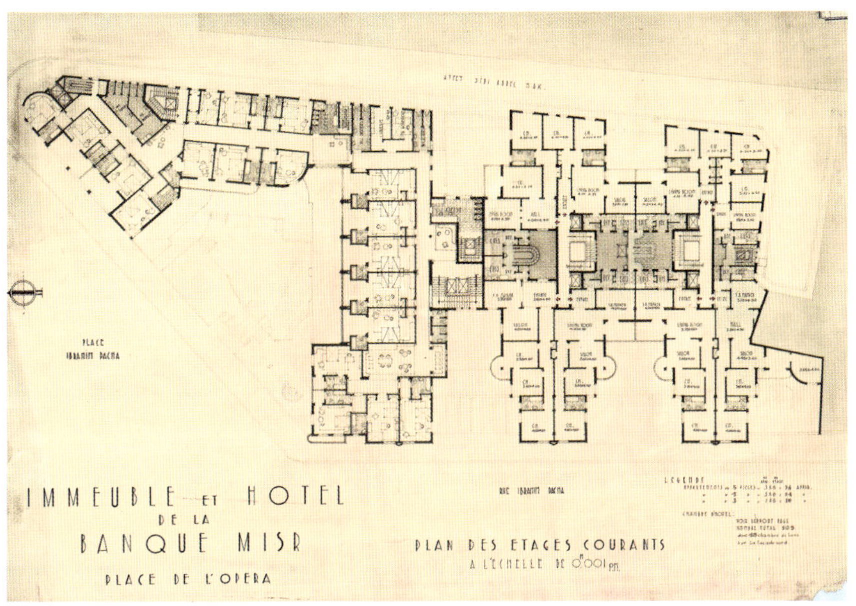

Typical floor.

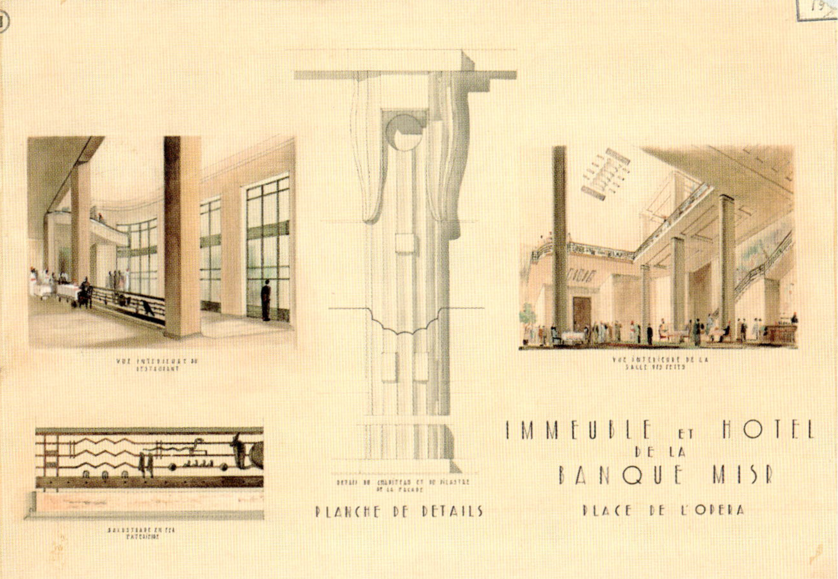

Interior renders and Art Deco details.

GARAGE AND ATELIER MAGAR

DATE: 1953
Location: al-Tahrir Street, Dokki/Bulaq al-Dakrur, Giza
Alternative names: Garage Magar, Garage Maqar, Awlad Maqar

Garage and Atelier Magar, now known as Magar Group, had a bus garage in Bulaq Abul-'Ila, and a car agency, repair and service center in Dokki, on that district's border with Bulaq al-Dakrur.[36] Most likely this project refers to the latter, as the only known drawing related to it depicts a car jack rather than a bus jack.[37]

Initially called Magar Bros., the Dokki establishment was inaugurated on 15 May 1953.[38] The company is owned by the family of Ina Makkar (aka Magar). It is unknown if Wissa Wassef designed only the jack or if he made other contributions. The architect of the building remains unidentified.

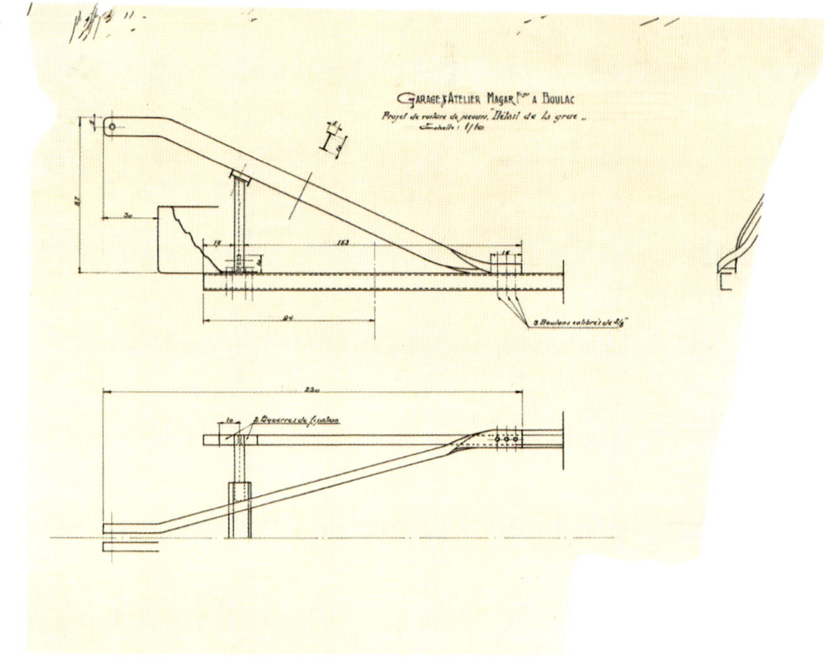

Section and elevation of car jack.

INTERIOR DESIGN AND STAINED-GLASS PANELS FOR THE GRAND RECEPTION HALL AT THE CAIRO GOVERNORATE HEADQUARTERS

Date: 1961
Location: Nile Corniche, Downtown, Cairo
Alternative names: Cairo Municipality Headquarters, Arab Socialist Union Headquarters, National Democratic Party Headquarters

This project—designed by Ramses Wissa Wassef, Shafiq Ahmed Hosni, Kamal al-Kafrawi, and Ahmed Bishindi, all members of the Faculty of Fine Arts in Cairo—is for the interior design of the reception hall at the Cairo Governorate building. The building itself was the work of the Egyptian modernist architect Mahmoud Riad and was built in 1958–59. Initially meant to be Cairo's Municipality Headquarters, it was immediately occupied by Gamal Abd al-Nasser's Arab Socialist Union until 1980, when it was taken over by the National Democratic Party (NDP) as its headquarters.[39] During its final phase of occupancy by the NDP, it also hosted other governmental and nongovernmental entities. A fire broke out in the building during the January 2011 revolution and devastated it. Its burnt ruins loomed over the Nile banks until it was demolished in 2015.[40]

The events reception hall was designed to occupy an area of 475 square meters with a height of 15 meters. The main entrance is 8.3 meters wide by 3 meters high and is topped by a stucco claustra pierced with triangular openings. On the opposite wall, mirroring the entrance, is a stage elevated by 30 centimeters. The room is clad in wood paneling up to a height of 3 meters, with evenly spaced triangular indentations into which 13-meter-long lighting units are embedded. Above the paneling, and evenly spaced between the lighting columns, are stained-glass panels measuring 9.5 meters long by 1.2 meters wide. The combination of all these vertical elements creates an atmosphere of grandeur within the hall. A folded-plane ceiling is suspended below the air-conditioning ductwork, and lighting strips are aligned with its folds; the folded design is replicated in copper as the door handles.

The design of the stained-glass panels reflects the diversity of Cairo. Each of the seven panels focuses on one of the following scenes: Cairo festivities, popular clothing and crafts, the famous Khan al-Khalili Suq, the minarets of Cairo, the Islamic Museum, the Coptic Museum, and the Egyptian Museum. Unfortunately, these were destroyed in the fire that consumed the building.

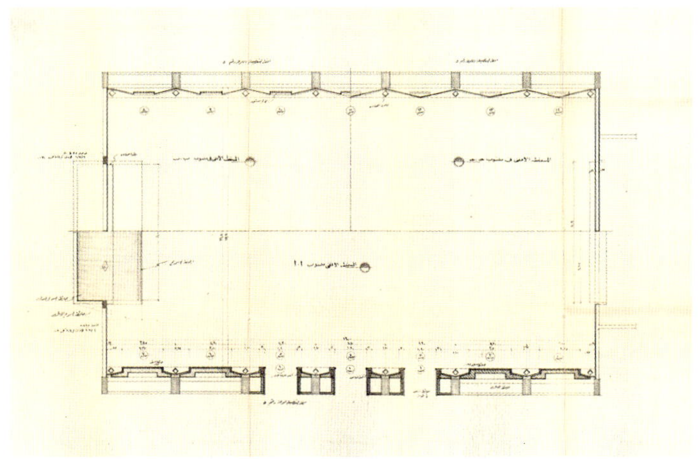

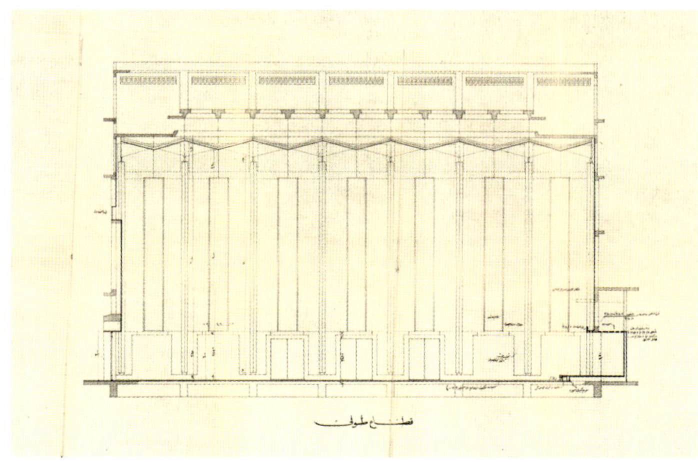

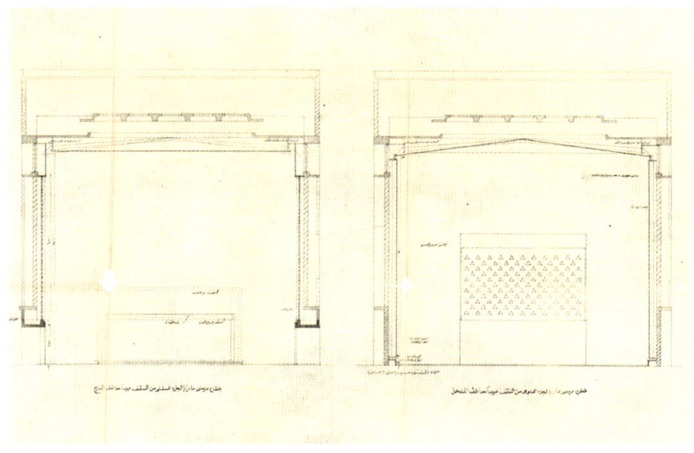

FROM TOP LEFT, CLOCKWISE:
Plan of the grand reception hall.
Longitudinal section through hall, showing interior elevations.
Cross sections through hall, showing entrance and stage at opposite ends.

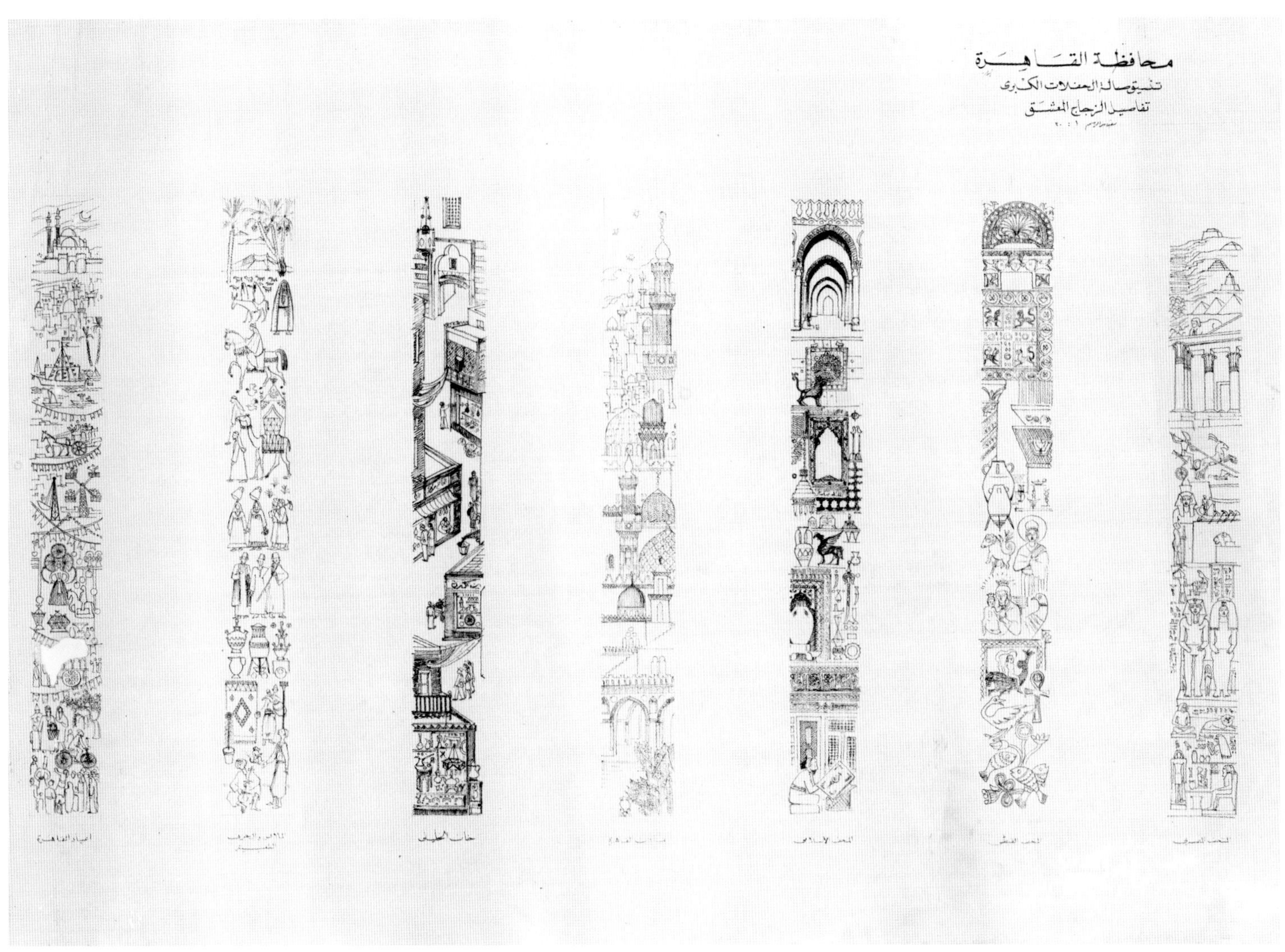

Drawings of the stained-glass panels, which depict scenes from Cairo.

Glossary

apse: semicircular recess behind the altar in a church.

arcade: roofed series of arches that provides cover.

arcature: arcade made up of several units.

archivolt: decorative elements around an arch.

atrium: courtyard surrounded by an arcade or colonnade, usually positioned in front of the church in a church complex.

basilica plan: rectangular church layout with a nave flanked by aisles.

bas-relief: a carving in which figures and scenes project at a shallow depth.

ciborium: freestanding dome situated above an altar and supported on four columns.

claustra: perforated wall or screen.

clerestory: windows located at the top of a wall.

cloister: covered walkway along the walls of a building, surrounding a courtyard or garden.

colonnade: row of columns.

dayr: monastery.

doksar: domed canopy in contemporary churches or domed room in historic churches, sheltering the entrance of a church.

durqa'a: covered court between *iwan*s, usually a step below their floor level.

felucca: traditional Egyptian narrow lateen-rigged sailing vessel.

hashmi: porous stone local to Egypt.

hawsh: courtyard within or adjacent to a building, enclosed by a fence.

haykal: sanctuary in Coptic churches, usually facing east.

iconostasis: screen separating the sanctuary from the main body of a church, usually embedded with icons; a curtain is usually drawn over the openings that lead to the altar.

iwan: vaulted room open from one side.

'izba: farm estate.

madyafa: reception room.

magaz: axially broken or bent entrance.

mangiliya: lectern.

mashrabiya: traditional window made from small turned-wood pieces fitted together to form a lattice; ornamental patterns are often integrated into its design.

mastaba: in Islamic and traditional Egyptian architecture, a built rectangular platform used for seating or sleeping; in ancient Egyptian architecture, a large flat-roofed rectangular tomb with sloped sides.

narthex: a church's entrance vestibule.

nave: main central area of a church where the congregation worships.

Nubian dome/vault: dome or vault typical of Nubia, with an almost parabolic section.

oculus (*pl.* oculi): round window.

portico: sheltered entrance porch supported by columns.

qa'a: traditional roofed reception hall in grand Islamic houses.

qamariya: carved stucco or stone grille panel creating an opening in a wall; in the case of the former, it may be combined with stained glass.

sanctuary: area in a church where the altar is located.

shukhshikha: skylight structure that protrudes from a ceiling/roof, with openings to allow warm air to escape.

takhtabush: receiving hall on the ground floor of Islamic houses, one of whose façades is open to a courtyard or garden and supported by a central column.

tibn: traditional material consisting of a mixture of mud and straw, from which mud bricks are made.

zugag mu'ashshaq: stained-glass windows.

Notes

Part 1: Ramses Wissa Wassef

Preface

1. Including the following books: *Woven by Hand*, photographs by Werner Forman and text by Ramses Wissa Wassef, 1972; *Egyptian Landscapes: 50 Years of Tapestry Weaving at the Ramses Wissa Wassef Art Centre Cairo*, by Yoanna Wissa Wassef, Suzanne Wissa Wassef, and Hilary Weir, 2006; *Fleurs du désert: tapisseries d'enfants égyptiens*, by Werner Forman, Bedrich Forman, and Ramses Wissa Wassef, 1961; *Threads of Life: A Journey in Creativity*, by E.A. De Stefano, 1991.

Introduction

1. Correspondence between Ramses Wissa Wassef and his mother Berlanty Youssef, undated, WW, Regional Architecture Collection, Rare Books and Special Collections Library, the American University in Cairo, Egypt. Ramses and his mother used to exchange letters in French.
2. Cérés Wissa Wassef, "Wissa Wassef," in *The Coptic Encyclopedia*, edited by Aziz Suryal Atiya (New York: Macmillan, 1991), vol.7, http://ccdl.libraries.claremont.edu/cdm/ref/collection/cce/id/1919
3. Wissa Wassef, "Wissa Wassef."
4. Interview with Sophie Habib Georgi, Harraniya, December 2012. In fact, Sophie Habib Georgi, the wife of Ramses Wissa Wassef, indicated that he was a good flautist and his older sister Cérés was an excellent pianist.
5. Ikram Nosshi, "Ramses Wissa Wassef: Architect, Artist, Stained Glass Window Designer and a Potter," in *Pre VERNADOC 2002, Ramses Wissa Wassef Art Centre—* Egyptian Earth Construction Association, (Helsinki: ICOMOS, 2013), 12–16.
6. Ikram Nosshi, "An Egyptian Architect," *Ramses Wissa Wassef Art Center - Egypt*, www.wissawassef.com/architecture
7. Interview with Sophie Habib Georgi, Suzanne and Yoanna Wissa Wassef, and Ikram Nosshi, Harraniya, March 2011.
8. Ikram Nosshi, Suzanne Wissa Wassef's husband and son-in-law of Ramses Wissa Wassef, reported that this residence, which Wissa Wassef El-Beblawi acquired in 1922, was built in 1909. In 1984, ten years after Ramses Wissa Wassef's passing, the family sold the house. And in 2003 the house was demolished to be replaced by a multi-level structure. The street is named Wissa Wassef, commemorating Wissa Wassef El-Beblawi.
9. Leïla el-Wakil, ed., *Hassan Fathy: An Architectural Life* (Cairo: American University in Cairo Press, 2018), 29.

10. El-Wakil, *Hassan Fathy*, 29.
11. Interview with members of the Wissa Wassef family, March 2011. During this conversation, an anecdote was given: A well-known French architect (whose name was not revealed) was asked to execute this project; he replied to the effect that having such a talented architect as Ramses Wissa Wassef, why were they asking him to design and build the kindergarten of the French School in Bab al-Luq? He asserted that this Egyptian architect (Wissa Wassef) would be capable of doing something truly extraordinary.
12. The family prefers this spelling of the name, but some sources spell it "Habib Gorgi."
13. John Feeney, "The Hidden Power," *Saudi Aramco World* (January/February 1982), 20–27. Aramco World, http://archive.aramcoworld.com/issue/198201/the.hidden.power.htm
14. Adelina Picone, *La casa araba d'Egitto: costruire con il clima dal vernacolo ai maestri contemporanei*, (Milan: Jaka Books, 2009), 214.
15. In spite of being an art teacher, Sophie never taught art to the children of Harraniya. A great collection of her watercolor pieces is displayed at the galleries of the Ramses Wissa Wassef Art Center in Harraniya.
16. Sherban Cantacuzino, ed. "Ramses Wissa Wassef Arts Center," in *Architecture in Continuity: Building in the Islamic World Today* (New York: The Aga Khan Award for Architecture, 2009), 131.
17. In some sources this award has been incorrectly attributed to Wissa Wassef's stained-glass windows in the Grand Reception Hall at the Cairo Governorate Headquarters, which has also been incorrectly referred to as the Egyptian National Assembly building.
18. Cantacuzino, ed. "Ramses Wissa Wassef Arts Center," 131.

Architect and Artist

1. El-Wakil, *Hassan Fathy*, 29–30, points this out when she compares Ramses Wissa Wassef's graduation project, 1935, with Hassan Fathy's, 1926, where the latter clearly replicated the dominant classicism that was purveyed by Egyptian schools of architecture.
2. A reference to the overbearing neoclassical style promulgated most famously by 'Baron' Georges-Eugène Haussmann in Paris under Napoleon III.
3. Photograph of clay model of School in Old Cairo. WW, Regional Architecture Collection, Rare Books and Special Collections Library, The American University in Cairo, Cairo, Egypt; Sherif Raouf Morgan, "Contemporary Coptic Orthodox Church Architecture: An Evaluative Model for Traditionalist Church Designs," PhD diss., Cairo University, 2016; photograph of clay model of the Church of the Virgin Mary in Zamalek, courtesy of the family of William Selim Hanna, the structural consultant. Aga Khan Award for Architecture, *Ramses Wissa Wassef Arts Center On-site Review Report.* The clay models were a tool for participatory design where the weavers were involved.
   For more information on the projects, see chapter 2, School in Old Cairo, Seven Weavers' Houses, and Church of the Virgin Mary in Zamalek, respectively.
4. Interview with Ikram Nosshi; Picone, *La casa araba d'Egitto*, 213; El-Wakil, *Hassan Fathy*, 109.
5. Hassan Fathy, *Architecture for the Poor: An Experiment in Rural Egypt* (Cairo: American University in Cairo Press, 2004), 6–7. Fathy does not mention Wissa Wassef by name in his book, in which he gives an account of this trip. However, in one of our interviews, members of the Wissa Wassef family described the experience lived by Ramses in 1941.
6. Picone, *La casa araba d'Egitto*, 218.
7. Yoanna Wissa Wassef. "The Story of Harraneya" (unpublished), cited in Picone, *La casa araba d'Egitto*, 216.
8. Picone, *La Casa Araba d'Egitto*, 216. In Ramses's system it would have taken some time for the children to put in practice and try at their own pace what they had in their

own imagination. He wanted them to feel free to explore their own images when weaving.

10. These windows, uniquely designed by Wissa Wassef following the Egyptian tradition of stained glass, are a common element in his projects.

Architectural Legacy

1. The term is interchangeable with 'self-sufficient' and 'green' as qualifiers for an architecture that is ecologically friendly and comfortable for users and that strives to reduce waste. It was coined in the 1970s, almost thirty years after Ramses put it into practice for the first time in Egypt.
2. James Steele, "An Architecture of Identity: Hassan Fathy and Rasem Badran," in *The Contemporary Arab Contribution to World Culture: An Arab–Western Dialogue*, ed. Magdi Youssef (Newcastle upon Tyne: Cambridge Scholars Publishing, 2018), https://books.google.com.eg/books?id=4HFmDwAAQBAJ; Picone, *La Casa Araba d'Egitto*, 213.
3. During this period many Europeans, particularly from France and Italy, came to Egypt seeking their fortune, among them architects. Perhaps many were also attracted by the romantic idea of living in a country that was considered sophisticated and mysterious, an attitude that was implanted and propagated through Orientalism. These architects with European origins, and their architectural influence, contributed to the new urban 'face' of Egypt.
4. Morgan, "Contemporary Coptic Orthodox Church Architecture," 119.
5. Ramses Wissa Wassef Archives, Rare Books and Special Collections Library, the American University in Cairo, Egypt. Unpublished, undated, and untitled documents.
6. El-Wakil, *Hassan Fathy*, 29.
7. Ikram Nosshi interview, December 2018. These children had no place to weave, so they were trained in mud-brick construction to build the chicken coops; later on, they were in charge of building the vaults of the six extra weaving studios for them to work in. The point is that after this experience they defined their vocation. One, whose name is Sha'aban, remained as a constructor. Another moved to creating pottery, and the rest of them followed the path to weaving wool and cotton tapestry.
8. William M. Rohe, et al., "The Social Benefits and Costs of Homeownership: A Critical Assessment of the Research," *Low-Income Homeownership Working Paper Series* (Cambridge, MA: Joint Center for Housing Studies of Harvard University October 2001), 4–8, http://www.jchs.harvard.edu/sites/default/files/liho01-12.pdf
   This is a natural tendency that has been proved to enhance psychological health and provide a feeling of security, solidifying an ownership relationship to the soil and structures that are possessed.
9. Ramses Wissa Wassef, Regional Architecture Collection, Rare Books and Special Collections Library, the American University in Cairo, Egypt.

Professorship

1. Nadia Radwan, "The Arts and Craftmanship," in *Hassan Fathy: An Architectural Life,* ed. Leïla el-Wakil (Cairo: American University in Cairo Press, 2018), 109–113.
2. Picone, *La casa araba d'Egitto*, 214, 287. Picone had come across a letter by Moheeb, a student of Ramses Wissa Wassef, in which he explains this major change to his approach in teaching by his professor at the School of Fine Arts in Cairo.
3. El-Wakil, *Hassan Fathy*, 29. El-Wakil cites Mercedes Voilat, who emphasizes the fact that Ramses Wissa Wassef was a product of the Roger-Henri Expert Studio. Several of Wissa Wassef's School Work drawings (WW.SW.01) include Expert's name as his professor and tutor.
4. George Bahgoury interviewed within an informal setting in an art exhibition, April 2004. At the mention of Ramses Wissa Wassef's name, Bahgoury's face brightened in happiness. He also gave testimony about the excellent traits with which Ramses was bestowed.

5. Qita'a al-funun al-tashkiliya, "Shady Muhamad Mahmud 'Abd al-Salam al-Sabah." http://www.fineart.gov.eg/arb/CV/CV.asp?IDS=2064
6. Interview with Adam Henein, Harraniya, May 2017.
7. Evidence of these projects exists in letters and notes in the Ramses Wissa Wassef documents, among which are projects that may have never passed the initial client-architect exchanges. Ramses Wissa Wassef, Regional Architecture Collection, Rare Books and Special Collections Library, the American University in Cairo, Egypt.

Part 2: A Descriptive Catalog

Extant

1. Aga Khan Award for Architecture, ed., *Ramses Wissa Wassef Arts Center On-site Review Report* (Cairo: Aga Khan Award for Architecture, 1983), https://archnet.org/sites/212/publications/335#item_associations
2. Ramses Wissa Wassef did not use *tibn*, a traditional binding and rendering material consisting of a mixture of mud and straw, because it was prone to attack from ants and termites.
3. Aga Khan Award for Architecture, *On-site Review Report.*
4. Aga Khan Award for Architecture, *On-site Review Report.*
5. Aga Khan Award for Architecture, ed., *Client's Record of Ramses Wissa Wassef Arts Center. Courtesy of Client (submitted to the Aga Khan Award for Architecture)* (Cairo: Aga Khan Award for Architecture, 1983), https://archnet.org/sites/212/publications/336
6. Aga Khan Award for Architecture, *On-site Review Report.*
7. Aga Khan Award for Architecture, *Client's Record of Ramses Wissa Wassef Arts Center.*
8. Aga Khan Award for Architecture, *On-site Review Report.*
9. Aga Khan Award for Architecture, *On-site Review Report.*
10. Aga Khan Award for Architecture, *On-site Review Report.*
11. Aga Khan Award for Architecture, *On-site Review Report.*
12. Morgan, "Contemporary Coptic Orthodox Church Architecture," 71.
13. Nessim Henein, discussion with Ehsan Abushadi, 15 November 2017.
14. Morgan, "Contemporary Coptic Orthodox Church Architecture," 12, 45, 93. Morgan identifies three categories for contemporary Coptic Orthodox church design: the 'modern' type, which does not relate to the Coptic tradition and heritage; the 'contemporary traditional,' which replicates the traditional without its essence; and the 'traditionalist' type, which integrates innovation while maintaining the essence and value of the traditional.
15. The existing iconostasis is different from the original, mainly in that it was extended beyond the three sanctuary arches to create the fluidity between it and the dado that was added. It is unclear if the existing iconostasis includes the original segments which were altered, or if it is a modified replica. The main alterations include modifying the configuration of icons; removing the upper part of the central segment which was reserved for icons and thereby reducing the height of the central segment to match the height of the other two parts; inserting icons to replace the window-like openings at either side of the central curtain; and adding crosses on top of each of the three segments of the iconostasis.
16. Morgan, "Contemporary Coptic Orthodox Church Architecture," 145, 147, 171.
17. Morgan, "Contemporary Coptic Orthodox Church Architecture," 141.
18. Morgan, "Contemporary Coptic Orthodox Church Architecture," 143, 164.
19. Ramses Wissa Wassef and Hussein el-Tahan, a glassblower from Bab al-Nasr, collected colored glass in the form of discarded perfume bottles, drink bottles, and more in order to recycle them. To aid this process, Ramses created a tool that would roll out the recycled glass into sheets to be used for stained-glass panels.
20. Interview with Wasseem Morcos, from the church of Archangel Michael Coptic Orthodox Church, Damanhur, 7 December 2018.

21. As per the architectural drawings found at the Archangel Michael Coptic Orthodox Church in Damanhur Archive, Damanhur, Egypt.
22. Archangel Michael Coptic Orthodox Church in Damanhur Archive, Damanhur, Egypt.
23. Discussions with Frère Jocelyn Dorvault revealed that he had seen Perret's name on the original plans of the priory.
24. Jean Druel, "Une « Nouvelle » Église pour le Caire," *Amitiés dominicaines: Précaires et fragiles* 47 (2010): 30–31.
25. The priory knows the icons are reproductions from a Coptic monastery, but not which one.
26. "Tarikh kanisat ra'is al-mala'ika al-jalil Mikha'il bi Tusun," Kanisat ra'is al- mala'ika al-jalil Mikha'il, http://www.elmalakmikhail.com/index.php?mypage=church_01
27. Mina Magid, "Kanisat Mar Mina bi Fleming," *al-Adyira wa-l-kana'is*, Group Ava Kyrillos, http://group-avakyrillos.rigala.net/t1-topic, excerpt obtained from *Kitab al-yuwbil li kanisat al-shahid al-'azim Mar Mina*.
28. Conchita Añorve-Tschirgi and Lesley Lababidi, "The Architect & the Artist: Ramses Wissa Wassef," *Obelisque* 15 (2013): 109. A photograph was recently discovered by Ikram Nosshi showing Sayyida Misak carving one of the panels.
29. Aga Khan Award for Architecture, ed., *Client's Record of Mohi Houssin Residence, Courtesy of Client* (Cairo: Aga Khan Award for Architecture, 1983), https://archnet.org/sites/213/publications/343
30. Aga Khan Award for Architecture, ed., *Mohi Houssin Residence Project Summary* (Cairo: Aga Khan Award for Architecture, 1983), https://archnet.org/sites/213/publications/341
31. Aga Khan Award for Architecture, ed., *Architect's Record of Mohi Houssin Residence, Courtesy of Architect (submitted to the Aga Khan Award for Architecture)* (Cairo: Aga Khan Award for Architecture, 1983), https://archnet.org/sites/213/publications/342
32. Giza Portal, "Museums," in which it is listed as "The Gallery of Mohy El Din Hussein," http://www.giza.gov.eg/English/Tourism/Agenda/TouristGuide/Museums.aspx
33. Humphrey Davies and Leslie Lababidi, *A Field Guide to the Street Names of Central Cairo* (Cairo: American University in Cairo Press, 2018), 223.
34. Tarek Mohamed Refaat Sakr, *Early Twentieth-Century Islamic Architecture in Cairo* (Cairo: American University in Cairo Press, 1992), 33–34. Frédéric Abécassis, "Les lycées de la Mission laïque française en Egypte (1909–1961): L'exportation d'un modèle français en Orient et ses contradictions," in *Lycées, lycéens, lycéennes, deux siècles d'histoire*, edited by Pierre Caspard, Jean-Noël Luc, and Philippe Savoie (Paris: Institut national de recherche pédagogique, 2005), 138, http://www.persee.fr/doc/inrp_0000-0000_2005_act_28_1_9246
35. Abécassis, "Les lycées," 135. Dario Miccoli, *Histories of the Jews of Egypt: An Imagined Bourgeoisie, 1880s–1950s* (London: Routledge, 2015), 62, https://books.google.com/books?id=rM4qBwAAQBAJ
36. Alain Farhi, Facebook comment on school page, 12 March 2016, https://www.facebook.com/LHC1930School/photos/a.174421679361110/174421682694443/?type=3&comment_id=746753608794578&comment_tracking=%7B%22tn%22%3A%22R%22%7D and https://www.facebook.com/LHC1930School/photos/a.174421679361110/174421682694443/?type=3&comment_id=746753298794609&comment_tracking=%7B%22tn%22%3A%22R%22%7D
37. As reported by the gatekeeper of the nursery.
38. Lycee El-Horreya, "About Us," http://www.lyceehelio.com/website/index.php?pg=about_us
39. As reported by the groundskeeper.
40. Lycée El-Horreya, "About Us."
41. St. Takla Haymanout Coptic Orthodox Website, "Tarikh kanisat al-Qiddisa Maryam bi-Qasriyat al-Rihan al-qibtiya al-urthudhuksiya, Misr al-Qadima, al-Qahira, Misr," https://st-takla.org/Coptic-History/places/africa/egypt/cairo/masr-el-adima/saint-mary-church-kasreyet-elrihan-history.html
42. Correspondence with S.G., September 2018.
43. Letter from Al-Chark, undated, WW, Ramses Wissa Wassef, Regional Architecture Collection, Rare Books and Special

Collections Library, the American University in Cairo, Egypt. The renovation appears to have followed Wissa Wassef's 1944 design, yet these drawings are not cosigned by Khayrat.

44. Both their signatures appear on the design for the logo.
45. Nadi al-Sayd al-Masri: al-mawqa' al-rasmi, "al-Marhala al-uwla: al-marhala al-ta'sisiya," http://www.egyptianshootingclub.net/index.php?option=com_content&view=article&id=136%3A2010-05-26-11-29-06&catid=961&Itemid=54. Islam Musa and Anas Muhamad, *"Antoine Selim Nahas (1901–1966)." Zamanyat Masriya: mi'at sana 'amara* (Cairo: Tarek Waly Center, 2015), 7, https://www.walycenter.org/images/stories/archives/TWC-Archives-Antoine.pdf
46. Drawings of these exist in Wissa Wassef's architecture collection, but they are fragmented and awaiting repair.
47. Interview with Kamal Maher, the cemetery caretaker, 19 May 2017.
48. As acknowledged to the authors by Kamal Maher, the cemetery caretaker, and Sami Shaker, dean of the Institute of Coptic Studies and professor of urbanism, Coptic art and architecture, and the history of architecture.
49. The inscription itself is unclear, as a repainting job has covered parts of the tile.
50. Helnan International Hotels, "History," http://www.helnan.com/en/Hotels/About/136
51. Nubar Hovsepian, *Palestinian State Formation: Education and the Construction of National Identity* (Newcastle upon Tyne: Cambridge Scholars Publishing, 2008), 37, https://books.google.com/books?id=-vwYBwAAQBAJ
52. Flagmakers, "Flags of the World," https://www.flagmakers.co.uk/national-flags/flags-world/. The flags used at the time by these countries have been identified in Wissa Wassef's design.
53. The lighting of the dome is not working, and in its unlit form, the Palestinian flag is identical to the Kuwaiti flag in shape; the colors of the stripes that determine the flag's country are indecipherable. Additionally, the only country from the summit with a missing flag is Palestine, but this displaced flag has a chamfered triangle like Kuwait's flag rather than Palestine's full triangle. This chamfering can be attributed to technical difficulties of working with the stucco.

Nonextant

1. Bishop Theodosius, via his secretary, to the authors in a phone call, 25 November 2018.
2. *Qibtiyat* (@Coptic W), "*Sharuwbiym and Farag Iqladiyuws,*" Facebook, June 15, 2013, https://www.facebook.com/CopticW/photos/a.197380660400580/264386693699976
3. Nabih Kamil Dawud, *Tarikh dayr Mar Girgis bi-Tura wa rahbanuh al-nisak bi qilali Jabal Tura* (Cairo: Kanisat Mar Girgis bi Kozzika al-Ma'adi, 2010), 17–18, 86, 93–97. The first known source mentioning the monastery dates to 1047.
4. Dawud, *Tarikh dayr Mar Girgis*, 98.
5. As per the original plan of the building found among Ramses Wissa Wassef's archive.
6. Heather Sharkey, *American Evangelicals in Egypt: Missionary Encounters in an Age of Empire*. (Princeton, NJ: Princeton University Press, 2008), 18. The American mission, also known as the American Presbyterian mission, established the Evangelical Church in Egypt, including many Evangelical teaching establishments.
7. St. Takla Haymanout Coptic Orthodox Website, "Mabna al-katidra'iya al-murqusiya al-jadida fi ard al-Anba Ruways bi-l-'Abbasiya fi-l-sitiniyat min al-qarn al-'ashrin," https://st-takla.org/Coptic-History/places/africa/egypt/cairo/hadayek-el-kobba--waily--abbasia/cathedral/new.html
8. Gawdat Gabra and Gertrud J. M. van Loon, *The Churches of Egypt: From the Journey of the Holy Family to the Present Day* (Cairo: American University in Cairo Press, 2012), 178.
9. St. Takla Haymanout Coptic Orthodox Website, "115: al-Baba Yusab al-Thani," https://st-takla.org/Saints/Coptic-Synaxarium-Orthodox-Saints-Biography-00-Coptic-Orthodox-Popes/Life-of-Coptic-Pope-115-Pope-Yusab-II.html
10. St. Takla Haymanout Coptic Orthodox Website, "Kanisatay al-'Adhra' Maryam (Anba Ruways wa Anba Bishuwi) asfal

katidra'iyat Mar Murqus bi-l-Anba Ruways, al-'Abbasiya, al-Qahira, Misr," https://st-takla.org/Coptic-History/places/africa/egypt/cairo/hadayek-el-kobba--waily--abbasia/cathedral/church-two.html

11. St. Takla Haymanout Coptic Orthodox Website, "Kinisat al-Sayyida Maryam, bi-dayr al-khunduq, al-'Abbasiya, al-Qahira, Misr," https://st-takla.org/Coptic-History/places/monasteries/africa/egypt/rouis-khandak/church-old-mariam.html
St. Takla Haymanout Coptic Orthodox Website, "Kanisat al-Sayyida al-'Adhra' Maryam wa-l-Anba Bishuwi al-qibtiya al-urthudhuksiya, asfal al-katidra'iya al-murqusiya bi-l-'Abbasiya, al-Qahira, Misr," https://st-takla.org/Coptic-History/places/africa/egypt/cairo/hadayek-el-kobba--waily--abbasia/cathedral/church-mary-bishoy.html
12. As indicated by the plans found in Wissa Wassef's archive.
13. Morgan, "Contemporary Coptic Orthodox Church Architecture."
14. Correspondence with Fikry Boutros's grandson Fikry Boutros, June 2017.
15. Christopher Buyers, "Genealogy," Egypt: The Muhammad 'Ali Dynasty, https://www.royalark.net/Egypt/egypt9.htm
16. Bill of Quantities from Sharubim and Farag Akladious for the construction of an upper story in the summer house of Habib Georgi in Abu Qir, 13 June 1953, WW, Ramses Wissa Wassef, Regional Architecture Collection, Rare Books and Special Collections Library, the American University in Cairo, Egypt.
17. Correspondence with Ikram Nosshi, May 2017.
18. Mona Khazindar, ed., *Adam Henein* (Milan: Skira Editore, 2005), 28.
19. Khazindar, *Adam Henein*, 39.
20. Aga Khan Award for Architecture, *Architect's Record of Mohi Houssin Residence*; Aga Khan Award for Architecture, *Client's Record of Mohi Houssin Residence.*
21. May Selim, "Les secrets de Hénein enfin dévoilés," *al-Ahram Hebdo*, January 29, 2014, http://hebdo.ahram.org.eg/NewsContent/1010/5/25/4934/Les-secrets-de-Hénein-enfin-dévoilés.aspx
22. Adam Henein Foundation, "The Artist," http://adamheneinmuseum.com/Pages/Inner/The_Artist/22/22
23. Jaklin Munir, "Bi-l-suwar . . . jawla wast 650 qit'a fi-l-ma'rad al-da'im li-l-fann al-sha'bi al-'arabi bi-l-Iskandariya," *al-yawm al-sab'a*, http://www.youm7.com/3234682
24. Mission Laïque Française. "Collège Français de Garçons." Advertisement. *La Revue du Caire: Revue de littérature et d'histoire paraissant tous les mois* (September 1942) http://www.cealex.org/pfe/diffusion/PFEWeb/pfe_002/PFE_002_059_w.pdf
Advertisements for Mission Laïque Française schools were placed in the magazine *La Revue du Caire* in September or October of each year, in anticipation of school enrollment. From 1941 to at least 1953 the "Collège Français de Garçons" was advertised with the address 45 rue du Daher, corresponding with the address mentioned in the *Revue de l'Enseignement Français - Hors de France: Mission Laïque Française* 108 (1934), https://www.tpsalomonreinach.mom.fr/Reinach/MOM_TP_129560/MOM_TP_129560_0001/PDF/MOM_TP_129560_0001.pdf
25. David Maslowski, "Les modèles culturels des Juifs d'Égypte de la fin de la domination ottomane (1882) jusqu'à la révolution des Officiers libres (1952)." Masters thesis, Université Paris 1 Panthéon-Sorbonne, 2013, 115, https://dumas.ccsd.cnrs.fr/dumas-00875326/document
26. *Revue de L'Enseignement Français*, 16.
27. Correspondence with Mervat Nasr, 2018.
28. Lawrence R. Murphy, *The American University in Cairo: 1919–1987* (Cairo: American University in Cairo Press, 1987), 70, 76.
29. Ramses College for Girls, "Home Page," http://rcgschool.com/
30. Murphy, *The American University in Cairo*, 36. Sharkey, *American Evangelicals in Egypt*, 35–36.
31. Murphy, *The American University in Cairo*, 98.
32. Murphy, *The American University in Cairo*, 76, 83, 98, 108, 119, 120, 126.
33. Correspondence from Ramses Wissa Wassef to Helen Martin, May 4, 1955, WW, Ramses Wissa Wassef, Regional Architecture Collection, Rare Books and Special Collections

Library, the American University in Cairo, Egypt. There is no evidence of correspondence with Cleland in Wissa Wassef's documents.

34. Basim 'Abd al-Latif, "Taht al-nazar asatdhat al-tasmim… 'indama yamtazij al-'azaf 'ala khutut al-'amara ma' al-bina'," *al-Bayt*, March 1, 2009, http://pw.ahram.org.eg/News/91294.aspx (item removed).
35. Nurhan Mustafa, "Qissat 'kazinu' kan yajlis bihi al-Malik Faruq: Asassathu raqisa mashhura wa attakhadhahu Nagib Mahfuz maqarran li nadawatihi," *al-Misri al-Yawm Layt*, October 27, 2016, https://lite.almasryalyoum.com/extra/117957/ Sharif 'Arif, "al-Misri al-Yawm takshaf 'an wathiqa tanshur li awwal marra hawl hariq al-Qahira (al-halaqa al-ula)," *al-Misri al-Yawm*, January 25, 2016, https://www.almasryalyoum.com/news/details/880632
36. Based on an interview with the company's gatekeeper, October 15, 2018.
37. The jack is too short for a bus; the other garage was exclusively for buses and did not contain a workshop.
38. LinkedIn, "Magar Group," LinkedIn, https://www.linkedin.com/company/magar-group/
39. Riad Architecture, "The Cairo Municipality Headquarters," https://www.riadarchitecture.com/cairomunipality; René Boer, "Erasing the Remnants of a Revolution," *Failed Architecture*, June 1, 2015, https://failedarchitecture.com/erasing-the-remnants-of-a-revolution/
40. Osman El-Sharnoubi, "Photo Gallery: The Demolition of Mubarak's NDP Headquarters," *Ahram Online*, May 31, 2015, http://english. ahram.org.eg/UI/Front/MultimediaInner.aspx?NewsContentID=131601&newsportalname=Multimedia

Bibliography

ʿAbd al-Latif, Basim. "Taht al-nazar asatdhat al-tasmim: ʿindama yamtazij al-ʿazaf ʿala khutut al-ʿamara maʿ al-binaʾ." *al-Bayt*, 1 March 2009. http://pw.ahram.org.eg/News/91294.aspx [item removed].

Abécassis, Frédéric. "Les lycées de la Mission laïque française en Egypte (1909–1961): L'exportation d'un modèle français en Orient et ses contradictions." In *Lycées, lycéens, lycéennes, deux siècles d'histoire*, edited by Pierre Caspard, Jean-Noël Luc, and Philippe Savoie, 131–43. Paris: Institut national de recherche pédagogique, 2005. http://www.persee.fr/doc/inrp_0000-0000_2005_act_28_1_9246

Adam Henein Foundation. "The Artist." http://adamheneinmuseum.com/Pages/Inner/The_Artist/22/22

Aga Khan Award for Architecture, ed. *Architect's Record of Mohi Houssin Residence. Courtesy of Architect (submitted to the Aga Khan Award for Architecture).* Cairo: Aga Khan Award for Architecture, 1983. https://archnet.org/sites/213/publications/342

———. *Client's Record of Mohi Houssin Residence, Courtesy of Client (submitted to the Aga Khan Award for Architecture).* Cairo: Aga Khan Award for Architecture, 1983. https://archnet.org/sites/213/publications/343

———. *Client's Record of Ramses Wissa Wassef Arts Center. Courtesy of Client (submitted to the Aga Khan Award for Architecture).* Cairo: Aga Khan Award for Architecture, 1983. https://archnet.org/sites/212/publications/336

———. *Mohi Houssin Residence Project Summary.* Cairo: Aga Khan Award for Architecture, 1983. https://archnet.org/sites/213/publications/341

———. *Ramses Wissa Wassef Arts Center On-site Review Report.* Cairo: Aga Khan Award for Architecture, 1983. https://archnet.org/sites/212/publications/335#item_associations

Añorve-Tschirgi, Conchita, and Lesley Lababidi. "The Architect & the Artist: Ramses Wissa Wassef." *Obelisque* 15 (2013).

Archangel Michael Coptic Orthodox Church in Damanhur Archive, Damanhur, Egypt.

ʿArif, Sherif. "al-Misri al-Yawm takshaf ʿan wathiqa tanshur li-awwal marra hawl hariq al-Qahira (al-halaqa al-ula)." *al-Misri al-yawm*, 25 January 2016. https://www.almasryalyoum.com/news/details/880632

Boer, René. "Erasing the Remnants of a Revolution." *Failed Architecture*, 1 June 2015. https://failedarchitecture.com/erasing-the-remnants-of-a-revolution/

Buyers, Christopher. "Genealogy." *Egypt: The Muhammad ʿAli Dynasty*. https://www.royalark.net/Egypt/egypt9.htm

Cantacuzino, Sherban, ed. "Ramses Wissa Wassef Arts Center." In *Architecture in Continuity: Building in the Islamic World Today.* New York: The Aga Khan Award for Architecture, 2009.

Davies, Humphrey, and Lesley Lababidi. *A Field Guide to the Street Names of Central Cairo.* Cairo: The American University in Cairo Press, 2018.

Dawud, Nabih Kamil. *Tarikh dayr Mar Girgis bi-Tura wa rahbanuh al-nisak bi qilali Jabal Tura.* Cairo: Kanisat Mar Girgis bi Kozzika al-Ma'adi, 2010.

Druel, Jean. "Une « Nouvelle » Église pour le Caire." *Amitiés dominicaines: Précaires et fragiles* 47 (2010): 30–31.

Fathy, Hassan. *Architecture for the Poor: An Experiment in Rural Egypt.* Cairo: The American University in Cairo Press, 2004.

Feeney, John. "The Hidden Power." *Saudi Aramco World* (January/February 1982): 20–27. Aramco World. http://archive.aramcoworld.com/issue/198201/the.hidden.power.htm

Flagmakers. "Flags of the World." https://www.flagmakers.co.uk/national-flags/flags-world/

Gabra, Gawdat, and Gertrud J.M. van Loon. *The Churches of Egypt: From the Journey of the Holy Family to the Present Day.* Cairo: The American University in Cairo Press, 2012.

Giza Portal. "Museums," Tourist Guide, Tourism in Giza. http://www.giza.gov.eg/English/Tourism/Agenda/TouristGuide/Museums.aspx

Hassan Fathy, HF. Regional Architecture Collection, Rare Books and Special Collections Library, The American University in Cairo, Egypt.

Helnan International Hotels. "History." Helnan Palestine Hotel. http://www.helnan.com/en/Hotels/About/136

Hovsepian, Nubar. *Palestinian State Formation: Education and the Construction of National Identity.* Newcastle upon Tyne: Cambridge Scholars Publishing, 2008. https://books.google.com/books?id=-vwYBwAAQBAJ

Khazindar, Mona, ed. *Adam Henein.* Milan: Skira Editore, 2005.

Kanisat Ra'is al-Mala'ika al-Jalil Mikha'il. "Tarikh kanisat ra'is al-mala'ika al-jalil Mikha'il bi-Tusun." http://www.elmalakmikhail.com/index.php?mypage=church_01

LinkedIn. "Magar Group." https://www.linkedin.com/company/magar-group/

Lycée El-Horreya. "About Us." http://www.lyceehelio.com/website/index.php?pg=about_us

Magid, Mina. "Kanisat Mar Mina bi-Fleming." *al-Adyira wa-l-kana'is.* Group Ava Kyrillos. http://group-avakyrillos.rigala.net/t1-topic Excerpt obtained from *Kitab al-yubil li-kanisat al-shahid al-'azim Mar Mina.*

Maslowski, David. "Les modèles culturels des Juifs d'Égypte de la fin de la domination ottomane (1882) jusqu'à la révolution des Officiers libres (1952)." Masters thesis, Université Paris 1 Panthéon-Sorbonne, 2013, https://dumas.ccsd.cnrs.fr/dumas-00875326/document

Miccoli, Dario. *Histories of the Jews of Egypt: An Imagined Bourgeoisie, 1880s–1950s.* London: Routledge, 2015. https://books.google.com/books?id=rM4qBwAAQBAJ

Mission Laïque Française. "Collège Français de Garçons." Advertisement. *La Revue du Caire: Revue de littérature et d'histoire paraissant tous les mois* (September 1942). http://www.cealex.org/pfe/diffusion/PFEWeb/pfe_002/PFE_002_059_w.pdf

Morgan, Sherif Raouf. "Contemporary Coptic Orthodox Church Architecture: An Evaluative Model for Traditionalist Church Designs." PhD dissertation, Cairo University, 2016.

———. "The Various Typologies of Historic Coptic Orthodox Church Design." *Engineering Research Journal 151* (September 2016): A1–A13.

Munir, Jaklin. "Bi-l-suwar: jawla wast 650 qit'a fi-l-ma'rad al-da'im li-l-fann al-sha'bi al-'arabi bi-l-Iskandariya." *al-Yawm al-sabi'*, May 15, 2017. http://www.youm7.com/3234682

Murphy, Lawrence R. *The American University in Cairo: 1919–1987.* Cairo: The American University in Cairo Press, 1987.

Musa, Islam and Anas Muhammad. "Antoine Selim Nahas (1901–1966)." *Zamaniyat misriya: mi'at sana 'amara.* Cairo: Tarek Waly Center, 2015. https://www.walycenter.org/images/stories/archives/TWC-Archives-Antoine.pdf

Mustafa, Nurhan. "Qissat 'kazinu' kan yajlis bihi al-malik Faruq: Assasathu raqisa mashhura wa attakhadhahu Nagib Mahfuz maqarran li-nadawatihi." *al-Misri al-yawm layt*, 27 October 2016. https://lite.almasryalyoum.com/extra/117957/

Nadi al-Sayd al-Misri: al-mawqa' al-rasmi. "al-Marhala al-ula: al-marhala al-ta'sisiya." *'An al-Nadi.* http://www.egyptianshootingclub.net/index.php?option=com_content&view=article&id=136%3A2010-05-26-11-29-06&catid=961&Itemid=54

Nosshi, Ikram. "Ramses Wissa Wassef: Architect, Artist, Stained Glass Window Designer and a Potter." In *Pre VERNADOC 2002, Ramses Wissa Wassef Art Centre*—Egyptian Earth Construction Association. Helsinki: ICOMOS, 2013.

———. "An Egyptian Architect." *Ramses Wissa Wassef Art Center, Egypt*. www.wissawassef.com/architecture

Picone, Adelina. *La casa araba d'Egitto: costruire con il clima dal vernacolo ai maestri contemporanei*. Milan: Jaka Books, 2009.

Qibtiyat (@Coptic W). "Sharubim and Farag Iqladiyus." Facebook, 15 June 2013. https://www.facebook.com/CopticW/photos/a.197380660400580/264386693699976

Qita'a al-funun al-tashkiliya. "Shadi Muhammad Mahmud 'Abd al-Salam al-Sabah." *al-Sira al-dhatiya*. http://www.fineart.gov.eg/arb/CV/CV.asp?IDS=2064

Ramses College for Girls. "Home Page," http://rcgschool.com/

Ramses Wissa Wassef, WW. Regional Architecture Collection, Rare Books and Special Collections Library, The American University in Cairo, Egypt.

Revue de l'Enseignement Français—Hors de France: Mission Laïque Française 108 (1934), https://www.tpsalomonreinach.mom.fr/Reinach/MOM_TP_129560/MOM_TP_129560_0001/PDF/MOM_TP_129560_0001.pdf

Riad Architecture. "The Cairo Municipality Headquarters." https://www.riadarchitecture.com/cairomunipality

Rohe, William M., et al. "The Social Benefits and Costs of Homeownership: A Critical Assessment of the Research." *Low-Income Homeownership Working Paper Series* (Cambridge, MA: Joint Center for Housing Studies of Harvard University, October 2001): 1–31. http://www.jchs.harvard.edu/sites/default/files/liho01-12.pdf

Sakr, Tarek Mohamed Refaat. *Early Twentieth-Century Islamic Architecture in Cairo*. Cairo: The American University in Cairo Press, 1992.

Selim, May. "Les secrets de Hénein enfin dévoilés." *al-Ahram Hebdo*, January 29, 2014. http://hebdo.ahram.org.eg/NewsContent/1010/5/25/4934/Les-secrets-de-Hénein-enfin-dévoilés.aspx

Sharkey, Heather. *American Evangelicals in Egypt: Missionary Encounters in an Age of Empire*. Princeton, NJ: Princeton University Press, 2008.

El-Sharnoubi, Osman. "Photo Gallery: The Demolition of Mubarak's NDP Headquarters." *Ahram Online*, 31 May 2015, http://english.ahram.org.eg/UI/Front/MultimediaInner.aspx?NewsContentID=131601&newsportalname=Multimedia

Steele, James. "An Architecture of Identity: Hassan Fathy and Rasem Badran." In *The Contemporary Arab Contribution to World Culture: An Arab–Western dialogue*, edited by Magdi Youssef. Newcastle upon Tyne: Cambridge Scholars Publishing, 2018. https://books.google.com.eg/books?id=4HFmDwAAQBAJ

St. Takla Haymanout Coptic Orthodox Website. "115: al-Baba Yusab al-Thani. Tarikh al-batarka fi-l-kanisa al-qibtiya." https://st-takla.org/Saints/Coptic-Synaxarium-Orthodox-Saints-Biography-00-Coptic-Orthodox-Popes/Life-of-Coptic-Pope-115-Pope-Yusab-II.html

———. "Kanisatay al-'Adhra' Maryam (Anba Ruways wa Anba Bishuwi) asfal katidra'iyat Mar Murqus bi-l-Anba Ruways, al-'Abbasiya, al-Qahira, Misr." *al-Kana'is wa-l-adyira wa-l-amakin al-qibtiya 'ala mustawa al-'alam*. https://st-takla.org/Coptic-History/places/africa/egypt/cairo/hadayek-el-kobba--waily--abbasia/cathedral/church-two.html

———. "Kanisat al-Sayyida al-'Adhra' Maryam wa-l-Anba Bishuwi al-qibtiya al-urthudhuksiya, asfal al-katidra'iya al-murqusiya bi-l-'Abbasiya, al-Qahira, Misr." *al-Kana'is wa-l-adyira wa-l-amakin al-qibtiya 'ala mustawa al-'alam*. https://st-takla.org/Coptic-History/places/africa/egypt/cairo/hadayek-el-kobba--waily--abbasia/cathedral/church-mary-bishoy.html

———. "Kanisat al-Sayyida Maryam al-'Adhra', bi dayr al-khunduq, al-'Abbasiya, al-Qahira, Misr." *al-Adyira al-qibtiya al-urthudhuksiya*, https://st-takla.org/Coptic-History/places/monasteries/africa/egypt/rouis-khandak/church-old-mariam.html

———. "Mabna al-katidra'iya al-murqusiya al-jadida fi ard al-Anba Ruways bi-l-'Abbasiya fi-l-sitiniyat min al-qarn al-'ishrin." *al-Kana'is wa-l-adyira wa-l-amakin al-qibtiya 'ala mustawa al-'alam*. https://st-takla.org/Coptic-History/places/africa/egypt/cairo/hadayek-el-kobba--waily--abbasia/cathedral/new.html

———. "Tarikh kanisat al-Qiddisa Maryam bi-Qasriyat al-Rihan al-qibtiya al-urthudhuksiya, Misr al-Qadima, al-Qahira, Misr." *al-Kana'is wa-l-adyira wa-l-amakin al-qibitya 'ala mustawa al-'alam*. https://st-takla.org/Coptic-History/places/africa/egypt/cairo/masr-el-adima/saint-mary-church-kasreyet-elrihan-history.html

El-Wakil, Leïla, ed. *Hassan Fathy: An Architectural Life*. Cairo: The American University in Cairo Press, 2018.

Wissa Wassef, Cérés. "Wissa Wassef." In *The Coptic Encyclopedia*, vol 7, edited by Aziz Suryal Atiya. New York: Macmillan, 1991. http://ccdl.libraries.claremont.edu/cdm/ref/collection/cce/id/1919

Wissa Wassef, Yoanna. "The Story of Harraneya." Unpublished. Cited in Adelina Picone, *La casa araba d'Egitto: costruire con il clima dal vernacolo ai maestri contemporanei*. Milan: Jaka Books, 2009.

Figure Credits

Figures © Nour El Refai except as noted below.
Photograph © Ehsan Abushadi: 34.
Photograph manipulated by Ehsan Abushadi, from Google Earth Pro, 2018, Ramses Wissa Wassef Art Center 29°58'08.37"N, 29°10'34.61"E, imagery captured October 27, 2018: 32.
Maps by Ehsan Abushadi, redrawn after Ahmad Abd al-Hamid, Ahmad Khaled, Ahmad al-Tulwany in "Ramses Wissa Wassef," Zamaniyat misriya: mi'at sana 'amara. Cairo: Tarek Waly Center, 2015: 66 (right), 211 (top right, bottom right).
Digitally combined image by Ehsan Abushadi. Courtesy of the Rare Books and Special Collections Library, The American University in Cairo: 189.
Photograph © Conchita Añorve-Tschirgi: 19 (left).
Photograph IAA0420 © Aga Khan Trust for Culture / Chant Avedissian (photographer): 59 (left).
Photograph IAA17965 © Aga Khan Trust for Culture / Chant Avedissian (photographer): 59 (right).
Photograph IAA1251 © Aga Khan Trust for Culture / Chant Avedissian (photographer): 121.
Photographs courtesy of the Dominican Institute for Oriental Studies, Cairo, Egypt: 78 (top right), 78 (bottom right).
Fayek Halim Gabra, from Amr El Komy's collection of postcards: 146.
J.F. Gout, courtesy of the Rare Books and Special Collections Library, The American University in Cairo: 49 (right), 55, 56, 64, 65, 116, 117, 158, 159, 210, 211 (left).
Photograph IAA17958 © Bassem Badie Gorgi / Badie Habib Gorgi (photographer). Aga Khan Trust for Culture: 58.
Photographs © Michel Hanna: 130, 131.
Lehnert & Landrock, from the author's collection of reprographic prints: 148 (left).
Map © Ramses Ikram Nosshi: 51.
Courtesy of the Rare Books and Special Collections Library, The American University in Cairo: 6, 9, 10, 11, 12, 14, 16, 19 (right), 22, 26, 29, 36, 37, 44, 49 (left), 50, 52, 57, 61, 62, 72, 79, 85, 86, 92, 94, 95, 96, 100, 101, 115, 118, 119, 120, 122 (bottom left), 122 (bottom right), 126, 127, 128, 129, 132, 133, 134, 135, 136, 138, 139, 143, 144, 145, 147, 148 (right), 149, 150, 151, 157, 160, 162 (right), 164, 165, 166, 167, 168, 169, 170, 171, 172, 173, 174, 176, 177, 178, 179, 180, 181, 182, 183, 184, 185, 186, 187, 188, 190, 191, 192, 193, 194, 195, 196, 197, 198, 199, 200, 201, 202, 203, 204, 205, 206, 207, 208, 212, 213, 214, 215, 216, 217, 218, 219, 220, 221, 222, 223, 224, 225, 226, 227, 228, 229, 230, 231, 232, 234, 236, 237, 238, 239, 240, 242, 243.
Courtesy of the Rare Books and Special Collections Library, The American University in Cairo, redrawn after Ahmad Abd al-Hamid, Ahmad Khaled, Ahmad al-Tulwany in "Ramses Wissa Wassef," Zamaniyat misriya: mi'at sana 'amara. Cairo: Tarek Waly Center, 2015: 66 (left).
Photograph © S.G.: 137 (top).